We all ⎯⎯⎯⎯⎯⎯⎯⎯ ⎯dy
a funny joke, but these jokes are quickly
forgotten and lost forever.

The purpose of this book is to create a repository
of clever and funny humour that has been
collected by me over the past fifty years and that
will last for the ages on your book shelf, rather
than disappearing forever in the digital realm.

When reading this book, to get the most out of it,
envisage yourself on stage entertaining a crowd
and acting out the characters and using their
language and situations that the characters find
themselves in.

CLEVER JOKES and WITTY DITTY'S is a gold
mine and a treasure trove of fun and laughter for
everyone who has a sense of humour, who is a
raconteur or office comedian or who is a 'life of
the party' person.

No obscene or vulgar language is used in this
book however some journalistic license has
been taken on occasions, to use colloquial and
commonly used Australianisms, to enhance the
comedic tone and essence of the story.

Please enjoy reading this book and especially
retelling some of the jokes to your friends.

This book is available in paperback form on
Amazon.com and in digital form on **Kindle
e-Book.**

Written, compiled and produced by Ian Nayda
2023

Luigi was an Italian immigrant, newly arrived in Australia, with a limited knowledge of the English language. He got himself a job working in the Kraft factory in South Melbourne. He was the happiest man because he was given a uniform to wear. This made him feel very important because it was the first time he had looked so good, even though he was just a cleaner.

One day on his way home, Luigi caught his usual tram into Flinders Street railway station, when a man got on the tram wearing a uniform even more resplendent than his. Luigi, in his broken English said, "What a beautiful'a uniform. What'a you do and where'a you work'a heh?"

The man, who worked for the Salvation Army, said, "I bring peace and tranquility to the human race. I help those in need and bring the gospel and the word of the Lord to mankind. I work for the Lord Jesus."

Luigi was flabbergasted with excitement. He grabbed the mans arm, shook it vigorously and blurted out, "We must'a work'a for da same'a family. I work'a for his'a brother, Kraft'a cheeses."

The missus shouted up the stairs this morning, "The sun's finally come out."
I thought, 'Brilliant'. Go to the beach, beer garden. So I threw some shorts and flip flops on and shot down the stairs.
I was rather shocked when I got down to find our lad holding hands with his mate Brian.

FUNNY WITTY ANALOGIES

She grew on him like she was a colony of E. Coli, and he was room-temperature Australian beef.

She had a deep, throaty, genuine laugh, like that sound a dog makes just before it throws up.

The little boat gently drifted across the pond exactly the way a bowling ball wouldn't.

McBride fell 12 stories, hitting the pavement like a hefty bag filled with vegetable soup.

Her hair glistened in the rain like a nose hair after a sneeze.

The hailstones leaped from the pavement, just like maggots when you fry them in hot grease.

Even in his last years, Grand dad had a mind like a steel trap, only one that had been left out so long it had rusted shut.

The plan was simple, like my brother-in-law Phil. But unlike Phil, this plan just might work.

He was as lame as a duck. Not the metaphorical lame duck, either, but a real duck that was actually lame, maybe from stepping on a land mine or something.

The ballerina rose gracefully en Pointe and extended one slender leg behind her, like a dog at a fire hydrant.

He was deeply in love. When she spoke, he thought he heard bells, as if she were a garbage truck backing up

Forgive me, Father, for I have sinned. Yesterday I made love to my wife."
The priest explained that there was nothing wrong with that.
"But Father, I did it with lust."
"That's alright", said the priest, "that was no sin."
"But Father, it was in the middle of the day."
"That's quite natural", replied the priest.
"But Father, I couldn't help myself. She leant over the deep freeze to get out a frozen chicken and I couldn't help myself so I jumped on her and we had sex right there. Am I banned from church?"
"Of course not!"
"What a relief, because the Woolworths manager banned us from his supermarket."

Three guys walk into a bar and have a drink. After about ten minutes of chatting and drinking, the first guy, a Frenchman says, "I was making zee love to my wife last night by dreebbling some French champagne on her navel and licking eet off and she enjoyed it so much that when I got off her, she rose 3 inches off zee bed!"
The second guy, an Englishman says, "Oh, that's nothing. When I made love to my wife last night, I sprinkled fine goose down on her

stomach and then gently blew them off and she enjoyed it so much that when I got off her, she rose 6 inches off the bed!"

The third guy, an Aussie battler, butts in and says, "That's nothing. When I screwed the old girl last night, I got off her, walked over to the window, wiped the end of me ol' fella on the satin curtains, and she hit the bloody roof!"

A grade-one teacher was welcoming her students back to school after their summer holidays.

She said, "Now class, before we begin work, would anyone like to share with the class anything interesting you may have done on your summer holidays?"

Nobody volunteered so she said, "How about you Mary?"

Mary said, "Well, Miss it was my birthday and for my birthday I received a Bow-Wow."

The teacher said, "Now Mary you are no longer in kindergarten, you are a big girl now, you don't say bow wow you can say dog."

The teacher then said, "How about you David?"

David said, "Miss, I went to visit a farm and at the farm I saw a moo-moo."

The teacher said, "Now David you are no longer in kindergarten, you are a big boy now so you don't say moo-moo, you say cow."

Johnny was waving his hand in anxious anticipation, saying "Miss, Miss."

The teacher said, "Yes Johnny would you like to share something with us?"

Johnny said, "Yes miss, I read a really good book over the summer."

The teacher said, "Good, what was the name of the book?"

Johnny said, "WINNIE THE DUMP."

Last year I replaced all the windows in my house with those expensive, double-pane, energy-efficient kind.
Today, I got a call from Bunnings who installed them. He complained that the work had been completed a year ago and I still hadn't paid for them.
Helloooo .... just because I'm blonde doesn't mean that I am automatically stupid.
So, I told him just what his fast-talking sales guy told me last year... that these windows would pay for themselves in a year. Helloooo? It's been a year, so they're paid for, I told him. There was only silence at the other end of the line, so I finally hung up.
He never called back. I bet he felt like an idiot.

WIFE: I have a bag full of my old clothes I would like to donate.
HUSBAND: Why not just throw them in the trash. That's much easier.
WIFE: But there are poor starving people who could really use these clothes.
HUSBAND: Honey, anyone who fits into your clothes is not starving.
With care and patience, husbands head injury and badly bruised left testicle are expected to make a slow but welcome recovery.

A wife was making a breakfast of fried eggs for her husband.
Suddenly, her husband burst into the kitchen. "Careful", he said, "CAREFUL! Put in some more butter! Oh my gosh! You're cooking too many at once. TOO MANY! Turn them! TURN THEM NOW! We need more butter. Oh my gosh! WHERE are we going to get MORE BUTTER? They're going to STICK! Careful. CAREFUL! I

said be CAREFUL! You NEVER listen to me when you're cooking! Never! Turn them! Hurry up! Are you CRAZY? Have you LOST your mind? Don't forget to salt them. You know you always forget to salt them. Use the! Salt. USE THE SALT! THE SALT!"

The wife stared at him.

"What in the world is wrong with you? You think I don't know how to fry a couple of eggs?"

The husband calmly replied, "I just wanted to show you what it feels like when I'm driving."

A young wife, recently married, decided to save money by making her own clothes. Her dismissive husband told her she would not have the faintest idea what to do. So to prove him wrong, she bought a cheap second hand sewing machine, a pattern and some cloth material. She laid everything out on the floor, pinned the pattern to the material, cut it out, sewed it up and produced a very lovely blowse.

Her husband on seeing the result scoffed, "That's nothing. Any one could make a blowse. I bet you couldn't make something difficult, like a pair of trousers for me."

And once again, to prove him wrong, she went out and bought a pattern, some material, took it all home, laid it out on the floor, cut it out and sewed it up.

Came the big day for the reveal and the man tried on his trousers. Well, either his wife cut the pattern out wrong or she sewed it up wrong, because when the man tried them on, it was as if the trousers had been turned ninety degrees to the left. His fly was running down the side of his leg and he had a pocket in front of him and a pocket in the back of him.

He wore them down the street one day and got arrested trying to find some change.

Paddy feared his wife Mary wasn't hearing as well as she used to and thought she might need a hearing aid. Not quite sure how to approach her, he called the family doctor to discuss the problem.

The doctor told him there is a simple informal test that paddy could perform to give the doctor a better idea about her hearing loss.

"Here's what you do", said the doctor. "Stand about 40 feet away from her and in a normal conversational speaking tone see if she hears you.

If not, go to 30 feet away and then 20 feet and so on until you get a response."

Later that day when Paddy gets home from the pub, he sees Mary in the kitchen cooking dinner and he was in the hallway,

He thinks to himself I'm about 40 feet away let's see what happens.

In a normal tone, he asks, "Mary what's for dinner my lovely?"

No response so he moves closer to 30 feet and he says, "Mary, what's for feckin dinner?".

Still no response.

He moves closer about 20 feet. "Mary, for Christ's sake can ye be telling me what's for dinner?" *Still nothing and again at 10 feet still nothing.*

So he walks up behind her and says, "Mary, can you tell me what's for dinner?"

FOR CRYING OUT LOUD PADDY FOR THE FIFTH TIME CHICKEN!!!

Man writing to advice columns

Guys, I have never written asking for your help before, but I really need your advice.

I have suspected for some time now that my wife has been cheating on me.

The usual signs; phone rings but if I answer, the caller hangs up.

My wife has been going out with "the girls" a lot recently although when I ask their names she always says, "just some friends from work, you don't know them."

I try to stay awake and look out for her when she comes home, but I usually fall asleep.

Anyway, I have never broached the subject with my wife.

I think deep down I just did not want to know the truth, but last night she went out again and I decided to finally check on her.

Around midnight, I hid in the garage behind my golf clubs so I could get a good view of the whole street when she arrived home from a night out with "the girls. "

When she got out of the car she was buttoning up her blouse, which was open, and she took her panties out of her purse and slipped them on.

It was at that moment, crouching behind my golf clubs, that I noticed a hairline crack where the grip meets the graphite shaft on my 3-wood.

Is this something I can fix myself or should I take it back to the pro-shop where I bought it?

Paddy the Irishman was talking to Mrs Dunne, enquiring as to the whereabouts of her son Michael.

"He went to London and I haven't seen or heard from him in five years. No phone call, no letter, no nothing", she moaned. "All I know is he might be at WC4", which is of course a London postcode.

The ever helpful but not too bright Paddy said, "I am going to London tomorrow and I will try and find him, Mrs Dunne."

So, Paddy wanders off to London and for several days looks for this elusive WC4, when one morning he sees a sign saying 'WC'. Paddy enters the public toilets and notes a line of cubicles down one side. Confident he has found where Michael lives, he counts down the doors until he gets to the fourth one. It's locked and there is a pair of feet inside.

Paddy bangs on the dunny door and yells "Oi!"

A gruff voice from the other side yells back, "Whatta ya' want."

Paddy says, "Are you Dunne?"

And the gruff voice says, "Am I done? Yeah! Why?"

To which Paddy replies, "Well why don't you write to your mother?"

Mick, from Dublin, appeared on the UK's 'Who Wants To Be A Millionaire'
and towards the end of the program had already won £500,000.

"You've done very well so far", said Steve Richards, the show's presenter, "but for One

Million Pounds, you've only got one life-line left, phone a friend. Everything is riding on this question. Will you go for it?"

"Sure", said Mick. "I'll have a go!"

"Which of the following birds does NOT build its own nest?

a) Sparrow

b) Thrush

c) Magpie

d) Cuckoo?"

"I haven't got a clue", said Mick, "so I'll use my last lifeline and phone my friend Paddy back home in Dublin."

Mick called up his mate, and told him the circumstances and repeated the question to him.

"Hell, Mick!" cried Paddy. "Dat's simple. It's a cuckoo."

"Are you sure?"

"Of course I'm sure."

Mick hung up the phone and told Chris, "I'll go with cuckoo as my final answer."

There was a long, long pause and then the presenter screamed, "Cuckoo is the correct answer! Mick, you've won £1 Million!"

The next night, Mick invited Paddy to their local pub to buy him a drink.

"Tell me Paddy? How in Heaven's name did you know it was da Cuckoo dat doesn't build its own nest?"

"Oi! Oi! Oi! Mick. You are just so much the dumbest. It's because everyone knows….. he lives in a clock!"

Celibacy can be a choice in life, or a condition imposed by circumstances.

While attending a Marriage Encounter Weekend, Walter and his wife Ann, listened to

the instructor declare:
"It is essential that husbands and wives know the things that are important to each other."
He addressed the men, "Can you name and describe your wife's favourite flower?"
Walter leaned over, touched Ann's arm gently and whispered,
"White Wings Self Raising flour isn't it?"
And thus began Walter's life of celibacy.

A couple in their nineties are both having problems remembering things. During a check-up, the doctor tells them that they'e physically okay, but they might want to start writing things **d**own to help them remember...

Later that night, while watching TV, the old man gets up from his chair. "Want anything while I'm in the kitchen?" he asks.

"Will you get me a bowl of ice cream?"

"Sure."

"Don't you think you should write it down so you can remember it?" she asks.

"No, I can remember it."

"Well, I'd like some strawberries on top, too. Maybe you should write it down, so as not to forget it?"

He says, "I can remember that. You want a bowl of ice cream with strawberries."

"I'd also like whipped cream. I'm certain you'll forget that, write it down?" she says.

Irritated, he says, "I don't need to write it down, I can remember it! Ice cream with strawberries and whipped cream - I got it, for goodness sake!"

Then he toddles into the kitchen. After about 20 minutes, the old man returns from the kitchen and hands his wife a plate of bacon and eggs. She stares at the plate for a moment.

"Where's my toast?"

Gay guy Frank goes into the doctor's office and has some tests run. The doctor says, "Frank, I am not going to beat around the bush, you have AIDS."

Frank is devastated. "Doc, what can I do?"

The doctor says, "I want you to go home and eat 5 kilos of spiced sausage, a head of cabbage, 20 un-peeled carrots drenched in hot sauce,10 Jalapeno peppers, 40 walnuts and 40 peanuts, 1/2 box of Kelloggs All Bran cereal, and top it off with a gallon of prune juice."

Frank asks, "Will that cure me, Doc?"

"No, but it should leave you with a better understanding of what your arse is for!"

Working people frequently ask retired people like me what they do to make their days interesting.

Well for example, the other day I went into the city and went to a shop in Latrobe Street Melbourne. I was only in there for about five minutes. When I came out there was a parking cop writing out a parking ticket. I went up to him and said, "Come on mate, how about giving a senior citizen a break?". He ignored me and continued writing the ticket. I called him a miserable bastard. He glared at me and started writing another ticket for having worn tyres. So, I called him a piece of stinking dog shit. He finished the second ticket and put it on the windshield with the first. Then he started writing a third ticket. This went on for about twenty minutes. The more I abused him, the more tickets he wrote.

Personally, I don't give a stuff. I came to town by bus. I try to have a little fun each day now that I'm retired. It's important at my age.

Two Americans decide to start a bungee jumping business in Mexico.

They're almost done setting up on a bridge by a city but first they have to test to see if the cord will work.

So, one of the men ties the cord to himself, jumps off, and comes back up with scratches on his face. Cord too long.

So, they get a shorter cord and the same guy tests it again.

Before he jumps, a large group of people from the city are standing at the bottom, staring up at him, with brooms in their hands.

He jumps and this time he comes back up with bruises and a broken bone.

The other guy says to him, "I thought that would be the perfect length that time."

The other guy that jumped replies, "It was. By the way, what the bloody hell is a pinata?"

A man went into a local tavern and took a seat at the bar next to a women patron.
He turned to her and said, "This is a special day, I'm celebrating."
"What a coincidence", said the woman, "I'm celebrating, too". She clinked glasses with him and asked, "What are you celebrating?"
"I'm a chicken farmer", he replied. "For years all my hens were infertile, but today they're finally fertile."
"What a coincidence", the woman said. "My husband and I have been trying to have a child. Today, my gynecologist told me I'm pregnant! How did your chickens become fertile?" she asked.
"I switched cocks", he replied.
"What a coincidence", she said.

Eric was lying on the bed naked with his girlfriend Wendy. She said to him, "Eric, how much do you love me?"

"Oh, heaps, really heaps luv", he nonchalantly answered.

"Well, I want you to display your love for me by having my name tattooed on your penis", she said.

Eric thought this was OK so next night, after he had the tattoo done, he was showing it to Wendy. But all she could see was the letters 'W' and 'Y'.

"No, No, give it a big rub", said Eric and sure as anything up it came and the name 'WENDY' appeared.

Several weeks later, Eric is out having beers with mates and he's taking a leak when a huge Afro American man walks into the toilet and stands at the urinals. Eric thinks, 'Hmmm, big black man, big dick.' He slyly looks at the black mans dick and there tattooed on it was the letters 'W' and 'Y'. Excitedly Eric says, "Er, excuse me, but I just happened to notice those letters on your dick. I have the same, see. But I bet you haven't got something like this", as he stretched his out to reveal 'WENDY".

In a deep guttural voice the huge dark guy said, "No man, I ain't got 'dat but I got 'dis."

And as he stretched his oversized member out, Eric read the tattoo which said,

'WELCOME TO THE CARRIBEAN HOPE YOU HAVE A NICE DAY'

A teacher asks the kids in her 3rd grade class: "What do you want to be when you grow up?"

Little Johnny says: "I wanna start out as a Fighter Pilot, then be a billionaire, go to the most expensive clubs, find me the finest prostitute, give her a Ferrari worth over a million bucks, an apartment in Rio de Janeiro, a mansion in Paris, a jet to travel throughout Europe, an Infinite Visa Card, and all the while bang her like a loose dunny door in a cyclone."

The teacher, shocked and not knowing what to do with this horrible response from little Johnny, decides not to acknowledge what he said and simply tries to continue with the lesson. "And how about you, Sarah?"

"I wanna be Johnny's prostitute."

A tour company was taking a coach load of elderly tourist on a trip through the Australian Outback. They turned off the main road and headed down a dusty dirt track for about twenty kilometres. The coach stopped next to an ancient very large ant hill and the tour guide told everyone to get off.

He then informed them that they were going for a hike into the bush to see an aboriginal carving. A great experience not to be missed. Everyone was eager to get moving except one elderly lady who was adamant she was not in any way interested.

When asked the reason for her reluctance to join the group she said, "I come from a dairy farm and I have seen a cow calving and no way known am I going to watch an aboriginal calving."

For her 40th birthday, my wife said, "I'd love to be ten again." So that Saturday, we had a heaping stack of chocolate-chip pancakes, her favourite childhood breakfast. Then we hit the playground and a merry-go-round. We finished the day with a banana split.

"So how did you enjoy being a kid for a day?" I asked.

"Great", she said. "But when I said I wanted to be ten again, I meant my dress size."

Over the last month I became a victim of a clever scam while out shopping. Here's how the scam works. Two very beautiful, university-age girls will come over to your car or truck as you are packing your purchases into your vehicle. They both start wiping your windshield with a rag and Windex, with their breasts almost falling out of their skimpy T-shirts. (It's impossible not to look). When you thank them and offer them a tip, they say 'No' but instead ask for a ride to McDonald's!

You agree and they climb into the vehicle. On the way, they start undressing. Then one of them starts crawling all over you, while the other one steals your wallet.

I had my wallet stolen February 4th, 9th, 10th, twice on the 15th, again on the 17th, 20th, 24th, and the 28th. Also, March 1st, 2nd, 8th, twice on the 9th &10th, and very likely again tomorrow and Wednesday. So, tell your friends to be careful. What a horrible way to take advantage of us older men. Warn your friends to be vigilant.

Big W has wallets on sale for $2.99 each. I

found even cheaper ones for $.99 at the Reject Shop and bought them out in three of their stores. Also, you never get to eat at McDonald's. I've already lost 5 kg just running back and forth from Big W, to Kmart, to Reject Shop. So please, be on the lookout for this scam. The best times are just before lunch and around 4:30 in the afternoon.

The Federal Government has been looking for a generic name for Viagra.

After careful consideration by a team of government experts, it recently announced that it has settled on the generic name of Mycoxafloppin. Also considered were Mycoxafailin, Mydixadrupin, Mydixarizin, and of course Dixafix.

Pfizer Corp announced today that Viagra will soon be available in liquid form, and will be marketed by Pepsi Cola as a power beverage suitable for use as a mixer. It wilow be possible for a man to literally pour himself a 'stiff one'.

Obviously. we can no longer call this a soft drink, and it gives new meaning to the names of 'cocktails', 'highballs' and just a good old-fashioned 'stiff drink'.

In addition, there is more money being spent on breast implants and Viagra today, than on Alzheimer's research. This means that by 2040, there should be a large elderly population with perky boobs and huge erections and absolutely no recollection of what to do with them.

A man escapes from a prison where he's been locked up for 15 years.

He breaks into a house and inside, he finds a young couple in bed.

He ties the man to a chair. While tying the wife to the bed, the convict gets on top of her, kisses her neck, then gets up and goes into the bathroom.

While he's in there, the husband whispers over to his wife,

"Listen, this guy is an escaped convict. Look at his clothes! He's probably spent a lot of time in jail and hasn't seen a woman in years.

I saw how he kissed your neck. If he wants sex, don't resist, don't complain. Do whatever he tells you. Satisfy him no matter how much he nauseates you. This guy is obviously very dangerous. If he gets angry, he'll kill us both. Be strong, honey. I love you!"

She responds: "He wasn't kissing my neck. He was whispering in my ear. He told me that he's gay, thinks you're cute, and asked if we had any Vaseline. I told him it was in the bathroom. Be strong honey. I love you, too."

The Irishman was walking through a field when he saw a man drinking water from a pool, using his hand as a scoop.

The Irishman shouted to him in his local Irish brogue, "Na ol an t-uisce, ta lan de chac bo" (Don't drink the water, it's full of cow shit.)

The man shouted back, "I'm English, speak the Queen's English you mindless idiot, I don't understand a damn word you are saying."

The Irishman replied, "Use both hands, you'll get more in."

A priest is driving back to Sydney when he gets pulled over for speeding.

The cop approaches the window and sees an empty wine bottle in the passenger's seat.

The priest rolls down the window and a strong smell of wine wafts out.

"Have you been drinking, Father?" asks the cop.

"Just water", replied the priest.

"I can smell wine, Father", said the cop.

The priest looks from the bottle to the heavens.

"Good Lord, he's done it again!"

A man was walking along the footpath one day quite sure that he was the unluckiest person in the world, when he noticed a strange lamp in the gutter. He picked it up, gave it a bit of a polish and suddenly, amidst a puff of smoke, a genie appeared.

The genie was relieved to be out of the lamp after several thousands of years, and granted the man two wishes. Thinking hard about this he said, "OK genie, first, I wish I was the luckiest man in the world and second, there is this gorgeous young Indian sheila living next door to me. I wish she would fall madly in love with me." The genie simply touched the man and vanished in a very bright light. It gave the man such a shock that he stumbled, fell over and landed next to a $100 note that was laying on the footpath. Picking it up he thought he would have a bet on a horse. The horse came home first and he won five thousand dollars. He was so happy with his good fortune that he bought a slab of beer to celebrate. As soon as he paid, a loud bell rang and staff came from everywhere because he was the millionth customer and was entitled to all the beer he could drink for a year.

He went home and began drinking his beer, thinking life could not get any better when there was a knock on the door. He opened the door and there was the Indian woman in a brief sheer outfit, wanting to come inside. He let her in and they adjourned to the bedroom where they had wonderful sex.

Lying back, with the young woman drowsing next to him on the bed, he contemplated that this must have been the result of the genie and most certainly he couldn't get any luckier, when he noticed the Indian red dot on the woman's forehead. "I have always wondered what that weird dot was for", he mused, so he leaned over and rubbed it off and saw some writing under the dot. He leaned closer to see it and it read, "Congratulations, you have just won a new car and a trip to Tasmania."

Seb and Davo were lifting a pint at the local pub. Davo said, "I haven't run into your Uncle Wally in a while. Whatever happened to him?"

Seb replied, "Dear Uncle Wally was busy trying to make a new kind of car. He took the wheels from a BMW, the radiator from a Lexus, the motor from a Ford and the seats from a Merc."

"What did he get?" asked Mick.

"Four years, but reduced to two for good behaviour."

At a wedding I whispered to a guy next to me, "Isn't the bride ugly?"

"Do you mind. That's my daughter you're talking about."

I said, "I'm sorry, I didn't know you were her father."

"I'm not, I'm her mother."

Finnigan went to the doctor for a physical exam and while he was there, he mentioned to the doctor that he was thinking about getting a vasectomy.

The doctor completed his examination and then commented to Finnigan about his question.

"Having a vasectomy is a pretty big decision", the doctor said. "Have you talked it over with your family?"

"Aye", Finnigan replied.

"And what did they think of the idea?" the doctor asked.

Finnigan said, "They are in favour of it, 15 to 2."

The young Indian brave approach his famous father Sitting Bull, and asked, "Father, why you call all your children such funny names?"

Sitting Bull thought for a moment then earnestly replied, "I get them from nature and from first thing I see when you born. Like when your brother, he born, I look out of tepee and first thing I see is deer, running through forest, so I call him Running Deer. And your sister, when she born, I look out of tepee and first thing I see is large white cloud floating in sky, so I call her Passing Cloud. And your other brother, when he born, I look out of tepee and first thing I see is wild horse kicking, spitting and jumping so I call him Crazy Horse."

Then he looked at his idiot son and said, "So tell me, why you ask me these questions Two Dogs Rooting?"

Two married women were walking home after a girl's night out, three parts boozed, weaving and giggling loudly along the footpath when they had to do a pee. So, they ducked into a cemetery. They had no toilet paper so one woman used her knickers and threw them away. The other used a ribbon from a wreath that had recently been laid on a grave. The next day their husbands were talking.

"We'd better keep an eye on our wives", one said. "Mine came home without her knickers."

"You think that's bad", said the other. "Mine had a card stuck up her backside saying, 'From all the lads at the Fire and Rescue Service, we'll never forget you'".

A woman told her husband that she was not happy with her small breasts and that she wanted to spend $5000 on breast implants.

"That's outrageous", said the man. "I know how you can increase the size for a fraction of the cost. All you have to do is, every morning, rub several pieces of toilet paper between your breasts and that will make them bigger."

"Don't be so stupid you idiot. That won't make my breasts larger", said the wife.

"Why not", said the man, "you've been doing the same thing between the cheeks of your butt for forty years and look at how big they are."

A crutchedy old General was interviewed on the radio recently regarding his upcoming sponsorship of a Boy Scout Troop visiting his military Headquarters.

FEMALE INTERVIEWER: So, General, what things are you going to teach these young boys when they visit your base?

GENERAL : We're going to teach them climbing, canoeing, archery and shooting.

FEMALE INTERVIEWER: Shooting! That's a bit irresponsible, isn't it?

GENERAL : I don't see why, they'll be properly supervised on the rifle range.

FEMALE INTERVIEWER: Don't you admit that this is a terribly dangerous activity to be teaching children?

GENERAL: I don't see how. We will be teaching them proper rifle discipline before they even touch a firearm.

FEMALE INTERVIEWER: But you're equipping them to become violent killers.

GENERAL : Well, Ma'am, you're equipped to be a prostitute, but you're not one, are you?

A dog lover, whose female dog came "in heat", was concerned about keeping it and her male separated. But she had a large house and she believed that she could keep the two dogs apart.

However, as she was drifting off to sleep, she heard awful howling and moaning sounds. She rushed downstairs and found the dogs locked together and unable to disengage, as frequently happens when dogs mate.
Unable to separate them, and perplexed as to what to do next, although it was very late at night, she called her vet, who answered in a very

grumpy voice.

After she explained the problem to him, the vet said, "Hang up the phone and place it down alongside the dogs.

I will then call you back and the noise of the ringing will make the male lose his erection and he will be able to withdraw."

"Do you think that will work?" she asked.

"Just worked for me." he replied

Two deaf people get married. During the first week of marriage, they find that they are unable to communicate in the bedroom when they turn off the lights because they can't see each other using sign language.

After several nights of fumbling around and misunderstandings, the wife proposes a solution.

"Honey", she signs, "why don't we agree on some simple signals? For instance, at night, if you want to have sex with me, reach over and squeeze my left breast one time. If you don't want to have sex, reach over and squeeze my right breast one time."

The husband thinks this is a great idea and signs back to his wife, "Great idea! Now if you want to have sex with ME, reach over and pull on my penis one time. And if you don't want to have sex, reach over and pull on my penis...FIFTY times."

I was having sex with this sheila over her kitchen table when we heard the front door open. She said, "It's my husband! Quick, try the back door!"

Thinking back, I really should have legged it – but you don't get offers like that every day.

An army major visits the sick soldiers in hospital one day.

He goes up to one private and asks him, "What's your problem, soldier?"

The soldier replies, "Chronic syphilis, Sir."

"And what treatment are you getting?"

"Five minutes with the wire brush each day."

"What's your ambition?"

"To get back to the front, Sir."

"Good man", says the Major.

He then goes to the next bed and asks the occupant, "And what's your problem, soldier?"

"Chronic piles, Sir."

"What treatment are you getting?"

"Five minutes with the wire brush each day."

"What's your ambition?"

"To get back to the front, Sir."

"Good man", says the Major.

He goes to the next bed and asks the soldier in it, "And what's your problem, soldier?"

"Chronic gum disease, Sir."

"What treatment are you getting?"

"Five minutes with the wire brush each day."

"What's your ambition?"

"To get the wire brush before the other two, Sir."

Three male bodies arrive at the morgue with big smiles frozen on their lifeless faces. The coroner calls the detective to ask what happened to the men.

"First body: French. Age 60. Died of Congestive Heart Failure while making love to his mistress. Hence the enormous smile", said the detective.

"Second body: Scottish. Age 25. Won one thousand dollars on the slot machines and spent it all on Old Single Malt Scotch Whiskey. Died of acute alcohol poisoning. Hence, going out with a smile."

The Coroner asked, "What about the third body; it's badly burned, but he still has a smile on his face?"

"Ah", said the detective, "This is the most unusual one: Justin Trudeau, Prime Minister of Canada. Age 45. He was struck by lightning."

"Why is he smiling then?" asked the Coroner.

"He thought someone was taking his picture!!"

A truck driver, on his way to Sydney, stopped at a road side truck stop for lunch. He ordered a cheeseburger, coffee, and a chocolate lamington.

As he was about to eat, three motorcycles pulled up outside. The bikers came in, and one grabbed the trucker's cheeseburger and took a bite from it. The second one drank the trucker's coffee, and the third wolfed down the lamington. The truck driver didn't say a word. He simply got up, paid the cashier, and left.

When he was gone, one of the motorcyclists said, "He ain't much of a man, is he?"

"He's not much of a driver, either", the cashier replied, "He just backed his B-Double over three motorcycles."

I was testing children in my Dublin Sunday School class to see if they understood the concept of getting to heaven.

I asked them, "If I sold my house and my car, had a big garage sale and gave all my money to the church, would that get me into heaven?" "NO!" the children answered.

"If I cleaned the church every day, mowed the lawns, raked the garden beds and kept everything neat and tidy, would that get me into heaven?" Again, the answer was a resounding "NO!"

"If I gave sweets to all the children, and loved my husband, would that get me into heaven?" Once again they all answered, "NO!"

I was just simply bursting with pride for them so I continued, "Then how can I get into heaven?"

A little boy not more than six years old shouted out: "YUV GOTTA BE FOOKIN' DEAD."

A South African Airways passenger cabin was being served by an obviously
gay flight attendant, who seemed to put everyone into a good mood as he
served them food and drinks. As the plane prepared to descend, he came
swishing down the aisle and announced to the passengers, "Captain Marvey Warvey has asked me to announce that he'll be landing the big scary plane shortly, lovely people, so if you could

just put up your trays, that would be super."

On his trip back up the aisle, he noticed that a well-dressed rather exotic looking woman hadn't moved a muscle. "Perhaps you didn't hear me over those big brute engines", he said. "I asked you to raise your trazy-poo so the main man can pitty-pat us on the ground." She calmly turned her head and said, "In my country, I am called a Princess. I take orders from no-one."

To which the flight attendant replied, without missing a beat: "Well,sweet-cheeks, in my country I'm called a Queen, so I outrank you. Tray-up, bitch."

An unemployed dimwit went for a job at the local blacksmiths. When he sat down for the interview, the blacksmith asked him, "Have you ever shoed horses?"

The dimwit thought about this for a couple of minutes and replied, "No, but I once told a donkey to go get stuffed."

This bartender is in a bar, when this really hot chick walks up and says in a sexy seductive voice, "May I please speak to your manager?" He says, "Not right now, is there anything I can help you with?"
She replies, "I don't know if you're the man to talk to...its kind of personal..."
Thinking he might get lucky, he says, "I'm pretty sure I can handle your problem, miss."
She then looks at him with a smile, and puts two of her fingers in his mouth...and he begins

sucking them, thinking, "I'm in!!!"
In a seductive husky voice she coos, "Can you give the manager something for me?"
The bartender nods...yes. "Tell him there's no toilet paper in the ladies restroom."

A super-hot woman arrived at a party. While scanning the guests, she spotted an attractive man standing alone. She approached him, smiled and said, "Hello. My name is Carmen." "That's a beautiful name," he replied. "Is it a family name?" "No", she replied. "As a matter of fact, I gave it to myself. It represents the things I enjoy the most – cars and men. Therefore, I chose 'Car-men.'"

"What's your name?" she asked.
He answered, "B.J. Titsnbeer."

The finals of the 'National Witty Ditty Contest' last year came down to two finalists. One was a Law School graduate from an upper crust Toorak family; well-bred, well-connected, and all that goes with it. The other finalist was an unemployed truck driver from Dandenong.
Each finalist was to be given a folded piece of paper with one word on it, the word being the same for both finalists. As soon as they read the word, they were required to compose a five-line witty ditty in thirty seconds or less, and the ditty had to contain the word that was on the piece of paper.

The unemployed truck driver wore ear muffs and the Law graduate went first.

He was given the piece of paper, opened it, and the word was TIMBUKTU. About twenty seconds after the clock started, he jumped up and recited the following ditty:

'Slowly across the desert sand
Trekked the dusty caravan
Men on camels
Two by two
Destination--Timbuktu.'

The audience went wild! How, they wondered, could the truck driver top that? The truck driver removed his ear muffs and he read the word. The clock started again and the truck driver sat in silent thought. Fifteen seconds gone. Twenty seconds gone. Finally, in the last few seconds, he jumped up and recited:

'Tim an' me, a-huntin' went
Met three whores in a pop-up tent
They was three
We was two
So I bucked one and Timbuktu.'

The phone rings and the wife answers.

A pervert breathing heavily and breathlessly says, "I bet you have a tight arse with no hair!"

The wife replies, "Yes, I do as a matter of fact. He's slouched on the couch drinking beer and watching TV...who shall I say is calling?"

Three Greeks and Three Turks are riding a train.

The Turks each buy one ticket, but the Greeks only buy one ticket total. The Turks are confused.

"How can you ride with one ticket?"

"Watch and you shall see."

The Greeks get on the train and pile into the bathroom. The Turks sit near the bathroom and observe.

The conductor knocks on the door and says, "Ticket please." The Greeks slide the ticket through the door.

The Turks think this is ingenious! They decide to try it, so on the ride back they buy only one ticket. But the Greeks don't buy any.

"How will you ride without any tickets?"

"Watch and you shall see."

They get on the train. The Turks pile into one bathroom, the Greeks into another. One Greek gets out of the bathroom, walks over to the bathroom the Turks are hiding in, and says: "Ticket please."

A guy brings his best golf buddy home, unannounced, for dinner at 6:30 PM after enjoying a day of golf.

His wife screams her head off while his friend sits at the kitchen table, open mouthed, listening to the tirade.

"My hair and makeup are not done. The house is a f__king mess and the dishes are still in the sink. I'm completely exhausted! I didn't get enough sleep last night. Can't you see I'm still in my f__king pyjamas? I can't be bothered with cooking tonight! Why the f__k did you bring him home without letting me know ahead of time, you stupid dumb inconsiderate asshole???"

"Because ... he's thinking of getting married..."

WITTY ABSTRACTED THOUGHTS

The fattest knight at King Arthur's round table was Sir Cumference. He acquired his size from too much pi.

I thought I saw an eye doctor on an Alaskan island, but he turned out to be an optical Aleutian.

She was only a whiskey maker, but he loved her still.

A rubber band pistol was confiscated from algebra class, because it was a weapon of math disruption.

No matter how much you push the envelope, it'll still be stationery.

A dog gave birth to puppies near the road and was cited for littering.

A grenade thrown into a kitchen in France would result in Linoleum Blownapart.

Two silk worms had a race. They ended up in a tie.

A hole has been found in the nudist camp wall. The police are looking into it.

Atheism is a non prophet organization.

Two hats were hanging on a hat rack in the hallway. One hat said to the other: 'You stay here; I'll go on a head.'

I wondered why the baseball kept getting bigger. Then it hit me.

A sign on the lawn at a drug rehab center said: 'Keep off the Grass.'

The midget fortune-teller who escaped from prison was a Small Medium at Large.

The soldier who survived mustard gas and pepper spray is now a seasoned veteran.

A backward poet writes inverse.

In a democracy it's your vote that counts. In feudalism it's your count that votes.

If you jumped off the bridge in Paris, you'd be in Seine

An Englishman, a Welshman and an Irishman were at a theme park and were about to go on a Roller Coaster when an old witch steps in front of them.

"This is a magic ride", she says. "You will land in whatever you shout out on the way down."

"I'm game for this", says Dai, the Welshman,

and takes off down the slide shouting "GOLD!" at the top of his voice. Sure enough, when he hit the bottom, he found himself surrounded by thousands of pounds worth of gold coins.

Nigel, the Englishman, goes next and shouts "SILVER!" at the top of his voice. At the bottom he lands in more silver coinage than he can carry.

Patrick, the Irishman, goes last and, launching himself from the top of the slide shouts "WEEEEEEE!"

A man was driving a large horse float to Flemington race course in Melbourne to pick up some horses after the last race. As he had plenty of time to spare, he decided to stop at a nearby hotel for a few beers. A few turned into many and he suddenly realized he would be late picking up the horses. He jumped into the horse float and sped towards the race course. A passing police patrol pulled him over and asked him why he was speeding. Rather dazed from too many beers he lied, "I have to get these horses to Flemington for the last race. They belong to Mr Bart Cummings and if I'm late I will be in big trouble."

The police officer didn't believe the story and asked the man to open the back of the float. Sitting in his cabin, the man activated the hydraulics and the large rear door opened. The policeman looked inside and the empty float was revealed. "So! What do we have here? I thought you said you had horses on board."

The drunk man walked to the back of the float, peered in and without missing a beat said, "Damn, wouldn't you know it. They've gone and given me the bloody 'scratchings' again."

Three men died on Christmas Eve. One was an American, one was an Englishman and one was an Irishman. They were met by Saint Peter at the pearly gates who said tiredly, "I'm terribly sorry guys but this is a very busy time for us up here. Pretty full up at the moment, however, in honour of this holy season, I am going to send you all back to Earth but you must bring back something that symbolizes Christmas in your country if you want guaranteed access into heaven."

So, with a wave of his hand, the three men were gone back to Earth.

The first man, the American, returned immediately with a piece of holly which he explained was hung everywhere at Christmas.

"Very good, you may pass through the pearly gates", Saint Peter said.

The second man, the Englishman was right behind the American with a piece of mistletoe which he explained was hung in doorways and people could kiss under it. "OK", said St Peter, "in you come", and the pearly gates were duly opened.

The third man, the Irishman, was nowhere to be seen. After about forty minutes he finally turned up with a smile on his face and acting very happy.

St. Peter looked at the man with a raised eyebrow and said, "You have taken forty minutes. What could have kept you so long? And just what have you managed to bring me back that symbolizes Christmas in Ireland?"

The Irishman reached into his vest and pulled out a pair of pretty pink, very sheer and very brief lace female knickers. Astounded, St Peter demanded, "Good Lord! What in heavens name are those things?" To which the smirking Irishman replied, "These are Carol's."

During his routine medical check, Paddy asked the doctor, "Do you think I'll live a long and healthy life?"

"I doubt it", said the doctor, "Mercury is in Uranus right now."

Paddy said, "I don't go in for any of that astrology nonsense."

"Neither do I", replied the doctor, "But my thermometer just broke off in your arse."

A new monk arrives at the monastery. He is assigned to help the other monks in copying the old texts by hand.

He notices, however, that they are copying copies, not the original books. So, the new monk goes to the head monk to ask him about this. He points out that if there were an error in the first copy, that error would be continued in all of the other copies.

The head monk says, "We have been copying from the copies for centuries and centuries, but you make a good point, my son." So, he goes down into the cellar with one of the copies to check it against the original.

Hours later, nobody has seen him. So, one of the monks goes downstairs to look for him. He hears a sobbing coming from the back of the cellar, and finds the old monk leaning over one of the original books crying. He asks what's wrong.

The old monk sobs, "The word is CELEBRATE!"

In parts of Eastern Europe there is a tradition that a person on their death bed can ask a question of anyone who is present and that person MUST answer that question honestly or else they will spend eternity in hell.

Papa was on his death bed surrounded by his wife and his four sons. Three of his sons were the largest men you could possibly meet while the fourth son was a pasty faced freckled runt called Guido.

Papa turned weakly to his wife and murmured, "Mama. I am almost on my way. It is time for the question."

His wife sniffed, wiped a tear from her eyes, and unsure of what was to follow, she whimpered, "Yes Papa, it is time. I am ready. What is the question?"

Papa looked her lovingly in the eye, wheezed heavily and haltingly asked, "Guido. The runt. Is he, Is he, Is he mine?"

Mama looked into Papa's eyes and earnestly said, "Yes Papa. He is yours."

A wan smile appeared on Papa's face and with one last contented gasp, Papa was gone.

The question had been asked and answered truthfully and his wife now knew she would not have to spend eternity in hell. As she wiped away a remaining tear, a small smile of relief appeared on her lips as she said quietly to herself, 'Thank God he didn't ask me about the other three.'

One year, I decided to buy my mother-in-law a cemetery plot as a Christmas gift.

The next year, I didn't buy her a gift. When she asked me why, I replied, "Well, you still haven't used the gift I bought you last year!"

And that's how the fight started.....

Nigel was telling friends how first-aid classes had prepared him for an emergency. "I saw a woman hit by a car", he said. "She had a broken arm, a twisted knee, a skull fracture and blood and guts everywhere."

"How horrible! What did you do?"

"Well, thanks to my high quality first aid training I knew exactly how to handle it. I sat on the curb and put my head between my knees, took long deep breaths and successfully managed to keep myself from fainting."

A man found two tennis balls while out jogging and put them in his pocket so he could give them to his dog back home.

As he stopped to wait at the traffic lights, a woman next to him couldn't help but notice the large bulge in his trouser pocket.

"Tennis balls" the man said.

"Oh, that must be painful," she replied. "I had tennis elbow once and it hurt like hell!"

A man in the Middle East wanted a camel that would last 10 days while he crossed the desert. He went to a camel market and the camel seller assured him this camel would last him 10 days provided he let the camel have a big drink beforehand. This was done and the man headed out across the dunes. After the ninth day the camel promptly lay down on the sand and died from dehydration.

The furious man eventually found his way back to the camel market and the camel seller and abused him for selling him a 9 day camel when he had paid for a 10 day camel.

"Ah my good friend", said the seller, "You do not understand the ways of the desert. There is no such thing as a 10 day camel. You have to make a 9 day camel into a 10 day camel."

"And just precisely how do you do that?" demanded the man.

"Well", said Ahmed the camel seller, "when the camel is having his big drink, you sneak up behind him with a brick in each hand. And when he has had enough water for nine days, you line up his testicles and clap them really hard between the bricks. The camel gets such a shock it goes SLUUUUUUUURP and takes in another days worth of water."

"Good heavens", said the astonished man, "doesn't it hurt."

"No, not if you keep your thumbs out of the way."

A young jackaroo from outback Queensland goes off to university,

but halfway through the semester he has squandered all of his money.

He calls home.

"Dad", he says, "you won't believe what modern education is developing...

they actually have a program here in Brisbane that will teach our dog Ol' Blue how to talk."

"That's amazing!", his dad says. "How do I get OL' Blue in that program?"

"Just send him down here with $2,000 and I'll get him in the course", the young jackaroo says,

So, his father sends the dog and $2,000.

About two-thirds through the semester, the money runs out again.

The boy calls home.

"So, how's OL' Blue doing, son?", his father wants to know.

"Awesome! Dad, he's talking up a storm... But you just won't believe this.

They've had such good results with talking, they've begun to teach the animals how to read."

"Read?", exclaims his father, "No kidding! How do we get OL' Blue in that program?"

"Just send $4,500. I'll get him in the class."

The money promptly arrives. But our hero has a problem.

At the end of the year, his father will find out the dog can neither talk nor read.

So, he shoots the dog.

When he arrives home at the end of the year, his father is all excited.

"Where's OL' Blue? I just can't wait to talk with him, and see him read something!"

"Dad", the boy says, "I have some grim news. Yesterday morning, just before we left to drive home, OL' Blue was in the living room, kicked back in the recliner, reading the Financial Review, when he suddenly turned to me and asked,

'So, is your daddy still bonking that little redhead barmaid at the pub?'"

The father groans and whispers,

"I hope you shot that bastard before he talks to your mother!"

"I sure did, Dad!"

"That's my boy!"

The kid went on to be a successful lawyer.

FUNNY INSIGHTFUL MOMENTS

Surprise sex is the best thing to wake up to. Unless you are in prison.

My wife says I only have two faults.
I don't listen and some other drivel she was prattling on about.

The speed at which a woman says "I'm fine" is directly proportional to the severity of the shit storm that's about to follow.

Funny how drinking 8 cups of water a day seems like it's impossible, but 8 beers and 6 shots in 3 hours go down like a fat kid on a see-saw.

Next time a stranger talks to me and I'm alone, I will just look at him shocked and just whisper quietly in a raspy voice, "You can see me?"

So, I was at the bar last night and the waitress screamed, "Anyone know CPR?"
I said, "Hell, I know the entire alphabet."
Everyone laughed....well except this one guy.

The Japanese have invented a camera that has a shutter speed so fast, that it can actually capture a picture of my mother in law with her mouth closed.

"Where do you want this big roll of bubble wrap?" I asked my boss.

"Just pop it in the corner", he said.

It took me three hours.

Two old men are sitting on the deck of a cruise ship.

The first one asks, "Have you read Marx?"

The other one replies, "Yes. I believe that comes from sitting on these wicker chairs."

A Frenchman walks into a bar with a toad on his head.

"What the hell is that?" asks the barman.

The toad replies, "I don't know – it started as a wart on my butt and just kept growing."

A penguin walks into a bar, goes to the counter and says to the barman, "Have you seen my brother?"

The barman says, "I don't know. What does he look like?"

It was so cold today, I saw a lawyer with his hands in his own pockets.

I'll never join one of those online dating services.

I prefer to meet someone the good old-fashioned way. You know, through alcohol, lies and poor judgement.

My computer said I had to change my password.

I entered "beefstew".

My computer said, "Sorry password not stroganoff."

As a boy, I was made to believe that earwigs lived in ears.

After that, I was terrified of cockroaches.

My girlfriend told me I'm her 32nd lover.

It turns out what she really meant was I'm her thirty second lover

It is true that a human fart can be louder than a trombone.

I discovered that at my daughter's school concert.

You may have been impressed with the hand sanitiser in the bathroom but it is not a good look coming out sniffing your fingers.

Remember the Swatch? A watch made in Switzerland? Thank God Croatia didn't come up with the idea first. Just imagine if someone were to ask you what time is it? "Oh, pardon me while I just look at my Crotch."

A rather senile old lady went to her doctor complaining of a feeling of fullness in her right ear.

After the examination, the doctor initiated a conversation that went as follows:

Doctor: Why madam, I think you have a suppository in your ear.

Lady: Eh?

Doctor: Madam - You have a SUPPOSITORY in your EAR!

Lady: EH?

Doctor: IN YOUR EAR! A SUPPOSITORY!

Lady: Oh, thank goodness. Now I think I know where I put my hearing aid.

An American, an Australian and a Japanese were stranded on a deserted island. The Yank took charge and said, "OK men. We need shelter from the elements, we need some water and supplies. I will be in charge of building a shelter. Aussie, you are in charge of the water and Jap, you are in charge of the supplies."

"No problems old cock", said the Aussie.

"Velly, velly good", said the Jap in his funny English.

Two hours later they had a shelter built and ample water but no Japanese with his supplies. Getting worried they decide to head off down the nearest trail and look for him. They hadn't gone far when they rounded a large forest tree and the Jap sprang out, arms spread wide yelling, "SUPPLIES!!!"

A judge asks a woman, "What did you steal, Mrs. Battanhatch?"

The woman looks down, "A can of peaches, Your Honour."

"And how many peaches were there in the can?" continues the judge.

"Six, sir", admits the woman.

"OK, you will serve 6 days in prison", rules the judge. Suddenly her husband shouts from the back of the court room, "Your Honour, she also stole a large can of peanuts!"

A tourist visiting the area drives through town, stops at the motel, and lays a $100 bill on the desk saying he wants to inspect the rooms upstairs to pick one for the night.

As soon as he walks upstairs, the motel owner grabs the bill and runs next door to pay his debt to the butcher. The butcher takes the $100 and runs down the street to retire his debt to the pig farmer.

The pig farmer takes the $100 and heads off to pay his bill to his supplier, the Co-op. The guy at the Co-op takes the $100 and runs to pay his debt to the local prostitute, who has also been facing hard times and has had to offer her "services" on credit.

The hooker rushes to the hotel and pays off her room bill with the motel owner. The motel proprietor then places the $100 back on the counter so the traveller will not suspect anything.

At that moment the traveller comes down the stairs, states that the rooms are not satisfactory, picks up the $100 bill and leaves.

No one produced anything. No one earned anything. However, the whole town is now out of debt and now looks to the future with a lot more optimism.

And that, ladies and gentlemen, is how a stimulus package works.

God is tired, worn out. So, he speaks to St. Peter, "You know, I need a vacation. Got any suggestions where I should go?" St. Peter, thinking, nods his head, then says, "How about Jupiter? It's nice and warm there this time of the year." God shakes His head before saying, "No. Too much gravity. You know how that hurts my back." "Hmmm", St. Peter reflects. "Well, how about Mercury?" "No way!" God mutters, "It's way too hot for me there!" "I've got it", St. Peter says, his face lighting up. "How about going Down to Earth for your vacation?" Chuckling, God remarks, "Are you kidding? Two thousand years ago I went there, had an affair with some nice Jewish girl, and they're STILL talking about it!"

I woke to go to the toilet in the middle of the night and noticed a burglar sneaking through next door's garden.

Suddenly my neighbour came from nowhere and smacked him over the head with a shovel killing him instantly. He then began to dig a grave with the shovel.

Astonished, I got back into bed.

My wife said, "Darling, you're shaking, what is it?"

"You'll never believe what I've just seen!", I said. "That tosser next door has still got my bloody shovel."

A teacher told her young class to ask their parents for a family story with a moral at the end of it, and to return the next day to tell their stories.

In the classroom the next day, Joe gave his example first, "My dad is a farmer and we have chickens. One day we were taking lots of eggs to market in a basket on the front seat of the truck when we hit a big bump in the road;

the basket fell off the seat and all the eggs broke. The moral of the story is not to put all your eggs in one basket."

"Very good", said the teacher.

Next, Mary said, "We are farmers too. We had twenty eggs waiting to hatch, but when they did, we only got ten chicks. The moral of this story is not to count your chickens before they're hatched."

"Very good", said the teacher again, very pleased with the responses so far.

Next it was Dave's turn to tell his story: "My dad told me this story about my Aunty Barbara…. Aunt Barbara was a flight engineer in the war and her plane got hit. She had to bail out over enemy territory and all she had was a bottle of whiskey, a machine gun, and a machete."

"Go on", said the teacher, intrigued.

"Aunt Barbara drank the whole bottle of whiskey on the way down to prepare herself. Then she landed right in the middle of a hundred enemy soldiers. She killed seventy of them with the machine gun until she ran out of bullets. Then she killed twenty more with the machete 'til the blade broke. And then she killed the last ten with her bare hands."

"Good heavens", said the horrified teacher, "What did your father say was the moral of that frightening story?"

"If you value your life, stay away from Aunt Barbara when she's been drinking."

A rather confident man walks into a bar and takes a seat next to a very attractive woman. He gives her a quick glance, then casually looks at his watch for a moment. The woman notices this and asks, "Is your date running late?"

"No", he replies, "I just bought this state-of-the-art watch and I was just testing it."

The intrigued woman says, "A state-of-the-art watch? What's so special about it?"

"It uses alpha waves to telepathically talk to me", he explains.

"What's it telling you now?" she asked.

"Well, it says you're not wearing any panties", he said.

The woman giggles and replies, "Well it must be broken then because I am wearing panties!"

The man explains, "Damn thing. Must be an hour fast."

A man was standing looking into a store window. He had just been to the bakery and was holding a loaf of bread in his right hand and had his other hand in his pocket.

The local vicar strolled past and noticed the man with the loaf of bread and said, "Ah my son! I see you have the staff of life in your hand."

To which the man replied, "Yes vicar I do. And I have a loaf of bread in the other one."

It's Saint Patricks Day and an armed hooded robber bursts into the Bank of Ireland and forces the tellers to load a sack full of cash.

As the robber is leaving with the loot, one brave Irish customer grabs his hood and pulls it off revealing his face.

The robber shoots the guy dead.

He then looks around the bank to see if anyone else has seen him.

One of the tellers is looking straight at him so the robber walks over and calmly shoots him dead too.

Everyone is now terrified and looking down at the floor.

The robber shouts angrily, "Did anyone else see my face?"

There's a brief silence then one elderly Irish man, still looking down, tentatively raises his hand and says, "I think me wife here may have caught a glimpse."

The Presbyterian church called a meeting to decide what to do about their squirrel infestation. After much prayer and consideration, they concluded that the squirrels were predestined to be there, and they should not interfere with God's divine will.

At the Baptist church, the squirrels had taken an interest in the baptistry. The deacons met and decided to put a water-slide on the baptistry and let the squirrels drown themselves. The squirrels liked the slide and, unfortunately, knew instinctively how to swim, so twice as many squirrels showed up the following week.

The Lutheran church decided that they were not in a position to harm any of God's creatures. So, they humanely trapped their squirrels and set them free near the Baptist church. Two weeks later, the squirrels were back when the Baptists took down the water-slide.

The Episcopalians tried a much more unique path by setting out pans of whiskey around their church in an effort to kill the squirrels with alcohol poisoning. They sadly learned how much damage a band of drunk squirrels can do.

But the Catholic church came up with a more creative strategy! They baptized all the squirrels and made them members of the church. Now they only see them at Christmas and Easter.

Not much was heard from the Jewish synagogue. They took the first squirrel and circumcised him. They haven't seen a squirrel since.

I met an older woman in a bar last night. She looked pretty good for a woman who must have been in her sixties. In fact, she wasn't bad at all.

I found myself thinking she probably had a hot daughter. We drank quite a few beers and then some spirits and then she asked if I had ever had a 'Sportsman Double'.

"What's that", I asked her.

"It's a mother and daughter threesome", she replied.

As my mind began to embrace the idea, and I wondered what her daughter might look like, I said, "No I haven't".

We drank a bit more and she winked at me and said sexily, "Tonight's going to be your lucky night big boy".

We went back to her place. I was nervous with anticipation of the fantastic night ahead, and an experience to always remember.

We walked in, she turned on the hall light and shouted upstairs……..

"Mother, you still awake?"

A wealthy man was having an affair with an Italian woman for a few years.

One night, during one of their rendezvous, she confided in him that she was pregnant.

Not wanting to ruin his reputation or his marriage, he paid her a large sum of money if she would go to Italy to have the child. If she stayed in Italy, he would also provide child support until the child turned 18.

She agreed, but wondered how he would know when the baby was born. To keep it discrete, he told her to mail him a post card, and write "Spaghetti" on the back. He would then arrange for child support.

One day, about 9 months later, he came home to his confused wife.

"Honey", she said, "you got a very strange post card today."

"Oh, just give it to me and I'll explain it later", he said.

The wife obeyed, and watched as her husband read the card, turned white, and fainted.

On the card was written "Spaghetti, Spaghetti, Spaghetti. Two with meatballs, one without."

Barry goes to the supermarket and notices a beautiful blond woman wave at him and say hello.

He's rather taken aback, because he can't place where he knows her from.

So he says, "Do you know me?"

To which she replies, "I think you're the father of one of my kids."

Now his mind travels back to the only time he has ever been unfaithful to his wife and says, "My God, are you the stripper from my bachelor party that I screwed on the pool table with all my buddies watching, while your partner whipped my butt with wet celery, tickled my balls with an egg beater and then stuck a carrot up my butt???"

She looks into his eyes and calmly says,

"No, I'm your son's maths teacher."

While reading an article last night about fathers and sons, memories came flooding back to the time I took my son out for his first pint.

Off we went to our local pub only two blocks from the cottage.

I got him a Guinness. He didn't like it, so I drank it.

Then I got him a Kilkenny's, he didn't like that either, so I drank it.

Finally, I thought he might like some Harp Lager? He didn't. I drank it.

I thought maybe he'd like whisky better than beer so we tried a Jameson's.

Nope!

In desperation, I had him try that rare Redbreast, Ireland's finest whisky.

He wouldn't even smell it. What could I do but drink it!

By the time I realised he just didn't like to drink, I was so shit-faced I could hardly push his stroller back home!!!

A big Texan stopped at a local restaurant following a day roaming around the countryside.

While sipping his tequila, he noticed a sizzling, scrumptious looking platter being served at the next table.

Not only did it look good, the smell was wonderful. He asked the waiter, "What is that you just served?"

The waiter replied, "Ah Senor, you have excellent taste! Those are called Cojones de Toro, bull's testicles from the bull fight this morning. A delicacy!"

The cowboy said, "What the heck, bring me an order."

The waiter replied, "I am so sorry, senor. There is only one serving per day because there is only one bull fight each morning. If you come early and place your order, we will be sure to save you this delicacy."

The next morning, the cowboy returned, placed his order, and that evening was served the one and only special delicacy of the day.

After a few bites, inspecting his platter, he called to the waiter and said, "These are delicious, but they are much, much smaller than the ones I saw you serve yesterday."

The waiter shrugged his shoulders and replied, "Eh, Senor. Sometimes ze bull, he wins."

When I was young, I wanted to be a doctor, so I took the entrance exam to go to Medical School.

One of the questions asked was to rearrange the letters PNEIS into the name of an important human body part which is most useful when it is erect.

Those who answered spine are doctors today. The rest of us are probably just sick or need a good talking to.

A soldier approached a nun. Out of breath he said, "Please, may I hide under your skirt, I'll explain later?" The nun agreed. A moment later, two Military Police came running up and asked, "Sister, have you seen a soldier?"

The nun replied, "He went that way." After the MP's ran off, the soldier crawled out from under the nuns skirt and said, "Thankyou so very much sister. You see, I don't want to go to Syria." The nun replied, "I understand completely."

The soldier added, "I hope I'm not being rude or forward, but you have a great pair of legs."

The nun replied, "Well! If you had looked a little higher, you would have seen a great pair of balls as well. I don't want to go to Syria either."

Three Irishmen were comparing parts of their bodies and realized that they all had something that was probably the smallest of anybody in the world. As luck would have it, the offices of The Guinness Book of Records were just over the road so each went in to see if they would be famous.

Paddy went in first with his incredibly small thumb and came out 30 minutes later, very happy and with a certificate saying he had the smallest thumb in the world.

Michael then went in with his really tiny nose and he also emerged with a certificate.

Shamus, very confident, went in with his extremely tiny and pathetic penis. He emerged about an hour later without a certificate and in a filthy mood exclaiming, "Who the bloody hell is ...." (use the name of the biggest idiot at your club who is listening to your joke)

Mrs. Sullivan returned home to Ireland from a vacation to France where she had taken a French Cooking class.

She tells her husband Seamus that she is going to prepare him a special meal for St. Valentine's Day, and that he is to go down to Murphy's Market and buy two dozen escargot, which she explains to Paddy are snails.

be no stops at the pub.

Well Seamus buys the snails and is on his way home, but alas his route takes him right past his favourite pub, and he can't bring himself to walk on by without stopping for a pint. Just one he tells himself. Well, perhaps another he says after having the first pint.

The company is good, the tales are tall, and Seamus finds himself having three or more pints, and the time passes...

As Seamus heads home in a rather alcoholic daze, he realizes it has become dark, and knows his lovely wife will be waiting and sharpening her tongue for him, never a pleasant experience, as Seamus rightly knows.

As he opens the gate to his home the porch light comes on, and he hears the door begin to open

Quickly, Seamus empties the bag of snails on the ground, and says in a loud voice, "Come on now lads! You're almost there."

.

A Russian communist in the 1970's went to the local car dealer to order a new car. Things were pretty tight under communism and luxuries hard to get. The car salesman said that the man had to pay a deposit of twenty percent of the purchase price right now and the car would then be ordered and would arrive in ten years time.

"Ten years", the man protested. "That's an awful long time to wait. Will it come in the morning or the afternoon?"

"How the hell would I know", said the salesman. "After ten years, what difference would it make."

"Because the plumber is coming in the morning."

WITTY SMART ALEC ONE LINERS

Why is it that the people with the smallest minds always have the biggest mouths?

What did the elephant say to the naked man? 'How do you breathe out of that thing?'

What is the difference between a Harley and a vacuum cleaner?
The location of the dirt bag.

You're not acting like yourself today. I noticed the improvement right away.

They said you were a great asset. I told them they were off by two letters.

Is that your nose or are you eating a banana?

I stood up for you the other day. Someone said you didn't have the brain of an ant. But I said you did.

You are such a smart ass I bet you could sit on a carton of ice cream and tell what flavour it is.

What's the difference between an Irish wake and an Irish wedding? One less drunk.

Politicians and baby's nappies have one thing in common: they should both be changed regularly… and for the same reason.

The other day my wife asked me, "Could you go to the shop for me on the way home from work and buy one litre of milk and if they have avocados, get 6."

When I got home with 6 litres of milk she asked me, "Why did you buy 6 litres of milk?"

I replied, "Because they had avocados."

A drunk gets up from the bar and heads for the toilet. A few minutes later, a loud, blood curdling scream is heard coming from that direction. A few minutes after that, another loud scream reverberates through the bar.
The bartender goes to investigate why the drunk is screaming.
"What's all the screaming about in there?" he yells. "You're scaring my customers!"
"I'm just sitting here on the toilet", slurs the drunk, "and every time I try to flush, something comes up and squeezes the hell out of my balls."
With that, the bartender opens the door where the screams are coming from, looks in and says, "You idiot! You're in the cleaner's room and sitting on the mop bucket!"

FUNNY AND RATHER SILLY

A woman bought some goods on the internet and when she came to pay, instead of giving her credit card details she gave her Organ Donor details. Wound up costing her an arm and a leg.

I would have loved to have played a part in one of those Clint Eastwood spaghetti westerns. Being a religious person, I think I could play the part of the local pasta.

Paddy goes on a first aid course. The instructor asks, "What would you do if your child swallowed the front door key?"

Paddy says, "I'd climb in through 'da window."

An idiot got a letter through the letterbox of his front door and it landed on the floor.

In big bold letters on the front was written, 'DO NOT BEND.'

The idiot is still there trying to work out how he is going to pick it up.

"Would you like anything on your chips?"

"Does it cost extra?"

"Fifty cents."

"Alright. I'll have that with four sausages and a steak pie."

Punched the doctor this morning.

"That's for saying my wife has a nice fanny."

The Doc screamed, "You idiot. I said she has acute angina."

Seamus says to Murphy, "Me mate came off his motor bike today."

"Oh really," Murphy said.

"Yes. He has brain damage, two broken ribs and is blind in one eye," replied Seamus.

"Bloody hell," says Murphy, "no wonder he came off."

Paddy is on the radio doing a live quiz. The presenter says, "Paddy, for $500, can you tell me, 'Who was the first woman on earth.'"

Paddy goes quiet for a few seconds and says, "Gimme a clue."

"Go on then", says the presenter. "Think of an apple."

Paddy's eyes light up and he blurts out, "That's easy. It's Granny Smith."

I had a really dodgy curry earlier and said to my wife, "My arseholes on fire."

She said, "Ring sting?"

"How the hell is HE going to help" I replied.

Just say "NO" to drugs. "Well, If I'm talking to my drugs....I probably already said "YES"

After looking for love in all the wrong places, a man returns from the Middle East and is feeling very ill. He goes to see his doctor, and is immediately rushed to the Hospital to undergo tests.

The man wakes up after the tests in a private room at the hospital. No one is around but there is a phone by his bed and it rings.

"This is your doctor. We've had the results back from your tests and we've found you have an extremely contagious and nasty STD called 'G.A.S.H.' It's a combination of Gonorrhea, AIDS, Syphilis, and Herpes!"

"Oh, my gosh," cried the man, "what are you going to do, doctor?"

"Well, we're going to put you on a diet of pizzas, pancakes, and pita bread."

"Will that cure me???" asked the man.

The doctor replied, "Well no, but....they're the only foods we can get under the door."

So, I'm driving down the highway south of Sydney with my girlfriend in my Mustang convertible, and we get stuck in heavy traffic. Glorious sunny day with the top down, not a care in the world. Me in just a pair of speedos and my girlfriend in a brief pink bikini. My girlfriend is blonde by the way, head full of hair, a stereo-typical blonde in many ways, and that's not just because we had the top down either, it's just the way she is. Anyhow, my girlfriend looks across at the car that is alongside, and says, "I think those people in the car next to us are foreigners."

Puzzled at this I said: "Really? Why do you think that?"

"Well, the young boys in the back are writing on the inside of their window and it says: 'stit ruoy su wohs'".

WITTY SHORT QUIPS

MAN: "Doc, I keep thinking I'm a pair of curtains."
DOC: "For heaven's sake man, pull yourself together."

STAN: "I regret the day I was married."
DAN : "Consider yourself lucky. I was married for a whole month."

MERYL: "I remember when my husband added some magic to our marriage."
BERYL : "That's so sweet. What did he do?"
MERYL "He disappeared."

HERB: "My uncle did his Christmas shopping really early."
MERV: "How early."
HERB: "Real early, about 5.00 am."
MERV: "Wow! That is early. What did he get?"
HERB: "Six months in jail. The store wasn't open yet."

MAX: "Doc, I'm feeling really suicidal. What should I do?"

DOC: "Pay me in advance."

MAY: "That handsome XRAY specialist is thinking of proposing to Jessica."

FAY: "Sigh! I wonder what he sees in her."

HERB: "So you haven't spoken to your wife for a month."

MERV: "No, she hates it when I interrupt her."

STAN: "A man came to the door today collecting for the new municipal swimming pool."

DAN: "What did you give him?"

STAN: "Two glasses of water."

MAN: "My good mate Gav died yesterday from taking heartburn tablets.

Can't believe Gavisgon."

BERT: "A police officer came to my door and asked me where I was between 5 and 6. He seemed irritated when I answered, 'Kindergarten'."

ME   : Please bring me a screwdriver

WIFE : Flat head, Phillips or Vodka.

And that was when I knew she was the one.

My girlfriend is very short and she gets fed up with me making fun of her height.

So tonight, I'm going to make it up to her.

I've got a good bottle of wine and I have downloaded a whole series of her favourite TV show on Netflix. When she gets in from work, I'm going to order her favourite takeaway which we'll sit and eat while we drink the wine and watch the downloaded TV show.

Then afterwards, I'm going to go upstairs and run her a nice hot sink.

On a beautiful deserted island in the middle of nowhere, the following group of people are ship wrecked:-

2 Italian men and 1 Italian woman
2 French men and 1 French woman
2 German men and 1 German woman
2 Greek men and 1 Greek woman
2 Bulgarian men and 1 Bulgarian woman
2 Japanese men and 1 Japanese woman
2 Chinese men and 1 Chinese woman
2 Australian men and 1 Australian woman
2 Irish men and 1 Irish woman and
2 English men and 1 English woman.

One month later on the same island in the middle of nowhere, the following things have occurred:

One Italian man killed the other Italian man for the Italian woman.

The two French men and the French woman are living happily together in a ménage-à-trois.

The two German men have a strict weekly schedule of alternating visits with the German woman.

The two Greek men are sleeping with each other and the Greek woman is cleaning and cooking for them.

The two Bulgarian men took one long look at the endless ocean, another long look at the Bulgarian woman, and started swimming.

The two Japanese men have faxed Tokyo, and are awaiting instructions.

The two Chinese men have set up a pharmacy, a liquor store, a restaurant and a laundry, and have got the woman pregnant in order to supply employees for their stores.

The two Australian men are contemplating suicide because the Australian woman keeps complaining about her body; the true nature of feminism; how she can do everything they can do; the necessity of fulfilment; the equal division of household chores; how sand and palm trees make her look fat; how her last boyfriend respected her opinion and treated her nicer than they do; how her relationship with her mother is improving, and how at least the taxes are low and it isn't raining.

The two Irish men have divided the island into North and South and have set up a distillery. They do not remember if sex is in the picture because it gets sort of foggy after the first few litres of coconut whisky. But they're satisfied because at least the English aren't having any fun.

And last but not least, the two English men are waiting for someone to introduce them to the English woman.

A high school English teacher reminds her class of tomorrow's final exam.

"Now class, I won't tolerate any excuses for you not being there tomorrow. I might consider a nuclear attack or a serious personal injury or illness, or a death in your immediate family, but that's it, no other excuses whatsoever."

A smart arse guy in the back of the room raises his hand and asks, "What would you say if tomorrow I said I was suffering from complete and utter sexual exhaustion?"

The entire class does its best to stifle their laughter and snickering. When silence is restored, the teacher smiles sympathetically at the student, shakes her head, and sweetly says, "Well, I guess you'd have to write the exam with your other hand."

An elderly Irish lady visits her physician to ask his advice on reviving her husband's libido.

"What about trying Viagra?" asked the doctor.

"Not a chance" she replied. "He won't even take an aspirin".

"Not a problem", said the doctor. "Give him an Irish Viagra."

"What on Earth is Irish Viagra?" she asked.

"It's Viagra dissolved in his morning cup of coffee. He won't even taste it.

Let me know how it goes", he said. She called the doctor the very next afternoon.

"How did it go?" he asked.

"Oh Jesus Doctor, it was terrible. Just horrid, I tell ya! I'm beside myself!"

"Oh, no! What in the world happened?" asked the doctor

"Well, I did the deed, Doctor, just as you advised.

I put the Viagra in his morning coffee, and he drank it.

Well, you know, it took effect almost immediately, and he jumped straight up out of his chair with a smile on his face, a twinkle in his eye and his pants a-bulging.

Then, with one fierce swoop of his arm, he sent the cups, saucers, and everything else that was on the table flying across the room ripped my clothes to tatters and passionately took me then and there, right on top of the table. T'was a nightmare, I tell ya, an absolute nightmare!"

"Why so terrible?" asked the doctor. "Wasn't the sex good?"

"Freakin jaysus, it was the best sex I've had in me last 25 years, but sure as I'm sittin' here, Doctor... I'll never be able to show me face in Starbucks again!"

At the end of the tax year the Tax Office sent an inspector to audit the
books of a synagogue. While he was checking the books he turned to the Rabbi and said, "I notice you buy a lot of candles. What do you do with the candle drippings?"
"Good question", noted the Rabbi. "We save them up and send them back to the candle makers, and every now and then they send us a free box of candles."

"Oh", replied the auditor, somewhat disappointed that his unusual question had a practical answer.
But on he went, in his obnoxious way: "What about all these bread-wafer purchases? What do you do with the crumbs "
"Ah, yes", replied the Rabbi, realizing that the inspector was trying to trap him with an unanswerable question, "we collect them and send them back to the manufactures, and every now and then they send us a free box of bread-wafers."

"I see", replied the auditor, thinking hard about how he could fluster the know-it-all Rabbi.

"Well, Rabbi", he went on, "what do you do with all the leftover foreskins from the circumcisions you perform?"

"Here, too, we do not waste", answered the Rabbi. "What we do is save all the foreskins and send them to the Tax Office, and about once a year they send us a complete dick."

Two young businessmen in Chadstone shopping Centre were sitting down for a break in their soon-to-be new store in the shopping mall.
As yet, the stores merchandise wasn't in -- only a few shelves and display racks set up.
One said to the other, "I'll bet that any minute now some halfwit senior is going to walk by, put his head in the door and ask what we're selling."
Sure enough, just a moment later, a curious senior

gentleman walked up to the door, looked around intensely and in a loud voice asked, "What are you selling here?"

One of the men replied sarcastically, "We're selling arse-holes."

Without skipping a beat, the old timer said, "You must be doing well. Only two left."

The pastor asked if anyone in the congregation would like to express praise for an answered prayer. Suzie stood and walked to the podium.

She said, "I have a praise. Two months ago, my husband, Phil, had a terrible bicycle wreck and his scrotum was completely crushed. The pain was excruciating and the doctors didn't know if they could help him."

You could hear a muffled gasp from the men in the congregation as they imagined the pain that poor Phil must have experienced.

"Phil was unable to hold me or the children", she went on, "and every move caused him terrible pain. We prayed as the doctors performed a delicate operation, and it turned out they were able to piece together the crushed remnants of Phil's scrotum, and wrap wire around it to hold it in place."

Again, the men in the congregation cringed and squirmed uncomfortably as they imagined the horrible surgery performed on Phil.

"Now", she announced in a quivering voice, "thank the Lord, Phil is out of the hospital and the doctors say that with time, his scrotum should recover completely."

All the men sighed with unified relief. The pastor rose and tentatively asked if anyone else had something to say.

A man stood up and walked slowly to the podium. He said, "I'm Phil." The entire congregation held its breath.

"I just want to tell my wife that the word is STERNUM."

AN ODE TO A FLY

There once was a fly and he flew into a store
He pooped on the ceiling, and he pooped on the floor
He pooped on the onions and he pooped on a can
And he pooped all over the grocer man.

Now the grocer man got his 'Mortein' gun
To shoot that fly on its little brown bum
But before you could count out nine or ten
He had jolly well pooped on the grocer again.

Now the fly flew here, and the fly flew there
He pooped while flying through the air
He pooped on the window and he pooped on the wall
He didn't care where he pooped at all.

So the grocer man chased him around and around
The fly pooped silently without a sound
Then all of a sudden, he flew out the door
Cos' that poor little fly couldn't poop no more.

A Scotsman is due to get married and he and his friend Archie are sitting in their local pub discussing Jock's forthcoming wedding.

"Ach, it's all goin' grand", says Jock. "I've got everything organised already: the flowers, the church, the cars, the reception, the rings, the minister, even ma stag night."

Archie nods approvingly.

"Heavens, I've even bought a kilt to be married in!" continues Jock.

"A kilt?" exclaims Archie, "that's braw, you'll look pure smart in that!"

"And what's the tartan?" Archie then enquires.

"Och", says Jock, "I'd imagine she'll be in white."

Three long serving dedicated Italian nuns were killed tragically in a car crash and went to heaven and were met by St Peter who said, "Ah, the three nuns from St Mary's. We've been expecting you. As a matter of fact, God here and myself have decided to send you all back to Earth for a short period as anyone you like."

The first nun was most excited and said, "I lika to go back asa Gina Lollabrigida because she sucha beautifula lady and doa gooda things for people." And poof, the nun was gone.

The second nun, equally excited said, "I lika to go back asa Sophia Loren because she sucha nicea woman and a very generous to a da sicka people." And poof, she was gone.

The third nun said, "I lika to go back asa Saharra Pippelini."

God looked at St Peter and then the nun and said, "Who is this person. I know everyone in the world and have never heard of a Saharra Pippelini. Can you give some clue as to who she is?"

With that the nun pulled a newspaper clipping from her habit, handed it to God who read, 'Sahara pipeline laid by two thousand men in 5 days.'

Hamish asked the bus conductor how much the bus fare was into Glasgow city centre.

"50p", said the bus conductor.

Hamish thought this was a bit much, so he decided to run behind the bus for a few stops.

"How much is it now?", he gasped.

"Still 50p", said the bus conductor.

Hamish ran three further stops behind the bus, and was barely able to ask the bus conductor again what the fare was now.

"75p", said the bus conductor.

"What! How the hell could that be?", gasps Hamish.

And the bus conductor says, "You idiot. You are running in the wrong direction."

Paddy the Irishman dies and is met at the pearly gates by Saint Peter. Paddy sees all the wonderful things inside and can't wait to get in.

"Just hang on a minute Paddy", the saint says, "we just don't let anyone in here you know. You are going to have to pass an I.Q. test by answering three questions."

Paddy says, "Oi, Oi, Oi. I'm not too good on them. But I'll give it a go."

Saint Peter said, "OK Paddy, first question. How many days of the week start with the letter 'T'?".

"Oi that's easy", says Paddy. "It's two."

"Very good Paddy, and what are they."

"Today and Tomorrow."

"No! No! Paddy, that's not quite what I had in mind but I'll let you off this time", said Saint Peter. "Now the second question is, 'How many seconds are there in a year'?"

"Oi! Oi! Oi! I've never been good at that sort of thing. I'll come back to you", said Paddy.

Thirty minutes later Paddy is back. "The answer is twelve", Paddy said.

"Twelve. How did you get twelve?" asked Saint Peter.

"Well, there's the second of January, the second of February........"

"No! No! Paddy. That's not what we are after. But because you have been a good person, I'll let you in if you can answer the third question. Are you ready? The question is, how many 'D's are there in the song Rudolph the Red Nosed Reindeer?" asked the saint.

"Oi! Oi!" said Paddy looking perplexed. "I'll have to have a count."

Ten minutes later Paddy was back. "I have the answer", said Paddy. "It's ninety four."

"Ninety four", exclaimed the Saint, "how did you get that answer?"

"Easy", said Paddy. As he flicked fingers in the air he started counting and singing to the tune of the song, "de de, de de de de de, de............"

The pastor stood before the congregation and said, "I have bad news, I have good news, and I have more bad news."

The congregation went quiet.

"The bad news is: the roof leaks water and we need a new roof." The congregation groaned… heard it all before.

"The good news is: we have enough money for the new roof."

A sigh of relief was heard rippling through the gathered faithful.

"The more bad news is: it's still in your pockets."

A barrister opened the door of his Aston Martin DB11, when suddenly a car came along and hit the door, ripping it off completely. When the police arrived at the scene, the barrister was complaining bitterly about the damage to his precious Aston Martin. "Officer, look what they've done to my DB11!!!", he whiningly said.

"You barristers are so materialistic, you make me bloody sick!!!" retorted the officer, "You're so worried about your stupid Aston Martin, that you didn't even notice that your right arm was ripped off!!!"

"Oh my god....", replied the lawyer, finally noticing the bloody right shoulder where his arm once was. And in a wild panic he screamed, "Where's my Rolex?"

Two cowboys are out on the range talking about their favourite sex position. One says, "I think I enjoy the rodeo position the best." "I don't think I have ever heard of that one", says the other cowboy. "What is it?" "Well, it's where you get your girl down on all fours, and you mount her from behind. Then you reach around, cup her breasts, and whisper in her ear, 'boy these feel almost as nice as your sisters.' Then you try and hold on for 30 seconds."

A popular bar had a new robotic bartender installed. A guy came in for a drink and the robot asked him, "What's your IQ?" The man replied, "130." So the robot proceeded to make conversation about physics, astronomy, and so on. The man listened intently and thought, "This is really cool." Another guy came in for a drink and the robot asked him, "What's your IQ?" The man responded, "120." So the robot started talking about football, dirt bikes, and so on. The man thought to himself, "Wow, this is really cool." A third guy came in to the bar. As with the others, the robot asked him, "What's your IQ?" The man replied, "40." The robot then said, "So, how are things in Canberra these days?"

Robin Hood was old, feeble and dying. King Richard had allowed him to see out his last days in a room high in one of the castle towers so he could overlook his beloved Nottingham Forest.

Gathered around Robin were his trusted merry men. "Little John", he wheezed out, "bring me my long bow and my straightest arrow. I will fire the arrow through the open window towards Nottingham Forest and where it lands, that is where I wish to be buried."

Knowing that Robin was very weak did not deter the men from conforming to their leader's request.

They sat Robin up in his bed, placed the long bow in his trembling feeble hands and placed the arrow onto the string. Robin slowly raised the bow and arrow, and with the last of his remaining strength, and shaking violently from the exertion, he pulled back on the bow and let the arrow go to his final resting place.

And that is why Robin Hood was buried..........on top of the wardrobe.

Once upon a time, a guy asked a girl, "Will you marry me?"

The girl said, "No!"

And the guy lived happily ever after and rode motorcycles and watched sport on a big screen TV, went fishing and surfing, and played golf a lot, and drank beer and scotch and had tons of money in the bank and left the toilet seat up and passed wind loudly whenever he wanted. Now how lucky is that?

Justine and Melissa were walking across a bridge over a small country stream.

"I'm dying to have a pee", she said, "but there's no toilets."

"Don't worry", said Justin, "just stick your butt over the bridge and I'll hold onto your hands."

She pulled up her skirt and sat with her butt over the edge.

"My God", she screamed, "there's a man in a canoe down there!"

Justine peered over the edge. "You fool, that's no canoe, that's your reflection."

FUNNY RELIGIOUS NONSENSE

A Sunday school teacher asked, "Johnny, do you think Noah did a lot of fishing when he was on the Ark?"

"What!" replied Johnny. "How the hell could he with just two worms?"

The Sunday School teacher was describing how Lot's wife looked back and turned into a pillar of salt, when little Jason interrupted, "My Mummy looked back once while she was driving", he announced triumphantly, "and she turned into a telephone pole!"

While driving in the backwoods of the Tasmanian highlands, a family caught up to an old couple driving a horse and carriage. The owner of the carriage obviously had a sense of humour, because attached to the back of the carriage was a hand printed sign..."Energy efficient vehicle: Runs on oats and grass. Caution: Do not step in exhaust."

And the Lord said unto John, "Come ye forth and ye will receive eternal life."
But John came fifth and won a toaster.

A redneck from the south of the USA, was sick and tired of hearing about how dumb people are in the South. So, he decided to take a maths test specially designed for Rednecks and to show the "so called smart people" just how smart he was.

The test follows. See how you go when it comes to this kind of maths.

-Calculate the smallest limb diameter on a persimmon tree that will support a 10 pound possum.

-Which of these cars will rust out the quickest when placed on blocks in your front yard?
(A) '65 Ford Fairlane
(B) '86 Dodge Diplomat
(C) '80 Ford pickup.

-If your uncle builds a still which operates at a capacity of 20 gallons of moonshine produced per hour, how many car radiators are required to condense the product?

-A woodcutter has a chainsaw which operates at 2700 RPM. The density of the pine trees in the plot to be harvested is 470 per acre. The plot is 2.3 acres in size. The average tree diameter is 14 inches. How many cold beers will be drunk before the trees are cut down?

-A front porch is constructed of 2×8 pine on 24-inch centres with a field rock foundation. The span is 8 feet and the porch length is 16 feet. The porch floor is 1-inch rough sawn pine. When the porch collapses, how many dogs will be killed?

- A man owns a house and 3.7 acres of land in a hollow with an average slope of 15%. The man has five children. Can each of his grown children place a mobile home on the man's land and still have enough property for their electric appliances to sit out front?

-A 2-ton truck is overloaded and proceeding 900 yards down a steep slope on a secondary road at 45 MPH. The brakes fail. Given average traffic conditions on secondary roads, what is the probability that it will strike a vehicle with a muffler?

-With a gene pool reduction of 7.5% per generation, how long will it take a town which has been bypassed by the Interstate to breed a country-western singer?

A man went to his proctologist for an anal examination with the intention of having a colonoscopy.

When the specialist opened the door and invited the patient into his office for the examination, the man noticed that the proctologist had a 30 centimetre rectal thermometer behind his ear. Amused at the sight he said to the proctologist, "Do you always go around with a long rectal thermometer wedged behind your ear?"

The proctologist gasped, grabbed the thermometer, looked at it and said, "Oh hell! Either I have just found a 30 centimetre rectal thermometer.... or some bums got my biro!"

A brash American from Texas was visiting the UK and while in London he realised that he had forgotten to pack any razor blades in his luggage.

He found a branch of 'Boots The Chemists' on the High Street, located the aisle with the men's shaving items, but he was unable to find what he wanted.

"Y'all got any American razor blades in here?" the Texan asked the pharmacist. "All ah' I see are these goddamn Wilkinsons."

"Sir", the Englishman patiently replied, "Wilkinson has been producing the finest surgical instruments, weapons and razors since before the Battle of Waterloo."

"Ah' don't give a damn if they passed them out on Noah's Ark, they ain't any good", the Texan retorted haughtily.

"I can assure you they are very good sir", the peeved pharmacist said. "Why just last year, my wife swallowed one. It gave her a tonsillectomy, an appendectomy, a hysterectomy, circumcised the gardener, emasculated a neighbour, cut two of a delivery boy's fingers off at the knuckle — and I still got 10 shaves out of it!"

A couple had been married to each other for many years and made a deal with each other that whoever died first would come back and inform the other of the afterlife. Their biggest fear was that there would not be any heaven. After a very long life, the husband was the first to go, and true to his word, he established contact.

As Mary lay dozing in her bed, she heard the curtains moving and rustling gently and then she heard a hoarse raspy, "Mary....Mary...."

Sitting bolt upright in bed she said, "Is that you, Fred?"

"Yes, I've come back like we agreed."

"What's it like there Fred?"

"Wonderful! I get up in the morning, and I have sex. I have breakfast, I have sex again, I bathe in the sun, then I have sex twice more. I have lunch, then sex pretty much all afternoon. After supper, I have sex until late at night. The next day it starts over again."

"Oh, Fred you must surely be in heaven!"

"Not exactly", says Fred. "I'm a rabbit somewhere out the back of Broken Hill".

WITTY THOUGHTFUL THOUGHTS

If you can't think of a word, then say, "I forgot the English word for it." That way people will think you're bilingual instead of stupid.

I'm at a place in my life where errands are starting to count as going out.

I just did a week's worth of cardio after walking into a spider web.

I don't mean to brag, but I finished my 14-day diet food supply in 3 hours and 20 minutes.

A recent study has found women who carry a little extra weight live longer than men who mention it.

Kids today don't know how easy they have it. When I was young, I had to walk 3 metres through shag carpet to change the TV channel.

A thief broke into my house last night. He started searching for money so I got up and searched with him.

I think I'll just put an "Out of Order" sticker on my forehead and call it a day.

Just remember, once you're over the hill you begin to pick up speed.

Having plans sounds like a good idea until you have to put on clothes and leave the house.

Never sing in the shower! Singing leads to dancing, dancing leads to slipping, and slipping leads to paramedics seeing you naked. So remember...Don't sing!

I see people about my age mountain climbing; I feel good getting my leg through my underwear without losing my balance.

My wife asked if she could have a little peace and quiet while she cooked dinner. So being an obliging caring husband, I took the battery out of the smoke alarm.

I took the shell off my racing snail to see if it would make him faster. If anything, it made him more sluggish.

The Queen visits a mental hospital and goes to the first ward. The first patient she sees is sitting up and with his left hand he seems to be grabbing something from the air. She asks, "What are you doing?" The patient replies, "I'm taking the stars from the sky!"
She then proceeds over to the second patient and he seems to be inserting something into the air. She asks, "What are you doing love?"
The second patient replies, "I'm putting the stars back in the sky!"
Finally, she reaches the third patient and he's sitting up pretending he's a rally driver and is making high speed noises.
She asks him, "What the hell are you up to?"
The patient replies, "I'm trying to get away from these two idiots, they're completely nuts."

Quasimodo, the Hunchback of Notre Dame, was learning how to ring the cathedral bells. One of the cathedral priests was his teacher, while the Abbot was on the ground watching. "Now Quasi", he said, "you need to grab this rope at shoulder height, and give it a strong pull."
Quasimodo did this and immediately went flying up in the air, smashed his nose on the big bell and fell back to the floor of the bell tower, moaning and groaning in agony and with blood everywhere.
"No, no Quasi! You have to hold the rope higher, pull harder, and this time look where you are going."
This Quasimodo did and immediately again went flying up in the air, smashed his chin on the big bell and fell back on to the bell tower floor groaning and dribbling profusely.
"No, no Quasi, you still haven't got it. Give it a really big pull this time."

Quasimodo did as requested, went flying up in the air, got his head caught between two bells smashing both cheek bones, fell to the floor, rolled over in agony straight out the open window and landed on his back on the ground thirty metres below, right at the Abbots feet.

Hearing all the commotion, the Bishop came out, saw the mangled head of Quasimodo and demanded of the Abbot, "What's that man's name?" To which the Abbot replied, "I don't know, but the face sure rings a bell."

An attractive young woman on a flight from Ireland asked the priest beside her, "Father, may I ask a favour?"

"Of course child. What may I do for you?"

"Well, I bought my mother an expensive hair dryer for her birthday. It is unopened but well over the customs limits and I'm afraid they'll confiscate it. Is there any way you could carry it through Customs for me? Hide it under your robes perhaps?"

"I would love to help you, dear, but I must warn you, I will not lie."

"With your honest face, Father, no one will question you", she replied.

When they got to Customs, she let the priest go first. The official asked, "Father, do you have anything to declare?"

"From the top of my head down to my waist I have nothing to declare."

The official thought this answer strange, so asked, "And what do you have to declare from your waist to the floor?"

Father replied, "I have a marvellous instrument designed to be used on a woman, which is, to date, unused."

Roaring with laughter, the official said, "Go ahead, Father. Next please!"

There was a young man called Shaun
Who was wondering why he'd been born
Well he wouldn't have been
If his father had seen
That the end of the rubber was torn.

FUNNY SMART SHORT ONES

Son complains to his mother, "Mummy, they told me at school that I have gigantic feet."
Mother strokes his head, "What utter nonsense. Let's talk about this later. Now, park your shoes in the garage, dinner is ready."

A guy runs with a machine gun into the local mens chess club and yells: "Which one of you nerdy sleazy scabs slept with my wife? I'm gonna kill ya."
A chess player looks up and says: "You know man, I think you're gonna need a bigger gun."

You know you're ugly when you get handed the camera every time they make a group photo.

If you donate a kidney, everybody loves you and you're a total hero.
But try donating five kidneys – people start yelling, police get called – sheesh.

The doctor gave me one year to live. So in the heat of the moment, I shot him. And the judge gave me 15 years. Problem solved.

If you need to break up with somebody, the best place to do so is McDonalds.
There are no plates or glasses to be broken over your head, no sharp knives or spiky forks, plus you can always hide behind a fat kid.

Why do hurricanes get such lame names, like 'Sandy' or 'Patty'? Name that thing 'Hurricane Death Megatron 900' and I guarantee folks will be evacuating like they need to.

When I see lover's names carved in a tree, I don't think it's sweet. I just think it's surprising how many people bring a knife on a date.

So, you think there's no good news about having Alzheimer's?
Well, not only can you buy and wrap your own surprise presents, but you are constantly making new friends every ten minutes or so.

Man to a butcher: "I'd like bull's testicles."
Butcher: "Hell, So would I."

The thing is, single women come home, see what's in the fridge, and go to bed.
Married women come home, see what's in the bed, and go to the fridge.

I pulled into the crowded parking lot at the local shopping centre, parked the car and rolled down the windows to make sure my Labrador Retriever Pup had fresh air.

She was laid there fully stretched out on the back seat and I wanted to impress upon her that she must remain there.

So, as I walked to the curb backward, I pointed my finger at the car and saying emphatically: "Now you stay. Do you hear me? Stay! Stay!"

An old geezer who saw me parking, gave me a strange look and said: "Why don't you just put it in PARK?"

An idiot walks into a pharmacy and asks for bottom deodorant.

The assistant, a little bemused, explains to the idiot they have never sold bottom deodorant.

The idiot, unfazed, assures the lady behind the counter, that he has been buying the stuff from here on a regular basis, and would like some more.

The shop assistant thinks for a minute, knowing full well that they don't stock or sell such an item, smiles at the idiot and says, "One moment please, I will get the pharmacist."

The pharmacist looks at the idiot and says, "Can I help you sir?"

"I would like to buy some bottom deodorant please", says the idiot.

"I'm sorry", says the pharmacist, "we don't have any."

"But I always get it here", says the idiot.

"Do you have the container it comes in?"

"Yes!" Said the idiot, "I will go and get it."

He returns with the container and hands it to the pharmacist who looks at it and says to the man, "This is just a normal stick of under-arm deodorant."

The annoyed idiot snatches the container back and reads out loud from the container, "To apply, push up bottom."

A Siamese princess from Baroda
Once built quite a remarkable pagoda
The halls and the walls
Were festooned with the balls
And the tools of the fools who bestrode her.

The priest in a small Irish village loved the rooster and ten hens he kept in the hen house behind the church. One Sunday morning, before mass, he went to feed the birds and discovered that the cock was missing. He knew about cock fights in the village, so he decided to question his parishioners in church. During mass, he asked the congregation, "Has anybody got a cock?" All the men stood up. "No, no", he said, "that wasn't what I meant. Has anybody seen a cock?" All the women stood up. "No, no", he said, "that wasn't what I meant. Has anybody seen a cock that doesn't belong to them?" Half the women stayed up. "No, no", he said, "that wasn't what I meant either. Has anybody seen MY cock?" Sixteen altar boys, two priests and a goat stood up. The priest fainted.

It only took the doctor about 2 seconds to say, "Give me a break, lady! Your daughter is pregnant!"
The mother turned red with fury, and she argued with the doctor that *her* daughter was a good girl, and would *never* compromise her reputation by having sex with a boy.
The doctor faced the window and silently watched the horizon.
The mother became enraged and screamed, "Quit looking out the window! Aren't you paying attention to me?"
"Yes, of course I am paying attention, ma'am. It's just that the last time this happened, a star appeared in the east, and three wise men came. I was hoping they'd show up again, and help me figure out who got your daughter pregnant."

An old man lived alone in Ireland. He wanted to dig his potato garden, but it was very hard work.

His only son, who would have helped him, was in prison for bank robbery.

The old man wrote a letter to his son and mentioned his predicament.

Shortly, he received this reply,

"For HEAVEN'S SAKE Dad, don't dig up that garden, that's where I buried the Money!"

At 4 A.M. the next morning, a dozen policemen showed up and dug up the entire garden, without finding any money.

Confused, the old man wrote another note to his son telling him what happened, and asking him what to do next.

His son's reply was: "Now plant your potatoes, Dad. It's the best I could do from here."

A man who smelled like a distillery flopped on a subway seat next to a priest.

The man's tie was stained, his face was plastered with red lipstick, and a half-empty bottle of gin was sticking out of his torn coat pocket.

He opened his newspaper and began reading.

After a few minutes the disheveled guy turned to the priest and slurs, "Shay, Father, what causes arthritis?"

"Mister, it's caused by loose living, being with cheap, wicked women, too much alcohol, and a contempt for your fellow man."

"Wow", the drunk muttered, returning to his paper.

The priest, thinking about what he had said, nudged the man and apologized. "I'm very sorry, I didn't mean to come on so strong. How long have you had arthritis?"

"I don't have it, Father. I was just reading here that the Pope does."

After my recent Prostate Exam, which was one of the most thorough and intrusive examinations I've ever had, the Doctor left and the nurse came in.

As she shut the door, she asked me a question I didn't want to hear....

She said...."Who WAS That Guy?"

A little boy goes to his dad and asks, "What is Politics?"

Dad says, "Well son, let me try to explain it this way:

I am the head of the family, so call me The Prime Minister.

Your mother is the administrator of the money, so we call her the Government.

We are here to take care of your needs, so we will call you the People.

The nanny, we will consider her the Working Class.

And your baby brother, we will call him the Future.

Now think about that and see if it makes sense."

So the little boy goes off to bed thinking about what Dad has said.

Later that night, he hears his baby brother crying, so he gets up to check on him.

He finds that the baby has severely soiled his nappy.

So the little boy goes to his parent's room and finds his mother asleep.

Not wanting to wake her, he goes to the nanny's room. Finding the door locked, he peeks in the keyhole and sees his father in bed with the nanny.

He gives up and goes back to bed. The next morning, the

little boy says to his father, "Dad, I think I understand the concept of politics now."

The father says, "Good, son, tell me in your own words what you think politics is all about."

The little boy replies, "The Prime Minister is screwing the Working Class while the Government is sound asleep. The People are being ignored and the Future is in deep shit."

I was stuck in a traffic jam outside Canberra this morning. No-one was moving at all.

Then this guy knocked on my window. I rolled it down and said, "What's happening?"

He said, "Terrorists have kidnapped the entire House of Representatives from inside the Houses of Parliament and they say they will douse them in petrol and set them all on fire if they are not paid a $100 million dollar ransom. We're going from car to car collecting donations."

"How much is everyone giving?" I asked.

He said, "About a litre but a lot of them are still siphoning."

Mr. Brown, the old history teacher, had a dirty mouth and lecherous mind. He was always saying something off-colour or suggestive.

One day after class, Sandra approaches his desk with a flock of girls in tow.

"Mr. Brown", she said, "We are tired of your filthy remarks and we aren't going to put up with it anymore! The next time you say something nasty in class, we are all going to complain to the principal."

Mr. Brown was silent and the girls stormed off thinking they had cowed him.

The next day as everyone arrives in class, Mr. Brown is reading the newspaper.

The bell rings, but he continues to read. Finally, he looks up and says, "Oh girls, you should find this interesting. The government is recruiting whores to go to Afghanistan and screw the servicemen over there for $100 a day."

All at once the girls get up and head for the door.

"Wait a minute!" shouted Mr. Brown. "The plane doesn't leave till Thursday!"

PETE THE PIDDLING PUP

A country dog once came to town his Christian name
was Pete
His pedigree was metres long and his looks were hard
to beat
He sauntered down the roadway, 'twas beautiful to see
His work on every corner, his work on every tree.

He watered every gateway, he watered every post
For piddling was his masterpiece, for piddling was his
boast
The city dogs looked longingly on in deep and jealous
rage
At this simple country dog, the piddler of the age.

They sniffed him over one by one, they smelled him
two by two
But noble Pete in high disdain stood still till they were
through
They sniffed beneath his stumpy tail, their praise for
him was high
But when one sniffed him underneath, Pete piddled in
his eye.

Then just to show the other dogs he didn't give a damn
Walked straight into a grocer's shop and piddled on
their ham
He piddled on the onions, he piddled on the floor
And when the grocer kicked him out, he piddled on the
door.

Behind him all the city dogs decided what to do
They'd hold a piddling carnival to see the stranger
through
They showed him all the piddling posts they knew
around the town
And started out with many winks to wear our hero
down.

Pete was with 'em every time, with vigour and with vim
A thousand piddles more or less were just the same to him
All along went noble Pete with hind leg kicking high
Most were lifting legs in bluff or piddling mighty dry.

On and on went noble Pete, he watered every sandhill
Till all the city piddling champs were piddled to a standstill
Then Pete an exhibition gave on all the ways to piddle
Like little drips and double flips and then the fancy dribble.

And all this time the country dog did neither wink nor grin
But gayly piddled out of town as he had piddled in
The city dogs said, "Off ya' go, you've brought us to our knees"
But no-one ever put them wise, that Pete had diabetes.

There was an old man in a nursing home who always fell out of his wheelchair. Finally, the nurses decided to do something about it, so they appointed a nurse to watch him all the time. He started to lean forward so the nurse stuck a pillow in front of him. Then he started to lean backward so she stuck a pillow behind him. Then he started to lean to the left so she stuck a pillow to the left of him. Then he leaned to the right and she stuck a pillow to the right of him. Later on that day, his son came to visit him and asked him how he was enjoying his new home.

"The food is good, the people are nice, it's quiet at night but there's one thing I hate." "What's that Dad?" said the son.

"Well, every time I want to pass wind, the nurses shove another bloody pillow under me."

My Polish neighbour, Stanislav, went into an optician's for an eye test.

The optician held up a card with CZWJNYSACZ on it and asked him if he could read it?

Stanislav said excitedly, "Read it? He's my best friend."

An American businessman goes to India on a business trip, but he hates Indian food, so he asks the concierge at his hotel if there's any place around where he can get American food. The concierge tells him he's in luck; there's a pizza place that just opened, and they deliver. The concierge gives the businessman the phone number, and he goes back to his room and orders a pizza. Thirty minutes later, the delivery guy shows up to the door with the pizza. The businessman takes the pizza, smells the familiar aromas deeply and starts sneezing uncontrollably. He asks the delivery man, "What the heck did you put on this pizza?" The delivery man bows deeply and says in his sing song accent, "We put on the pizza what you ordered sir, pepper only."

One evening a couple were at home watching television and the man was eating peanuts.

He would toss them in the air, one at a time, then catch them in his mouth.

Having just thrown one peanut, his wife asked him a question, and as he turned his head to answer her, the peanut fell in his ear.

He tried and tried to dig it out, but unfortunately only succeeded in pushing it in deeper.

He called his wife for assistance, and after hours of trying to dislodge the peanut, they became worried and decided to go to the hospital.

As they were getting ready to go out the door, their daughter came home with her latest date.

After being informed of the problem, the young man said he could get the peanut out.

The young man told the father to sit down, then proceeded to shove two fingers up the father's nose and told him to blow hard.

When the father blew his nose, the peanut flew out of his ear.

The mother and daughter jumped and yelled for joy.

The young man insisted that it was nothing and the daughter took the young man out to the kitchen for something to eat.

Once he was gone, the mother turned to the father and said, "That's so wonderful! Isn't he smart? What do you think he is going to be when he grows older?"

The father replied, "From the smell of his fingers, our son in-law."

Stan and Dan were friends for more than 30 years. Their friendship had weathered innumerable arguments. However, Stan being the more intelligent one, had fared better than Dan in business, which was a constant source of irritation to Dan.
Stan was on his death bed with Dan hovering over him. Apparently in his last few moments, Stan called Dan close to him and said, "Dan, you know we've been friends for 30 years now, and even though we have had numerous disagreements, I have this one last wish which only you, my friend, can grant. "Will you do it?"
"Just tell me what it is Stan", said Dan, "and I'll do it happily. Anything for you my friend."

"You know Dan, there's this bottle of the finest 20 year old single malt whisky which I have been saving for the last 15 years. I want you to pour it over my grave when I'm gone. Will you do it?"
"Sure thing Stan", said Dan. And remembering all the put-downs and insults he had received over the years he added, "but would you mind if I passed it through my kidneys first?"

An Englishman, a Scotsman, and an Irishman all walk into a pub with their wives.

They all sit down and order a cup of tea. The Englishman looks to his wife and says, "Could you pass the honey, honey?"

The Scotsman thinks to himself how clever that was, then turns to his wife and says, "Could you pass the sugar, sugar?"

The Irishman, not wanting to be out witted by the other two men, looks over at his very ordinary wife and says, "Could you pass me the tea.....bag?"

At a parole hearing, the officer asked, "Tell me, why should you be released early?"

The inmate responded, "It's bec..."

Officer: "Yes?"

Inmate: "I think I have…."

Officer: "Go on."

Inmate: "Can I please finish my sentence?"

Officer: "Sure. Parole denied. Next prisoner!"

There was a young pirate called Bates
Who did the fandango on skates
But a slip on his cutlass
Rendered him nutless
And totally useless on dates.

NEW YEARS EVE PARTY INVITATION

FAIRY LIGHTS, LAIRY TIGHTS, STEAMY NIGHTS, LOVE BITES,

DANCIN' SHOES, NUMBER TWOS, BOYFRIEND BLUES, CARROT SPEWS,

JOCK RAIDS, FRENCH MAIDS, SEX AIDES, GET LAID,

LOVE STARES, UNDERWEARS, TRUTH AND DARES, HELL WHO CARES,

BUSH BASHIN', GATE CRASHIN', TYRE SLASHIN', TONGUE PASHIN',

ROOTIN' TOOTIN', HOG SHOOTIN', TAN BOOTIN', BIRTHDAY SUITIN',

COCKTAIL FRANKS, SCHOOLYARD PRANKS, SEPTIC TANKS, SLEAZY WANKS,

BULLSHIT LINES, CASKED WINES, SIXTY NINES, PARKING FINES,

SHORT SKIRTS, DIRTY FLIRTS, HAWAIIAN SHIRTS, JUST DESSERTS,

DRINKING GAMES, DIZZY DAMES, FAMOUS NAMES, HOME JAMES,

ROCKIN' EDDIE, SURFIN' FREDDIE, ROUGH AND READY, BACKYARD HEADY,

FRILLS AND BOWS, BLOODY NOSE, BATHROOM THROWS, CURLED TOES,

BROKEN HEARTS, BODY PARTS, MUSIC CHARTS, SMELLY FARTS,

LOUD NOISE, SEX TOYS, STYLE N POISE, BLONDE BOYS,

GRABBIN' TITS, CRACKIN' SHITS, PINKY BITS, ONE SIZE FITS,

HARD ROCKIN', TIK-TOKKIN', CROWDS FLOCKIN', NIK-NOCKIN',

ROOF RAISIN', HELL BLAZIN', KNEE GRAZIN', SO AMAZIN',

ARTY-FARTYS, TOUGHS AND TARTYS,

......COME AND JOIN THE NEW YEARS PARTY......

FUNNY WITTY AND QUICK

Got the wife a pug dog yesterday. Despite the squashed nose, the bulging eyes and the rolls of fat......the dog seems to like her.

Dirty Derek, our local flasher, was thinking about retiring.
But he's decided to stick it out for another year.

I've just pulled up on our driveway to see some thieving bastard run out our back door and jump over the fence.
The wife must have put up a damn good fight though....she's half naked, drenched in sweat and can hardly bloody walk.

Paddy says to Mick, "I found this pen, is it yours?"
Mick replies, "I don't know. Give it here." He then tries it and says, "Yes, it is."
Paddy says, "How do you know?"
Mick replies, "That's my hand writing."

I walked into a restaurant and asked an obviously very effeminate male for a table for two.
He lisped, "Thertainly thir, walk thith way."
He sashayed his way to a table with his little quick short steps and I said, "Mate, if I 'walked that way', I would need baby powder in my undies to stop the chafing."

As the coffin was being lowered into the ground at a Parking Officer's funeral, a voice from inside screams:
"I'm not dead, I'm not dead. Let me out!"
The Vicar smiles, leans forward, sucking air through his teeth and mutters,
"Too late, mate, the paperwork's already done."

AN ODE TO MY WILLY

My nookie days are over
My pilot light is out
What used to be my pride and joy
Is now my water spout.

Time was when, on its own accord
From my trousers it would spring
But now I've got a full-time job
To find the friggin' thing.

It used to be embarrassing
The way it would behave
For every single morning
It would stand and watch me shave.

But now as old age creeps up fast
It sure gives me the blues
To see it hang its little head
And watch me tie my shoes!!

A man walks into a bar in Sydney and orders a glass of Irish whisky. As the bartender slides the drink to the patron, a man sitting next to him remarks, "That's a coincidence, I, too, am enjoying an Irish whisky. Since I arrived from the old country, this is the only bar in which I have found this particular brand."

To which the first replies, "Old country, I'm from the old country. Let me buy you another!"

As the drinks are being poured, one of the men asks, "What part of the old country are you from?"

"Dublin", replies the other.

"This is weird", says the first, "I, too, am from Dublin! Let's get another shot."

After the new round arrives, the first asks, "So, pal, what did you do back in Dublin?"

"Not much, really, I came here right out of high school. I graduated from Michael O'Leary Technical Academy in '81."

"This is so eerie", replies the other, "I'm O'Leary Tech, '81. Let's get another shot."

But the bartender says, "Slow down fellas, I gotta make a call."

The bartender calls his wife and tells her that he'll be late getting home. When she inquires as to the cause, he replies, "Oh bloody hell. The friggin' idiot O'Reilly twins are here again."

The Chief Financial Officer for a large corporation had some highly confidential documents that he needed to be processed. He waited until everyone had gone home, such was the secrecy of these documents. He headed to the machine room and was confronted by an array of printers, scanners, video equipment, faxes, PCs and was rather overawed.

Not being tech savvy, he had no idea what machine to use when he espied a young geeky lad pounding away on a computer. He approached the young man and thought he would know all about these machines and he said to him, "I have some documents here. Highly confidential. No one is allowed to see them. I need to process them but don't know which machine to use." Eager to help, the young lad grabs the highly confidential documents and says, "No worries sir, I know exactly what to do. Leave it to me." With that, the young man proceeded to feed them in to the shredding machine, careful not to even glance at the all important documents, while the CFO browsed around the room looking at all the unfamiliar machines.

The CFO stood back, thinking how good it was to be in charge and to be able to rely on lesser people to do the hard work, when the young man yelled over the noise, "Won't be long now Sir. Almost finished." To which the officer replied, "No worries son. Take your time. I only need ONE copy of each page."

There was an elderly man who wanted to make his younger wife pregnant. So, he went to the doctor to have a sperm count done.
The doctor told him to take a specimen cup home, fill it, and bring it back the next day.
The elderly man came back the next day and the specimen cup was empty and the lid was on it.
Doctor: "What was the problem?"
Elderly man: "Well, I tried with my right hand... nothing. So, I tried with my left hand...nothing. My wife tried with her right hand... nothing. Her left hand... nothing. Her mouth...nothing. Then my wife's friend tried. Right hand, left hand, mouth.... still nothing."
Doctor: "Wait a minute. You mean your wife's friend too?"
Elderly man: "Yeah, and we still couldn't get the damn lid off of the specimen cup."

WITTY SHORT AND HUMOROUS

Murphy says to Paddy, "What ya talkin' into an envelope for?"
"I'm sending a voicemail ya fool!"

Paddy says, "Mick, I'm thinking of buying a Labrador."
"Blow that", says Mick, "have you seen how many of their owners go blind?"

19 paddies go to the cinema and the ticket lady asks, "Why so many of you?"
Mick replies, "The film said 18 or over."

I went to the cemetery yesterday to lay some flowers on a grave.
As I was standing there I noticed 4 grave diggers walking about with a coffin, 3 hours later and they're still walking about with it.
I thought to myself, they've lost the plot!!

My daughter asked me for a pet spider for her birthday, so I went to our local pet shop and they were $70!!!
Blow this, I thought, I can get one cheaper off the web.

Statistically, 6 out of 7 dwarfs are not Happy.

My neighbour knocked on my door at 2:30am this morning, can you believe that, 2:30am?!
Luckily for him I was still up playing my Bagpipes.

Two Muslims have crashed a speedboat into the Thames barrier in London .
Police think it might be the start of Ram-a-dam.

Sat opposite an Indian lady on the train today, she shut her eyes and stopped breathing.
I thought she was dead, until I saw the red spot on her forehead and realised she was just on standby.

When I was in the pub, I heard a couple of halfwit idiots saying that they wouldn't feel safe on an aircraft if they knew the pilot was a woman.
What a pair of sexists. I mean, it's not as if she'd have to reverse the bloody thing!

Local Police hunting the 'knitting needle nutter' who has stabbed six people in the rear in the last 48 hours, believe the attacker could be following some kind of pattern.

Just got back from my mate's funeral. He died after being hit on the head with a tennis ball.
It was a lovely service.

At a wedding party recently, someone yelled, "All married people, please stand next to the one person who has made your life worth living."
The bartender was almost crushed to death.

I had far too many drinks the other night, so I left my car and took a bus instead. Thought I was doing the right thing.
Turns out I'm just as hopeless at driving a bus when I'm drunk as I am driving a car.

An eighty-year-old man was having an annual physical. As the doctor was listening to his heart with the stethoscope, he began muttering, "Oh Oh!"
The man asked the doctor, "What's the problem?"
"Well", said the doc, "you have a serious heart murmur. Do you smoke?"
"No", replied the man.
"Do you drink in excess?"
"No", replied the man.
"Do you have a sex life?"
"Yes, I do!"
"Well", said the doc, "I'm afraid with this heart murmur, you'll have to give up half your sex life."
Looking perplexed, the old man said, "O.K. Which half are we talking about. The looking or the thinking?"

Apparently, 1 in 5 people in the world are Chinese. There are 5 people in my family, so it must be one of them. It's certainly not me. It's either my Mum or my Dad, or my older Brother Colin, or my younger Brother Ho-Cha-Chu? But I think it's Colin.

Little Johnny is out trick or treating on Halloween dressed as a pirate. He walked up to a house and said "trick or treat". The little old lady just gushed over his costume. She says to Johnny, "What a cute costume, but let me ask you, where are your buccaneers?" Little Johnny says straight back, "On the side of me buckin' head lady."

A man is out shopping and discovers a new brand of condoms called 'Olympic Condoms'. Clearly impressed, he buys a pack.

Upon getting home he announces to his wife the purchase he just made.

"Olympic condoms?" she blurts out. "What makes them so special?"

"They come in three colours", he replies, "Gold, Silver and Bronze."

"What colour are you going to wear tonight?" she asks cheekily.

"Gold of course", says the man proudly.

The wife responds wryly, "Why don't you wear Silver? It would be nice if you came second for a change."

Two elderly gentlemen from a retirement centre were sitting on a bench under a tree when one turns to the other and says:

"George, I'm 83 years old now and I'm just full of aches and pains. I know you're about my age. How do you feel?"

George says, "I feel just like a newborn baby."

"Really!? Like a newborn baby!?"

"Hell yeah! No hair, no teeth, and I think I just peed in my pants."

THE OFFICIAL AUSTRALIAN POO LIST

GHOST POO :

You know you've pooed. There's poo on the toilet paper but none in the toilet.

TEFLON COATED POO :

It comes out so slick and clean that you don't even feel it. No trace of poo on the toilet paper. You have to look in the toilet to be sure you did it.

GOOEY POO :

This has the consistency of hot fresh tar. You wipe 12 times and you still don't come clean.

You end up putting toilet paper in your underwear so you don't stain them. The poo leaves permanent skid marks in the toilet.

SECOND THOUGHT POO :

You're all done wiping and you're about to stand up when you realise it......you've got some more.

POP A VEIN IN YOUR FOREHEAD POO :

This is the kind of poo that killed Elvis. It doesn't want to come out until you are sweaty, trembling and purple from straining so hard.

WEIGHT WATCHERS POO :

You poo so much, you lose several kilograms.

Right NOW POO :

You'd better be within 30 seconds of a toilet. You burn rubber getting to the toilet.

Usually has its head out before you can get your pants down.

King KONG OR DUNNY CHOKER POO :

This one is so big that you know it won't go down the toilet unless you break it into smaller chunks.

A wire coat hanger works well. This kind of poo usually happens at someone else's house.

Cork POO (Also known as floaters) :

Even after the third flush, it's still floating in the bowl. My God! How do I get rid of it?

Wet CHEEKS POO :

The poo hits the water sideways and makes a big splash that gets you all wet.

Wish POO :

You sit there all cramped up, fart a few times. But no poo.

Cement BLOCK POO (with extra blue metal) :

You wish you'd gotten a spinal block before you pooed. Usually has rough bits of undigested food sticking out the side of it.

Snake POO :

This poo is fairly soft and about as thick as your thumb and at least 3 feet long.

BEER DRINK AND MEAT PIE POO :

This happens the day after the night before. Normally your poo doesn't smell too bad, but this one is BAD......usually this one happens at someone else's house and there's someone standing outside waiting to use the bathroom.

MEXICAN FOOD POO :

You'll know it's alright to eat again when your bum stops burning.

FRIGHTENINGLY REAL, ISN'T IT

Derek the drunk, rode to the liquor store on his bicycle and bought a bottle of Jameson Whiskey that he then put in the bicycle basket.
As he was about to peddle home, he thought, "If I fall off the bicycle, the bottle will fall out of the basket and break." To avoid such a catastrophe Mick decided to drink the bottle of whiskey before he travelled. It turned out to be a very good decision, because he fell off the bike seven times on the way home.

Bert saw his neighbour Alf, heading down the street with a suitcase in his hand and asked where he was going.
  "I'm off to see my sister in Sydley", he said.
  "Sydley!! There's no such place", said Bert.
  "Of course there is. You know, with the opera house and harbour bridge."
  "You idiot. You mean SydNEY not SydLEY."
  "Yeah. That's what I said diddle I."

A man came home from work one day to find his wife on the front porch with her bags packed.

"Just where the heck do you think you're going!', said the man.

"I'm going to Las Vegas", said the wife. "I just found out I can get $400 a night for what I give you for free!"

The man said, "Wait a minute!", and then ran inside the house only to come back a few minutes later with his suitcases in hand.

"Where the heck are you going?", said the wife.

The man said, "I want to see how you're gonna live on $800 a year!"

Two doctors, a psychiatrist and a proctologist, opened an office in a small town and put up a sign reading: "Dr. Smith and Dr. Jones: Hysterias and Posteriors." The town council was not happy with the sign, so the doctors changed it to read: "Schizoids and Hemorrhoids."

This was not acceptable either, so in an effort to satisfy the council, they changed the sign to: "Catatonics and High Colonics." No go.

Next, they tried: "Manic Depressives and Anal Retentives." Thumbs down again.

Then came: "Minds and Behinds." Still no good.

Another attempt resulted in: "Lost Souls and Butt Holes." Unacceptable again!

So they tried: "Analysis and Anal Cysts." Not a chance. "Nuts and Butts." No way. "Freaks and Cheeks." Still no go. "Loons and Moons." Forget it.

Almost at their wit's end, the doctors finally came up with: "Dr. Smith and Dr. Jones, Odds and Ends."

Everyone loved it.

The Prime Minister of New Zulland, is awoken at 4am by the telephone.

"Sir, it's the Hilth Munister here. Sorry to bother you at this hour but there is an emergency. I've jist received word thet the condom factory en Aucklind hes burned to the ground. It is istimated that the entire New Zulland supply of condoms will be gone by the ind of the week."

PM: "Shut. The economy wull niver be able to cope with all those unwanted babies. We will be ruined."

Hilth Munister: "We're going to haf to shup some in from Brutain?"

PM: "No chence. The Poms will have a field day on thus one."

Hilth Munister: "What about Australia?"

PM: "I'll call the Aussies. Tell them we need one million condoms, ten enches long and four enches thuck. That way they'll continue to respect the 'All Blacks'."

Three days later, a delighted PM rushes out to open the boxes that arrived at the Pust Office.

He finds one million condoms - 10 enches long, 4 enches thuck, all coloured green and gold with small writing on each one.

"MADE IN AUSTRALIA - SIZE: SMALL"

A little old man shuffled slowly into an ice cream parlour and pulled himself slowly, painfully, up onto a stool. After catching his breath, he lifted a gnarled and crooked finger and pointed at the menu on a board on the wall and ordered a banana split with whipped cream and chocolate flavouring on top.

The waitress enquired kindly, "Crushed nuts?"

"No," he replied, "Arthritis."

A drunken man staggers in to a Catholic church and wanders over to the confessional box. He opens the door, sits down and says nothing.

The bewildered priest waits for a few minutes, allowing the drunken man some time to collect his thoughts.

Growing impatient, the priest coughs to attract his attention, but still the man says nothing.

The priest then knocks on the wall three times in a final attempt to get the man to speak.

Finally, the drunk replies: "No use knockin' mate, there's no paper in this one either."

A politician visited a small town in outback Queensland and asked what their needs were.

"We have 2 basic needs, sir", replied the local mayor. "Firstly, we have a hospital, but there's no doctor."

On hearing this, the politician whipped out his mobile phone, and after speaking for a while he reassured the mayor that the doctor would be there the next day.

He then asked about the second problem.

"Secondly sir, there is no mobile phone coverage anywhere in this area."

An idiot walked into a green grocers shop and was cheerfully approached by the grocer. When asked what he would like, the idiot said, "I would like a water melon, a pineapple and a coconut." This was duly placed in a bag and the grocer asked if there was anything else he wanted. The man said, "Oh yes. A kilo of tomatoes."

"Terribly sorry sir", said the grocer, "but we haven't got any tomatoes, can't get them anywhere. However, I believe the supermarket down the street has some."

With that the idiot left only to return ten minutes later. Thinking the man had forgotten something the amiable grocer asked him what he wanted. "Er, a kilo of tomatoes please", said the idiot. The bemused grocer told him he must not have heard him before, that he did not have any tomatoes but the supermarket had some.

The idiot disappeared again only to return shortly and again ask for a kilo of tomatoes.

"Listen", an increasingly agitated grocer said, "I have told you, there are no tomatoes here!! None what so ever!! All gone!! Can't get them!! Go to the supermarket."

Once again the idiot left but returned within ten minutes. Very agitated, the grocer gritted his teeth and asked, "What-do-you-want?"

"Kilo of tomatoes please."

The grocer lost it and roared, "I have told you three times we have no tomatoes. We can not get them. We have nil, nought, nix, none." Thinking how he could convince the idiot once and for all there were no tomatoes, he grabbed the idiots bag, reached in and dragged out the water melon and red faced and angry said, "Listen you idiot, if I take this water melon and take out the WATER in it, what have I got?"

And the idiot said, "Duh, melon."

"Right!!!! And if I take this pineapple, and I take out the PINE in it, what have I got?"

"Duh, apple."

Right!!! And if I take this coconut, and take out the COCO in it, what have I got?"

"Duh, nut."

"Right!!!", the grocer screamed. "And if I take a tomato, and I take out the FRIG in it, what have I got?"

And the idiot said, "Duh, HUH!!! But there's no frig in tomatoes."

"That's right", roared the grocer. "There's no FRIGGIN' tomatoes."

Mick was meeting a friend at the pub and as he went in, he noticed two pretty girls looking at him.

"Nine," he heard one whisper as he passed them.

Feeling arrogantly pleased with himself, he swaggered over to his pal and told him a girl had just rated him a nine out of ten.

"I don't want to ruin it for you", his friend said, "but when I walked in, they were speaking German."

A man and his wife were supposed to go to a costume party together one New Years Eve, but when the time came to go to the party, the woman told him to go on without her, because she said she had a terrible headache.

The man reluctantly did, and the suspicious wife decided to see just how faithful her man really was. She put on a different costume and went to the party.

When she got there, she saw her husband in his costume dancing with a young girl in a sexy costume. Now, even more suspicious, she decided to really put him to the test. She danced with him and whispered that they should sneak into a bedroom. She insisted they leave the masks on and had sex with him.

Fuming, she ran home to wait for his return. When he got there, she innocently asked if he'd had fun. He told her he hadn't.

He said that after a few minutes at the party, he and some guys had gone across the street to play poker.

He added, "The guy who borrowed my costume said he had a hell of a time, though!"

The old bloke was a bit embarrassed, but he had to see the doctor.

"I'm worried, doc", he said. "I met this twenty five year old woman last night and she made passionate love to me. Since then, my old fella has swollen to twice its normal size, it's become red and itchy and there's a discharge beginning to appear."

The doctor examined him.

"You'd better sit down", he said. "You're about to cum."

The new priest was so nervous at his first mass, he could hardly speak. Before his second appearance in the pulpit, he asked the monsignor how he could relax. The Monsignor said, "Next Sunday, it may help if you put some vodka in the water pitcher. After a few sips, everything should go smoothly."

The next Sunday the new priest put the suggestion into practice and was able to talk up a storm. He felt great.

However, upon returning to the rectory, he found a note from the monsignor. It read:

1. Next time, sip rather than gulp.
2. There are 10 commandments, not 12.
3. There are 12 disciples, not 10.
4. We do not refer to the cross as the big 'T'.
5. The recommended grace before meals is not "rub-a-dub-dub, thanks for the grub, yeah God."
6. Do not refer to our saviour, Jesus Christ and his apostles as "J.C. and The Boys".
7. David slew Goliath. He did not kick the crap out of him.
8. The Father, Son, and Holy Spirit are never referred to as "Big Daddy, Junior and, The Spook".
9. It is always the Virgin Mary, never "Mary with the Cherry".
10. Jesus was Consecrated, NOT constipated.
11. David was hit by a rock and knocked off his donkey, he wasn't "stoned off his ass."

A sexually active, middle-aged woman informed her plastic surgeon that she wanted her vaginal lips reduced in size because, over the years, they had become loose and floppy.

Out of embarrassment, she insisted that the surgery be kept a secret and, of course, the surgeon agreed.

Awakening from the anaesthesia after surgery, she found 3 roses carefully placed beside her on the bed.

Outraged, she immediately called in the surgeon. "I thought I specifically asked you not to tell anyone about my operation!"

The surgeon told her he had carried out her wish for confidentiality and that the first rose was from him:

"I felt so sad for you, because you went through this all by yourself."

"The second rose is from my nurse. She assisted me in the surgery and understood perfectly, as she had the same procedure done some time ago."

"And what about the third rose?" the woman demanded.

"That's from a man upstairs in the burns unit - he wanted to thank you for his new ears."

Very sad news has just been reported by CNN News in America today, that Walt Disney's new film called "Jet Black," the African American version of "Snow White" has been cancelled.

All of the seven dwarfs: Dealer, Stealer, Mugger, Forger, Drive-By, Homeboy and Shank have refused to sing "Hi Ho, Hi Ho" because they say it offends black prostitutes.

They also say there ain't no way in hell they're gonna sing.....

"It's off to work we go."

Harold and Jenny have been married for forty years, and during all that time Harold had always wanted to own an expensive pair of cowboy boots.

He had been a fan of the old Western movies and television shows about cowboys since he was a young lad, so seeing some cowboy boots on sale one day, he buys a pair and proudly wears them home.

He swaggers into the kitchen, doing his best cowboy walk, and asks Jenny, trying to put on his best John Wayne accent, "So Jenny, do you notice anything different about me?"

"What's different? It's the same shirt you wore yesterday and the same pants. What's different?", says Jenny.

Frustrated, Harold goes into the bathroom, undresses and comes out completely naked, wearing only his new boots.

Again he asks Jenny, "Do you notice anything different?"

"What's different, Harold? Its hanging down today, it was hanging down yesterday, and it will be hanging down tomorrow."

Angrily, Harold yells at her, "Do you know why it's hanging down? Cause it's looking at my NEW BOOTS."

Jenny replies, "You should have bought a hat."

During a recent meeting in Heaven, God, Moses and Saint Peter concluded that the behaviour of former President Clinton had brought about the urgent need for an eleventh commandment, particularly since there is a chance that Bill would get into the White House again if Hilary wins.

They worked long and hard in a brain-storming session, trying to settle on the wording of the new commandment, because they realized that it should have the same style, majesty and dignity as the original ten.

They persevered and, after many revisions, finally agreed that the eleventh Commandment should be:

"Thou shalt not comfort thy rod with thy staff."

…Amen!

A man walks into a bar, notices a very large jar on the counter,

and sees that it's filled to the brim with $10 notes.

He guesses there must be at least ten thousand dollars in it.

He approaches the bartender and asks, "What's with the money in the jar?"

"Well., you pay $10, and if you pass three tests, you get all the money in the jar and the keys to a brand new Lexus."

The man certainly isn't going to pass this up, so he asks, "What are the three tests?"

"No! No! No! You gotta pay first", says the bartender, "those are the rules."

So, after thinking it over a while over five or six schooners, the man gives the bartender $10 which he stuffs into the jar.

"Okay", says the bartender, "here's what you need to do:

First - You have to drink a whole bottle of tequila, in 60 seconds or less, and you can't make a face while doing it and you must keep it in."

"Second - There's a pit bull dog chained in the back with a bad tooth. You have to remove that tooth with your bare hands."

"Third - There's a 90-year old lady upstairs who's never had sex. You have to take care of that problem."

The man is stunned. "I know I paid my $10 -- but I'm not an idiot. I won't do it.

You'd have to be nuts to drink a bottle of tequila and then do all those other things."

"Your call", says the bartender, "but, your money stays where it is."

As time goes on, the man has a few more drinks, eyeing off the huge horde of money on offer and finally says, "OK! Where's the damn tequila?"

He grabs the bottle with both hands and drinks it as fast as he can. Tears stream down both cheeks but he doesn't make a face -- and he drinks it in 58 seconds.

Next, he staggers drunkenly out the back door where he sees the pit bull chained to a pole.

Soon, the people inside the bar hear loud growling, screaming, and sounds of a terrible fight, then nothing but silence.

Just when they think that the man surely must be dead, he staggers back into the bar. His clothes are ripped to shreds and he's bleeding from bites and gashes all over his body.

He looks at the barman through heavily glazed eyes and drunkenly slurs,

"Now...., wheresh dat old sheila wiff da' bad tooth?"

The executive was interviewing a young nerdy graduate for a position in his company.

He wanted to find out something about their personality so he asked, "If you could have a conversation with any person, living or dead, who would that be?"

The nerd quickly responded, "The living one."

An attractive blonde from Cork, Ireland arrived at the casino. She seemed a little intoxicated and bet twenty-thousand Euros on a single roll of the dice.

She said, "I hope you don't mind, but I feel much luckier when I'm completely naked."

With that, she stripped from the neck down, rolled the dice and with an Irish brogue yelled, "Come on, baby, Mama needs new clothes!"

As the dice came to a stop, she jumped up and down and squealed: "YES! YES! I WON, I WON!"

She hugged each of the dealers and then picked up her winnings, and her clothes, and quickly departed.

The dealers stared at each other dumbfounded. Finally, one of them asked, "What did she roll?"

The other answered, "I don't know - I thought you were watching the dice."

These two idiots are building a house. One of them is putting on the siding. He picks up a nail and hammers it in. Picks up another nail, throws it away. Picks up a nail, hammers it in. Picks up another, throws it away.

This goes on for a while, and finally his friend comes over and asks him why he is throwing half of the nails away.

He replies, "Those ones were pointed on the wrong end."

The idiot buddy gets exasperated and says, "You dribbling mindless halfwit, those are for the other side of the house!"

My neighbour found out that her dog, a schnauzer, could hardly hear, so she took it to the veterinarian. The vet found that the problem was hair in the dog's ears. He cleaned both ears, and the dog could then hear fine. The vet then proceeded to tell the lady that, if she wanted to keep this from recurring, she should go to the chemist and get some "Nair" hair remover and rub it in the dog's ears once a month.

The lady went to the chemist and bought some "Nair" hair remover. At the register, the pharmacist told her, "If you're going to use this under your arms, don't use deodorant for a few days."

The lady said, "I'm not using it under my arms."

The pharmacist said, "If you're using it on your legs, don't shave for a couple of days."

The lady replied, "I'm not using it on my legs either. If you must know, I'm using it on my schnauzer."

The pharmacist said, "Oh dear. Well, in that case, stay off your bicycle for at least a week."

There was a young plumber from Coo-gee
Who was plumbing his girl by the sea
She said stop your plumbing
I can hear someone coming
He said, "My God you've got good ears, that's me."

Two dim wits were sipping their Starbucks when a truck went past loaded up with rolls of instant turf.

"I'm going to do that when I win the lottery", announced the first dim wit.

"Do what?" asked the second dim wit.

"Send my lawn out to be mowed."

An attorney arrived home late, after a very tough day trying to get a 'Stay Of Execution'. His last-minute plea for clemency to the judge had failed and he was feeling worn out and depressed.

As soon as he walked through the door at home, his wife started on him about, 'What time of night to be getting home is this? Where have you been? Dinner is cold and I'm not reheating it'. And on and on and on.

Too shattered to play his usual role in this familiar ritual, he poured himself a shot of whiskey and headed off for a long hot soak in the bathtub, pursued by the predictable sarcastic remarks as he dragged himself up the stairs.

While he was in the bath, the phone rang. The wife answered and was told that her husband's client, James Wright, had been granted a 'Stay of Execution' after all. Wright would not be hanged tonight.

Finally realizing what a terrible day he must have had, she decided to go upstairs and give him the good news.

As she opened the bathroom door, she was greeted by the sight of her husband, bent over naked, drying his legs and feet.

"They're not hanging Wright tonight", she said.

He whirled around and screamed, "FOR THE LOVE OF GOD WOMAN, DON'T YOU EVER STOP?!"

FUNNY SMART ARSE ANSWERS

SMART ARSE ANSWER 1

It was mealtime during a flight on a British Airways plane:

"Would you like dinner?" the flight attendant asked the man seated in the front row.

"What are my choices?" the man asked.

"Yes or no," she replied.

SMART ARSE ANSWER 2

A lady was picking through the frozen Chickens at a Woolworths store but she couldn't find one big enough for her family.

She asked a passing assistant, "Do these chickens get any bigger?"

The assistant replied, "I'm afraid not, they're dead."

SMART ARSE ANSWER 3

The policeman got out of his car and the teenager he stopped for speeding rolled down his window. "I've been waiting for you all day," the Cop said.

The kid replied, "Well I got here as fast as I could."

SMART ARSE ANSWER 4

A truckie was driving along on a country road. A sign came up that read "Low Bridge Ahead."

Before he realised it, the bridge was directly ahead and he got stuck under it.

Cars were backed up for miles. Finally, a police car arrived.

The policeman got out of his car and walked to the lorry's cab and said to the driver, "Got stuck, eh?"

The lorry driver said, "No, I was delivering this bridge and ran out of diesel!"

A priest decides to take a walk to the pier near his church. He looks around and finally stops to watch a fisherman load his boat. The fisherman notices, and asks the priest if he would like to join him for a couple of hours. The priest agrees. The fisherman asks if the priest has ever fished before, to which the priest says no. He baits the hook for him and says, "Give it a shot father."

After a few minutes, the priest hooks a big fish and struggles to get it in the boat.

The fisherman says, "Whoa, what a big Bugger!"

Priest: "Uh, please sir, can you mind your language?"

Fisherman: (THINKING QUICKLY) "I'm sorry father, but that's what this fish is called - a Bugger!"

Priest: "Oh, I'm sorry - I didn't know."

After the trip, the priest brings the fish to the Bishop.

Priest: "Look at this big Bugger!"

Bishop: "Please, your language, this is a house of God."

Priest: "No, you don't understand - that's what this fish is called, and I caught it. I caught this Bugger!"

Bishop: "Hmmm. You know, I could clean this Bugger and we could have it for dinner."

So the Bishop takes the fish and cleans it, and brings it to the head mother.

Bishop: "Could you cook this Bugger for dinner tonight?"

Head Mother: "My lord, what language!"

Bishop: "No, sister, that's what the fish is called - a Bugger! Father caught it, I cleaned it, can you cook it?"

Head Mother: "Hmmm. Yes, I'll cook that Bugger tonight."

The Pope stops by for dinner with the three of them, and they all think the fish is great. He asks where they got it.

Priest: "I caught the Bugger!"

Bishop: "And I cleaned the Bugger!"

Head Mother: "And I cooked the Bugger!"

The Pope stares at them for a minute with a steely gaze, but then takes off his hat, puts his feet up on the table, lights up a cigarette and takes a deep drag, leans back on his chair, lets rip a savage fart and says, "You know what? You bastards are bloody allright."

Three elderly men were sitting at the table discussing funny things that were happening to them. The first man said, "You know, I was standing on the stairs the other day and I couldn't remember if I was going up or going down."

The second one said, "How unusual, I found myself this morning standing in the middle of the room with my bath towel and I couldn't remember if I was on my way to the showers or whether I was coming from them."

The third gent said, "Oh for heavens sake, You two are going nuts. I'm so glad I don't suffer from your short-term memory, knock on wood."

And just as he rapped on the table he looked up and said, "Oh! Would that be the front door or the back door?"

I decided to go to the local mosque at Lakemba in western Sydney for the first time to see what it was all about.

I sat down and the Imam came up to me, laid his hands on my hand and said:

"By the will of Allah and the prophet Mohammed - you will walk today."

I told him I wasn't paralyzed, I only had a small bunion on my left foot.

He came back and laid his hands on me and looking skywards, earnestly repeated his mantra:
"By the will of Allah and the prophet Mohammed - you will walk today."

Once again, I told him there was nothing wrong with me.

After prayers I stepped outside, and stuff me rotten.....
MY CAR WAS GONE!

Retired Irishmen were playing poker in O'Leary's apartment when Paddy Murphy loses $500 on a single hand, clutches his chest, and drops dead at the table. Showing respect for their fallen brother, the other five continue playing standing up.

Michael O'Connor looks around and asks, "Oh, me boys, someone's got to tell Paddy's wife. Who will it be then?" They draw straws. Paul Gallagher picks the short one. They tell him to be discreet, be gentle, don't make a bad situation any worse. "Discreet??? I'm the most discreet Irishmen you'll ever meet. Discretion is me middle name. Leave it to me."

Gallagher goes over to Murphy's house and knocks on the door. Mrs. Murphy answers, and asks what he wants. Gallagher declares, "Your husband just lost $500, and is afraid to come home."

"Tell him to drop dead!", says Murphy's wife.

"I'll go tell him." says Gallagher.

A hell raising evangelist faith healer was ranting to a crowd of would-be believers at a suburban hall.

"My friends", he bellowed, "I can heal the wounded, the sick, the infirmed and the afflicted just by praying to the good Lord. If there is one amongst you who wants to be healed, then come ye forth?"

A lady stood up and walked to the stage. "My friends, we have a believer", the faith healer again bellowed. "Madam, what is your name?"

"My name ith Thmith. I've had thith lithp thinth birth and I want it fixthed."

"Go behind the curtain Mrs Smith and ye shall be healed by the power of the Lord", the healer wailed.

"Is there another believer in our midst?"

A man with two crutches stumbled to the stage and the healer said, "We have a believer. Sir, what is your name?"

"My name is Brown and I have not been able to walk without these crutches since birth."

"Mr Brown, go behind the curtain with Mrs Smith and we shall pray to the Lord for you."

So, the faith healer got into his act. There was a gospel choir and loud music and fervent praying by the healer and the crowd and then suddenly it all stopped and with great theatrics the healer said, "Mr Brown, Mr Brown. Throw away your left crutch." And over the curtain came the left crutch.

"Mr Brown, Mr Brown. Throw away your right crutch." And over the curtain came the right crutch. Now on a roll the preacher enthralled, "And now Mrs Smith. Mrs Smith. Speak to us Mrs Smith." And from behind the curtains in a lispy voice came, "Hey reverend, Mithter Brown hath jutht fallen over!"

Bad Bernie was in prison for seven years. The day he got out, his wife and son were there to pick him up. He came through the gates and got into the car.
The only thing he said was, "F.F."
His wife turned to him and answered, "E.F."
Out on the highway, he said, "F.F."
She responded simply, "E.F."
He repeated, "F.F."
She again replied, "E.F."
"Mum! Dad!" their son yelled. "What's going on?"
Bad Bernie answered, "Your mother wants to Eat First!"

Three men were in a bar comparing who had experienced the most excruciating pain.

The first man said, "I was living in the outback a number of years ago when I had a tooth that was causing me extreme pain. The only person who could take it out was an old aboriginal and the only tools he had was a screwdriver and pliers and no anaesthetic.

Having that pulled out was the most painful thing I have experienced.

The second man chipped in with, "I was wounded by a mine in Vietnam in '73. I had two broken legs, a broken arm and shrapnel through my body. I had to crawl through snake infested jungle for five days to get help. That was the most painful experience I have experienced.

The third man, not to be outdone, recounted, "I was rabbit trapping in the bush one day when I suddenly had this great urge to have a really urgent crap. So, I dropped the trousers and squatted in an old rabbit run near an old burrow. Suddenly a large rabbit darted out of the burrow and gave me such a scare that I fell backwards into the burrow, right on an old rabbit trap that snapped loudly right around my knackers. That was the second most painful thing I have experienced."

"Hang on", said one of the men. "We aren't talking about the second most painful. When did the most painful thing happen?"

To which the man replied, "Oh!. That happened when the length of chain holding the trap in the ground, ran out."

There's a girl living across the street from me. Single and very attractive. I can see her place from my kitchen window. I watched as she got home from work this evening.

I was surprised when she walked across the street, up my driveway and knocked on the door.

I opened the door, she looked at me and said, "I just got home, and I have this strong urge to have a good time, dance, get drunk, and get laid tonight. Are you doing anything?"

I quickly replied, "Nope, I'm free!"

"Great", she said. "Can you watch my dog?"

Being a senior citizen really sucks!

One night, Tom does what he normally does --- he kisses his wife, crawls into bed and falls asleep. All of a sudden, he wakes up with an elderly man dressed in a white robe sitting next to him!

"What the heck are you doing in my bedroom...and who are you?" he asked.

"This is not your bedroom", the man replied. "I am St. Peter, and you are in heaven."

"WHAT! Are you saying I'm dead? I don't want to die! I'm too young", said Tom. "I want you to send me back immediately."

"It's not that easy", said St.Peter. "You can only return as a dog or a hen. The choice is your own."

Tom thought about it for a while, and figured out that being a dog would be too tiring, but a hen would probably have a nice and relaxed life. Running around with a rooster can't be that bad.

"I want to return as a hen", Tom replied.

And in the next second, he found himself nicely feathered and in a chicken farm. But now he felt like his rear end was going to blow. Then along came the rooster.

"Hey, you must be the new hen St. Peter told me about", he said. "How do you like being a hen?"

"Well, OK I guess, but it feels like my butt is about to explode."

"Oh that!" said the rooster. "That's only the ovulation going on. You need to lay an egg."

"How do I do that?" Tom asked.

"Cluck twice, and then you push all you can."

Tom clucked twice and pushed more than he was good for, and then 'plop' an egg was on the ground.

"Wow" Tom said. "That felt really good!" So he clucked again and squeezed. And just like that, there was yet another egg on the ground.

The third time he clucked, he heard his wife shout:

"Bloody hell Tom! Wake up you idiot! You're foulin' up the bed sheets again!"

An Englishman, a Frenchman and an Irishman were in a pub talking about their children.

"My son was born on St George's Day", postured the Englishman, "so we obviously decided to call him George."

"That's a real coincidence", observed the Frenchman. "My daughter was born on Valentine's Day, so we decided to call her Valentine."

"Now dat's really incredible", drawled the Irishman. "Exactly da' same t'ing 'appened wif me son Pancake."

An elderly couple had been experiencing declining memories, so they decided to take a power memory class where one is taught to remember things by association. A few days after the class, the old man was outside talking with his neighbor about how much the class really helped him.

"What was the name of the instructor?" asked the neighbor.

"Oh, ummmm, let's see", the old man pondered. "You know that flower, you know, the one that smells really nice but has those prickly thorns, what's that flower's name?"

"A rose?" asked the neighbor.

"Yes, that's it", replied the old man. He then turned toward his house and shouted, "Hey, Rose, what's the name of the instructor we took the memory class from?"

FUNNY MENS SENSITIVITY

I was devastated to find out my wife was having an affair but, by turning to religion, I was soon able to come to terms with the whole thing. I converted to Islam, and we're stoning her in the morning!

The wife suggested I get myself one of those penis enlargers, so I did.
She's 25, and her name's Kathy.

I went to our local bar with my wife last night. Locals started shouting "pedophile!" and other names at me, just because my wife is 24 and I'm 50. It completely spoiled our 10th anniversary.

My son was thrown out of school today for letting a girl in his class give him a hand-job. I said, "Son, that's three schools this year! You'd better stop before you're banned from teaching altogether."

The cost of living has now gotten so bad that my wife is having sex with me because she can't afford batteries.

I was explaining to my wife last night that when you die you get reincarnated, but must come back as a different creature. She said she would like to come back as a cow. I said, "You obviously haven't been listening."

The Red Cross just knocked on my door and asked if we could contribute towards the floods in Pakistan. I said we'd love to, but our garden hose only reaches the driveway.

A professor of mathematics sent a fax to his wife. It read:

"Dear wife, you must realize that you are 54 years old and I have certain needs which you are no longer able to satisfy. I am otherwise happy with you as a wife, and I sincerely hope you will not be hurt or offended to learn that by the time you receive this letter, I will be at the Grand Hotel with my 18-year-old teaching assistant. I'll be home before midnight. - Your Husband"

When he arrived at the hotel, there was a faxed letter waiting for him that read as follows:

"Dear Husband. You too are 54 years old, and by the time you receive this, I will be at the Breakwater Hotel with the 18-year-old pool boy. Being the brilliant mathematician that you are, you can easily appreciate the fact that 18 goes into 54 a lot more times than 54 goes into 18. Don't wait up."

After being married for 50 years, I took a careful look at my wife one day and said, "Fifty years ago we had a cheap house, a junk car, slept on a sofa-bed and watched a 10-inch black and white TV. But hey I got to sleep every night with a hot 23-year-old girl.

Now ... I have a $750,000 home, a $45,000 car, a nice big bed and a large screen TV, but I'm sleeping with a 73-year-old woman."

So I said to my wife, "It seems to me, that you're not holding up your side of things."

My wife is a very reasonable woman. She told me to go out and find a hot 23 year old girl and she would make sure that I would once again be living in a cheap house, driving a junk car, sleeping on a sofa bed and watching a 10-inch black and white TV.

Aren't older women great?

They really know how to solve an old guy's problems!

WITTY MARRIAGE INSIGHTS

Husbands are like lawn mowers? They're hard to get started, emit foul odours and don't work half the time!

The FIVE most essential words for a healthy, vital relationship are "I apologize" and "You are right."

Why did the Mormon cross the road? So he could get to the other bride.

The man hadn't spoken to his mother-in-law for eighteen months…. He didn't like to interrupt her.

My wife and I were happy for 20 years. Then we met.

The secret to having your husband come home from work on time? Tell him sex starts at 6 P.M. sharp….whether he's there or not.

A man placed an ad online saying "Wife wanted." He got hundreds of messages the next day saying, "You can have mine."

Marriage is a three-ring circus: engagement RING, wedding RING, and suffeRING.

Men. If you yawn while arguing with your wife, it is because you merely thought it was your turn to speak.

Arguing with your partner is like trying to read the "Terms of Use" on the internet. Eventually, you just give up and say, "I Agree."

A tourist was walking through a small Italian village when he noticed an old man sobbing on a park bench. Touched by this, the tourist wandered over and asked what could be the matter.

The old man looked at the tourist and explained, "Looka down there at all those beautifula boats. You know who builda them? It was I, Mario, the greata boata builder. But when I walka downa da street you think alla da people stop and stare and say, 'Hey look. There goes Mario, the greata boata builder.' No. They notta say that."

"And looka over there at all those beautifula houses. You know who builda them? It was I, Mario, the greata housea builder. But when I walka downa da street you think alla da people stop and stare and say, 'Hey look. There goes Mario, the greata housea builder'. No, they notta say that."

"And looka at that beautifula bridge. You know who builda that? It was I, Mario, the greata bridge builder. But when I walka downa da street you think alla da people stop and stare and say, 'Hey, look, there goes Mario the greata bridgea builder.' No, they notta say that." "But a man, he goes out and hasa da sex with one lousy little goat........."

Maria, a devout Catholic, got married and had 15 children.

After her first husband died, she remarried and had 15 more children.

A few weeks after her second husband died, Maria also passed away.

At Maria's funeral, the priest looked skyward and said, "At last, they're finally together."

Her sister sitting in the front row said, "Excuse me, Father, but do you mean she and her first husband, or she and her second husband?"

The priest replied, "Neither. I mean her legs."

A young Sydney woman was so depressed that she decided to end her life by throwing herself into the Harbour.

Just before she could throw herself off Circular Quay, a handsome young man stopped her.

"You have so much to live for", said the man. "I'm a sailor, and we are off to Italy tomorrow. I can stow you away on my ship. I'll take care of you, bring you food every day, and keep you happy."

With nothing to lose, combined with the fact that she had always wanted to go to Italy, the woman accepted.

That night the sailor brought her aboard and hid her in a small but comfortable compartment in the hold.

From then on, every night he would bring her three sandwiches, a bottle of red wine, and make love to her until dawn.

Two weeks later she was discovered by the captain during a routine inspection. "What are you doing here?" asked the captain.

"I have an arrangement with one of the sailors", she replied. "He brings me food and I get a free trip to Italy."

"I see", the captain says.

Her conscience got the best of her and she added, "Plus, he's screwing me."

"He certainly is", replied the captain. "This is the Manly Ferry."

One day, a rather inebriated ice fisherman drilled a hole in the ice and peered deeply into the hole examining it for fish. Suddenly, a loud voice boomed, "THERE ARE NO FISH UNDER THE ICE!"

Surprised, but not discouraged, the fisherman continued on. He walked and swayed several yards away, drilled another hole and peered deeply into it. Again, out of nowhere, a voice suddenly boomed, "THERE IS NO FISH DOWN THERE!"

A bit nervous now, the fisherman managed to continue. He walked about 50 yards away and drilled yet another hole, peered long and deep into the hole, hoping for some fish. Suddenly, the voice boomed again, this time louder than ever, "THERE IS NO FISH UNDER THE ICE!"

The fisherman, quite frightened at this point, looked up into the sky and asked, "Lord!? Is that you?"

"No, you idiot", the voice said. "This is the manager of the ice rink."

He was eager to go out with the boys for their usual Friday night drinks at the club but was stopped at the door by his wife. Having a reputation for getting himself hopelessly drunk, his wife warned him, "If you go out and embarrass yourself, and me, and your family, and come home smashed, you will not want to be living with what I will do to you."

"No, my dear", he said to her. "We are just having a few rounds of snooker and a few drinks and then home."

On notice from his wife to behave, he headed out to the club. It was a great night with a heap of the boys there and the man successfully managed to get hopelessly intoxicated once again, to the point where he vomited on the sleeve of his jacket.

Hearing his wife's warning in his ear, he temporarily panicked with the thought of her temper. But the guy next to him said, "Simple fix. Get a ten dollar note, put it in a jacket pocket and tell your wife it was the bloke next to you at the bar who vomited and that he gave you ten dollars to get the jacket dry cleaned." Happy with this, the guy continued his drinking.

Next morning the man awoke in bed with a fearful pounding hangover and through his haze he saw his wife standing near the bed with a vicious glare and the jacket and pointing to the stain.

Realizing he had been found out he gathered his thoughts and smugly blurted out, "No my dear, that was not me. That was the bloke sitting next to me at the bar and he was so sorry that he gave me ten dollars to get it cleaned. Have a look. The ten dollars is in the pocket."

His wife reached into the pocket and pulled out two ten dollar notes.

Holding a ten dollar note in each hand, she held out the one in her left hand and said, "OK! So this one is from the guy who vomited on your sleeve, who's the other one from?"

To which the smug man said, "Oh! That's from the guy who shat in my pants."

A new psychiatrist is making rounds, getting acquainted with his new patients, and asks one of them, "So how did you get here, anyways, Mr. Schleppel?" "Well, doctor, it started with me getting married, a thing I never should have done. I married a widow with an adult daughter who thus became my step-daughter. When my father came to visit us at Christmas, he fell in love with her and they eventually married. So my step-daughter became my step-mother. Then my wife gave birth to our son who of course was my father's brother-in-law, because he was the brother of his wife. And because my step-daughter was my step-mother, my son was also my uncle. That means that my wife, being the mother of my step-mother, is my grandmother and I am her grandson. But that's not everything, because I'm married to my step-grandmother, I'm not only her husband and grandson, but also my own grandfather. I think that's enough to make anybody go nuts, wouldn't you agree?"

A little boy was lost at a large shopping mall. He approached a uniformed policeman and said, "I've lost my dad!"

The cop asked, "What's he like?"

The little boy replied, "Beer, and women with big tits."

There was a young man from Brighton
Who said to his girl, "You're a tight one"
She said, "Bless my soul
You're in the wrong hole
There's plenty of room in the right one."

A man is spread across three seats of a theatre.

The usher comes along and says, "Sorry sir, it is only one seat allowed per person."

The man groaned but didn't budge. "Sir", the usher said, "if you do not get up from there, I shall have to call the manager."

Again, the man just groaned infuriating the usher who immediately went to get the manager.

Together, the usher and manager repeatedly tried to move him to no avail.

So, they called the police who arrived and surveyed the situation.

"Mate, what's your name?"

"Barry", the man moaned.

"Where are you from Barry?" the cop asked.

"The balcony."

Three men: one American, one Japanese, and an Australian were sitting naked in the sauna. Suddenly there was a beeping sound.

The American pressed his forearm and the beep stopped. The others looked at him questioningly.

"That was my pager", he said. "I have a microchip under the skin of my arm."

A few minutes later a phone rang. The Japanese fellow lifted his palm to his ear. When he finished, he explained, "That was my mobile phone. I have a microchip in my hand."

Bruce felt decidedly low-tech. So as not to be outdone, he decided he had to do something just as impressive. He stepped out of the sauna and went to the toilet. He returns with a piece of toilet paper hanging out of his backside. The others raised their eyebrows. "It's OK", says Bruce, "Just getting a fax coming through."

A man appeared before St. Peter at the Pearly Gates.

"Have you ever done anything of particular merit?" St. Peter asked.

"Well, I can think of one thing", the man offered.

"On a trip to the Outback I was in Alice Springs, when I came upon a gang of bikers who were threatening a young woman. I told them to leave her alone, but they wouldn't listen. So, I approached the largest and most tattooed biker and smacked him in the face, kicked his bike over, ripped out his nose ring, and threw it on the ground. Then I yelled, 'Now, back off or I'll beat you all unconscious.'"

Saint Peter was impressed, "When did this happen?"

"Couple of minutes ago."

A man was quietly having a beer in a bar, minding his own business, when one of the men drinking next to him decided to leave for the day. The bloke leaving turned to his mate still at the bar and said to him, "See you Donkey, same time tomorrow."

The stranger turned to the drinker left behind and asked, "That wasn't very nice. Why did he call you donkey?"

And the drinker replied, "I don't know. HeAw, HeAw, he always calls me that."

A man and a woman, who have never met before, find themselves assigned to the same sleeping room on a transcontinental train.

Though initially embarrassed and uneasy over sharing a room, the two are tired and fall asleep quickly...he in the upper bunk and she in the lower.

At 1:00 AM, he leans over and gently wakes the woman saying, "Ma'am, I'm sorry to bother you, but would you be willing to reach into the closet to get me a second blanket? I'm awfully cold."

"I have a better idea," she replies. "Just for tonight, let's pretend that we're married."

"Wow! That's a great idea!!" he exclaims.

"Good", she replies. "Get your own damn blanket!"

After a moment of silence, he farted loudly.

Mahatma Ghandi, as you know, walked barefoot most of the time, which produced an impressive set of calluses on his feet. He also ate very little, which made him rather fragile, and with his odd diet, he suffered from bad breath.

This made him a super callused fragile mystic hexed by halitosis.

A young woman bought a mirror at an antique shop, and hung it on her bathroom door. One evening, while getting undressed, she playfully said, "Mirror, mirror, on my door, make my bustline forty four."

Instantly, there was a brilliant flash of light, and her breasts grew to enormous proportions. Excitedly, she ran to tell her husband what happened, and in minutes they both returned.

The husband crossed his fingers and said, "Mirror, mirror on the door, make my penis touch the floor!"

Again there was a bright flash......... and his legs fell off.

Little Freddie was called by his mother who said, "Freddie, I want you to go to the butcher and get me six lamb chops for dinner. And make sure they are lean."

Little Freddie was eight years old but thought he was the equal of a twelve year old. He walked into the butcher shop and the butcher said, "Hello little man. And what would you like today?"

'Little man', thought Freddie. I'll show him who's big and grown up here. So he puffed his scrawny chest out and real tough like, he said, "I want six lamb chops. And I want you to make them lean."

The butcher just smiled and said, "Certainly little man. And which way would you like me to make them lean? To the left or to the right?"

Little Johnnie was playing in the gutter with a bottle of liquid that he had found, when the local vicar came past.

"What's that you are playing with Little Johnnie?" asked the vicar.

"It's a bottle of magic water. See, when I pour some on these ants, they shrivel up and die." The vicar took the bottle and had a sniff and thought to himself, 'This is sulphuric acid.' He said to Little Johnnie, "Come with me and I will show you some water that is much more powerful than this but is completely safe."

So off to the church vestry the pair went and the vicar pulled out a bottle of water and said to Little Johnnie, "Do you know what this is? This is a bottle of Holy water. This is so powerful that only last week, I sprinkled some of this over a pregnant lady's tummy, and she 'passed' a baby."

Totally unimpressed, Little Johnnie said, "Jeez vicar, that's nothing. Just yesterday I sprinkled some of my magic water over our dog's knackers, and he 'passed' a bloke on a motor bike."

FUNNY QUICKIES

"IT'S A BOY", I shouted. "A BOY, I DON'T BELIEVE IT, IT'S A BOY". And with tears streaming down my face I swore I'd never visit another Thai Brothel.

In the first few days of the Olympics the Romanians took gold, silver, bronze, copper, lead, chairs......

A boy asks his granny, "Have you seen my pills, they were labelled LSD?'"

Granny replies, "Stuff the pills, we have to get out of here. Have you seen the size of the dragons in the kitchen?"

Wife gets naked and asks hubby, "What turns you on more, my pretty face or my sexy body?"

Hubby looks her up and down and replies, "Your sense of humour."

The wife's back on the warpath again.

She was up for making a sex movie last night, and all I did was suggest we should hold auditions for her part.

I've accidentally swallowed some Scrabble tiles. My next trip to the toilet could spell disaster.

The other night, my wife asked me how many women I'd slept with. I told her, "Only you. All the others kept me awake all night!"

My missus packed my bags, and as I walked out the front door, she screamed,

"I wish you a slow and painful death, you bastard!"

"Oh," I replied, "so now you want me to stay!"

A government survey has shown that 91% of illegal immigrants come to this

country so that they can see their own doctor.

A man is just like a ceramic tile.

Lay them properly the first time and you can walk all over them for the rest of your life.

Felt uncomfortable driving into the cemetery the other day.

The GPS blurted out, 'You have reached your final destination.'

I was in the supermarket with my wife when she said she would like to buy some things that reminded her of me. Thinking she was in a romantic mood, I said, "Oh, do you mean like honey, sugar or cream puffs." She said, "No. They are all here in aisle four. Nuts, crackers and fruitcake."

God said to Adam, "I've got some good news and some bad news. First the good news. I have given you a brain and a penis. The bad news... I've only given you enough blood to work one of them at a time!"

My mate Rodney, who had a really bad stutter, was telling us about his Nana.
By the end of it we were all singing Hey Jude.

Day 284 without sex.
Went jogging this morning in flip flops just to remember the sound.

When I married my wife, her father promised me a cow and an acre of land....
20 years later, I'm still waiting for the land!

Luigi Spagatini was the most famous portrait artist in the whole of Italy.
His fame was known widely and people from all over came to him to have their portraits painted by such a talented artist.
One day, Luigi was in his studio when the door opened and a gorgeous middle
aged woman came in. Tall and slim with bright red lipstick and a slinky walk,

"I would like'a for you to paint'a me in'a da nude", she breathlessly said.

Luigi was a bit taken aback by this request from such a beautiful woman.

"Senora", he said. "I have never painted such a beautiful'a woman in'a da nude.

I must'a ask'a my wife Maria if it is'a OK?"

Ten minutes late Luigi comes back and says, "Senora. My wife'a she say it is OK. But on'a one'a condition."

Slightly confused, the gorgeous woman queried, "Oh!, And what is'a that'a condition Senor?"

"If I, Luigi Spagatini, the most'a famous painter in'a da whole of Italy is to paint'a you in'a da nude, then you must at least allow'a me to wear'a my socks so I have some'a where to wipe'a my brushes."

George and Bert met everyday for 'elevenses' at their local pub and would drink all afternoon. One day George was already there and saw Bert coming. "Hey Bert. Over here", he said.

"Don't call me Bert. Call me Lucky", said Bert.

"What? But Bert is your name. Why am I calling you Lucky?"

"Because", said Bert, "you wouldn't believe what happened to me last night. I left here, I walked down the street and a car came sliding around a corner and missed by only 6 inches."

"Gee", said George, "that WAS lucky." They drank on as usual and the next day met at the pub where Bert was late again. When he came in, Bert thought he would do the right thing and said, "Hey Lucky, over here."

"Don't call me Lucky. Call me Lucky Lucky", said Bert.

"Why am I calling you Lucky Lucky?" asked George.

Bert said, "You wouldn't believe what happened to me last night. I left here, walked across the road and a huge truck went through a red light and it only missed me by three inches."

"Now that is really lucky", said George. They drank on and again met at the pub next day. When Bert came in, George thought he better do the right thing and said, "Hey Lucky Lucky, over here."

"Don't call me Lucky Lucky. Call me Lucky Lucky Lucky".

Exasperated, George said, 'Ok, why am I calling you Lucky Lucky Lucky?"

Bert explained. "You wouldn't believe what happened to me this morning. There I was, on the bed, making mad passionate love to my wife when someone walked down our driveway, threw a house brick through our bedroom window and it hit me right in the arse."

"What's so lucky about that?" said George.

"What's so lucky about that you ask? Five minutes earlier it would have hit me right in the back of the head."

A middle-aged man went to his doctor for his regular physical check-up. The doctor asks about the man's daily activity level.

The patient said: "Well, yesterday afternoon, I waded along the edge of a lake, drank eight beers, escaped from wild dogs in the heavy brush, marched up and down several rocky hills, stood in a patch of poison ivy, crawled out of quicksand, jumped away from an aggressive snake and took four leaks behind big trees."

Inspired by the story, the doctor said, "You must be one hell of an outdoorsman!"

"No", he replied, "I'm just a lousy golfer."

A woman rushed up to the manager of the movie theatre and complained that she had been molested in the front stalls.

The manager calmed her down and was ushering her to another seat when another woman complained to him that she had been molested in the front stalls too. The manager went down to the front and shone his torch along the floor where he saw a bald man crawling along on his hands and knees.

"What are you doing?" demanded the manager.

The bald man looked up. "I've lost my toupee. It fell off in the dark. I had my hand on it twice but it got away!"

It was a blinding snowstorm in Cooma in the Australian alps and Mick was lost. However, he didn't panic, because he remembered his father's instructions, "If you ever get lost in a snowstorm, just wait for a snow plough to come by and follow it." Sure enough, pretty soon a snow plough came by, and Mick started to follow it. He followed the plough for about forty-five minutes. Finally, the driver of the truck got out and asked him what he was doing. Mick explained that his dad had told him to follow a plough if he ever got lost in a snowstorm. The driver nodded and said, "Well, I'm done with the Bunnings parking lot, do you now want to follow me over to Woolworths?"

A wife, being the romantic type, sent her husband a loving text.

"If you are sleeping, send me your dreams" she wrote.

"If you are laughing, send me your smile.

If you are eating, send me a bite.

If you are drinking, send me a sip.

If you are crying, send me your tears. I love you."

The husband, not the romantic type, texted back:

"I am on the toilet. Please advise."

Three soldiers were back from duty in the jungles of Vietnam and were being debriefed by the quartermaster. The quartermaster started, "As a gesture of goodwill towards your bravery, we have decided to monetarily reward you. In a change to the calculation of payments, we have decided to take a measurement of a given part of your body as decided by you, and then give you $1000 for every inch of that measurement."

The first man was a very portly man and said, "You can measure the distance from my navel, around my belly and back to my navel. This was done, and as his girth was 60 inches he received $60,000.

The second man, a tall person, said he wanted to be measured from head to toe. He was 6 feet 3 inches so he received $75,000.

The third man said, "I want you to measure the distance from the end of my dick to my balls." Taken aback, the quartermaster queried this but the soldier was adamant.

So the soldier dropped his trousers and the quartermaster put the tape on the end of his dick and brought it towards his balls.

"I don't seem to be able to finds your balls", said the quartermaster. "Where are they?"

The soldier just smiled and said, "I lost them in a rice paddy in Vietnam."

A young journalist was sent to interview the renowned explorer and British army colonel, Lord Ponsonby. The journalist was feeling a bit intimidated having to interview this pompous, ancient and grumpy old man. But having done his research on the man, said to him, "Lord Ponsonby. You indeed have had a very exciting career, especially in India, could you tell our readers about one of your most dangerous exploits."

Happy to relive and recount his past achievements he started, "Ah yes, I remember it was back in the conflict of '48 when I was leading a column of men along this narrow mountain trail in the Khyber Pass. We rounded a very sharp bend and I was confronted by this enormous mountain lion. Ten feet long from its nose to its tail. It reared up on its hind legs, bared its enormous teeth and went, 'RAAAAAAH! RAAAAAAH!'. I fouled my knickers."

The astounded young journalist said, "Good heavens Lord Ponsonby, if I had been confronted by such a ferocious lion, I too would have fouled my pants." The Lord huffed and fluffed and snorted, "What? No not with the lion you fool, just before, when I went 'RAAAAAAH.'"

Lord Nelson was on his ship the HMS Victory , cruising the Atlantic ocean off the coast of France when a frantic call came from the crows nest, high up the top of one of the masts.

"Lord Nelson!!. Lord Nelson!! Three Froggie war ships on the port side."

"Thank you crows nest", said Lord Nelson as he turned to his bosun and said, "Bosun, go down to my rooms and get me my crimson coat for me to wear while we take care of these annoying Frenchmen."

"But Sir", said the bosun, "If you wear your crimson uniform, you will stand out like a beacon for the enemy to be able recognize you and to shoot you."

Lord Nelson, full of confidence said, "Yes I am aware of that but as improbable as that will be, if it should happen, then my men will not see that I have been shot as my blood will be the same colour as my clothes, and my men will continue fighting the Froggies with the same endeavour and courage as before."

Just then the crows nest shouted out in panic, "Lord Nelson!! Lord Nelson!!. Thirty five Froggie warships on the port side."

"Thank you crows nest." Then Nelson turned to his bosun and said, "Oh busun. While you are down in my quarters getting my crimson jacket, you had better bring me my brown trousers."

An old married couple are in church one Sunday when the woman turns to her husband and says, "I've just let out a really long, silent fart. What should I do?"

The husband turned to her and said, "Replace the battery in your hearing aid."

A primary school teacher asks her prep students which job they would like to do when they grow up.

From the front row, Chloe said, "I'd like to be a doctor so I can fix sick people."

"Very good, Chloe. What about you Ryan?"

Ryan stood upright and said, "Well Miss, I'd like to be an astronaut and visit the moon and Mars."

"Excellent", said the teacher. "Would anybody else like to tell us what they would like to do?"

Little Ronnie from the back of the class said, "I would like to be a lollipop man at a school crossing."

The teacher was aghast. "Why in heavens name would you want to be one of those?"

Ronnie grinned and said, "From what I've seen, Miss, most of those lucky buggers don't start work until they are 70."

The day after his mother-in-law disappeared in a kayaking accident, a man from Launceston in Tasmania, answered his door to find two grim-faced police officers.

"We're sorry Mr. Flynn, but we have some information about your mother-in-law", said one of the officers.

"Tell me. Did you find her?" Cedric Flynn asked.

The police officers looked at each other.

One said, "We have some bad news, some good news, and some really great news. Which would you like to hear first?"

Fearing the worst, Mr. Flynn said, "Give me the bad news first."

The police officer said, "I'm sorry to tell you, sir, but this morning we found your mother-in-law's body in the bay."

"Lord sufferin' Jaysus!" exclaimed Flynn.

Swallowing hard, he asked, "What could possibly be the good news?"

The officer continued, "When we pulled her up, she had 12 of the best looking Tasmanian lobsters that you have ever seen clinging to her. Haven't seen lobsters like that since the 1960's, and we feel you are entitled to a share in the catch."

Stunned, Mr. Flynn demanded, "If that's the good news, then what's the great news?"

The officer replied, "We're gonna pull her up again tomorrow."

A nun at a Catholic school asked her students what they want to be when they grow up.

Little Mary declares, "I want to be a prostitute."

"What did you say?" asks the nun, totally shocked.

"I said I want to be a prostitute", Mary repeats.

"Oh, thank heavens", says the nun. "I thought you said a Protestant!"

An elderly couple had been dating for some time and decided it was finally time to marry.
Before the wedding they embarked on a long conversation regarding how their marriage might work. They discussed finances, living arrangements and so on. Finally, the old man decided it was time to broach the subject of their connubial relationship.
"How do you feel about sex?" he asked, rather hopefully.
"Well, I'd have to say I like it infrequently", she responded.
The old guy paused . . . then he asked, "Was that one word or two?"

An American tourist walks out of a Mexican train station when he notices he isn't wearing his watch. A Mexican man is resting under a sombrero under a nearby tree. The American approaches the Mexican and asks, "Excuse me, do you know what time is?" The Mexican looks at the donkey, grabs its balls, and replies, "4:30." The American, clearly impressed by this local custom, asks, "How do you know that?" The Mexican replies, "Well you get a handful of the donkey's balls, lift them gently up and slightly to the left and then you can see that clock across the street you idiot."

Two guys grow up together, but after university one moves to Sydney and the other to Tasmania. They agree to meet every ten years on the Gold Coast, Queensland, to play golf and catch up with each other.
At age 32 they meet, finish their round of golf and head for lunch.
"Where you wanna go?"
"Hooters."
"Why Hooters?"
"They have those broads with the big knockers, the tight shorts and the gorgeous legs."
"You're on."
At age 42, they meet and play golf again.
"Where you wanna go for lunch?"
"Hooters."
"Again? Why?"
"They have cold beer, big screen TVs, and side action on the games."
"OK."
At age 52 they meet and play again. "So where you wanna go for lunch?"
"Hooters.

"Why?"
"The food is pretty good and there's plenty of parking."
At age 62 they meet again.
After a round of golf, one says, "Where you wanna go?"
"Hooters."
"Why?"
"Wings are half price and the food isn't too spicy."
"Good choice"
At age 72 they meet again.
Once again, after a round of golf, one says, "Where shall we go for lunch?"
"Hooters."
"Why?"
"They have six handicapped parking spaces right by the door and they have senior discounts."
"Great choice."
At age 82 they meet and play again. "Where should we go for lunch?"
"Hooters."
"Why?"
"Because we've never been there before."
"Okay. Let's check it out. Might be good"

An elderly woman told her friend, "I feel like my body has gotten totally out of shape, so I got my doctor's permission to join a fitness club and start exercising."
She said, "So, I decided to take an aerobics class for seniors. I bent, twisted, gyrated, jumped up and down, and perspired for an hour."

"And did that make you feel better?" asked the friend.

"Don't know", said the elderly woman. "By the time I got those damn leotards on, the class was already over."

A Chinese couple, who ran a very busy take away restaurant offering a rather extensive numbered menu, were at home after a busy day at work. After a nice hot shower, it was time to go to bed.

The man was in bed waiting for his wife and feeling rather horny. The wife came in looking rather bedraggled after a day taking orders and dealing with customers.

She climbed into bed and her husband tenderly touched her with his hand and said, "How about we have a sixty niner."

She sat upright in bed, looked at him and scowled, "If you think I am going to get out of bed and make lemon chicken this time of night, you can go and get stuffed!!!"

An elderly man, walking and weaving down the street around 2:00am, is stopped by the police and is asked where he is going at this time of night.

The man replies, "I am on my way to a lecture about alcohol abuse and the effects it has on the human body, as well as smoking and staying out late."

The officer then asks, "Really? Who is giving that lecture at this time of night?"

The man replies, "That would be my wife then."

First-year students at Med School were receiving their first anatomy class with a real dead human body.

They all gathered around the surgery table with the body covered with a white sheet.

The professor started the class by telling them, "In medicine, it is necessary to have 2 important qualities as a doctor: The first is that you not be disgusted by anything involving the human body."

As an example, the Professor pulled back the sheet, stuck his finger in the butt of the corpse, withdrew it, and stuck his finger in his mouth.

"Go ahead and do the same thing", he told his students.

The students freaked out, hesitated for several minutes, but eventually took turns sticking a finger in the butt of the dead body and sucking on it.

When everyone finished, the Professor looked at them and told them, "The second most important quality is observation. I stuck in my middle finger and sucked on my index finger.

Now, "LEARN TO PAY ATTENTION!"

A lawyer and a zoologist were walking through the woods and attracted the attention of a vicious looking bear. The bear noticed them, and started to walk toward them. The lawyer immediately opened his briefcase, pulling out a pair of sneakers, and started putting them on. The zoologist looked at him and said, "You're crazy! You'll never be able to outrun that bear!" The lawyer smiled and looked at him "Oh, I know that. Bears are much faster than humans. I have no hope of ever being able to outrun a bear." The zoologist was confused. "If you know that, why are you changing shoes?" "Well, the way I figure it", the lawyer replied, "I don't have to outrun the bear. I only have to outrun YOU ."

A doctor and a lawyer were talking at a party. Their conversation was constantly interrupted by people describing their ailments and asking the doctor for free medical advice.
After an hour of this, the exasperated doctor asked the lawyer, "What do you do to stop people from asking you

for legal advice when you're out of the office?"
"I give it to them", replied the lawyer, "and then I send them a bill."
The doctor was shocked, but agreed to give it a try.
The next day, still feeling slightly guilty, the doctor prepared the bills.
When he took the bills to the post office to be sorted and sent out, he looked in his own postal box and he found a bill from the lawyer.

When our lawn mower broke and wouldn't run, my wife kept hinting to me that I should get it fixed. But somehow I always had something else to take care of first ... the shed, the boat, making beer. Always something more important to me. Finally, she thought of a clever way to make her point. When I arrived home one day, I found her seated in the tall grass, busily snipping away with a tiny pair of sewing scissors. I watched silently for a short time and then went into the house. I was gone only a minute, and when I came out again, I handed her a toothbrush. I said, "When you finish cutting the grass, you might as well sweep the driveway and then probably polish the car."

The doctors say I will walk again, once my testicles descend, but I will always have a limp.

A young lad had a burning desire to become a big-time wrestler. He finally got his chance but it was a bout against the most feared wrestler around called Killer Gorilla. His father was adamant he should not do it because this man had the dreaded 'killer hold' which left other wrestlers maimed for life.

But the lad would not hear of it. This was his big chance and so the bout went ahead. Killer Gorilla was a towering hairy apelike man and it looked like a total mismatch. Twenty seconds into the match the big hairy 'apeman' grabbed the lad, turned him upside down and put him in the dreaded 'killer hold'. The crowd was hushed and the father couldn't watch.

Next moment, the crowd erupted, the father opened his eyes and there was Killer Gorilla upside down in the fifth row and the lad had won the match.

The father rushed to the ring and gasped, "Son, son what happened? I couldn't look."

"Well dad", said the lad, "that big hairy ape man had me in the 'killer hold'. He had me upside down and bent over double and I was almost gone when I glanced up and saw this big pair of hairy knackers dangling from their shorts. So, I craned and stretched with all my might, opened my mouth wide and went 'CRUNCH' right on those big hairy nuts. And you know what dad?"

"No son, what?" asked the dad.

"Jeez it makes you strong when you bight yourself on your balls."

It is the week before Christmas.

An elderly man in Melbourne calls his son in London and says, "I hate to ruin your day, but I have to tell you that your mother and I are divorcing; forty-five years of misery. Enough is enough."

"Dad, what are you talking about?" the son screams.

"We can't stand the sight of each other any longer," the old man says. "We're sick of each other, and I'm sick of talking about this, so you call your sister in Oxford and tell her", and he hangs up.

Frantic, the son calls his sister, who explodes on the phone. "Like heck they're getting divorced", she shouts, "I'll take care of this."

She calls her dad immediately, and screams at the old man, "You are NOT getting divorced! Don't do a single thing until I get there. I'm calling my brother back, and we'll both be there tomorrow. Until then, don't do a thing, DO YOU HEAR ME?" and hangs up.

The old man hangs up his phone and turns to his wife. "Okay," he says, "they're coming for Christmas and paying their own airfares."

A man walks into a pharmacy with his 8-year-old son. They happen to walk by the condom display, and the boy asks, "What are these, Dad?" To which the man matter-of-factly replies, "Those are called condoms, son. Men use them to have safe sex." "Oh, I see.", replied the boy, pensively. "Yes, I've heard of that in health class at school." He looks over the display and picks up a package of 3 and ask, "Why are there 3 in this package?" The dad replies, "Those are for high-school boys. One for Friday, one for Saturday and one for Sunday." "Cool!" says the boy. He notices a 6-pack and asks, "Then who are these for?" "Those are for university men", the dad answers. "TWO for Friday, TWO for Saturday and TWO for Sunday." "WOW!" exclaimed the boy, "Then who uses THESE?" he asks, picking up a 12-pack. With a sigh, the dad replied, "Those are for married men, One for January, one for February, one for.........."

A boy asks his dad one day, "Dad, why is my sister called Paris?"
   His Dad replies, "Because she was conceived in Paris."
   The boy says, "Ahh, thanks Dad."
   His Dad says, "You're welcome, Backseat."

I was a very happy man. My wonderful Italian girlfriend and I had been dating for over a year, and so we decided to get married. There was only one little thing bothering me....It was her beautiful younger sister.
   My prospective sister-in-law was twenty-two, wore very tight miniskirts, and generally went bra-less. She would regularly bend down when she was near me, and I always got more than a nice view. It had to be deliberate. Because she never did it when she was near anyone else. One day this 'little' sister called and asked me to

come over to check the wedding invitations. She was alone when I arrived, and she whispered to me that she had feelings and desires for me that she couldn't overcome. She told me that she wanted me just once before I got married and committed my life to her sister.

Well, I was in total shock, and couldn't say a word. She said, 'I'm going upstairs to my bedroom, and if you want one last wild fling, just come up and get me.' I was stunned and frozen in shock as I watched her go up the stairs. Her slender hips sensually moved from side to side and I then noticed that she wasn't wearing any panties.

I stood there for a moment, then turned and made a beeline straight for the front door. I opened the door, and ran straight towards my car.

Lo and behold... my entire future family was standing outside, all clapping! With tears in his eyes, my father-in-law put down his shotgun and hugged me and said, "We are very happy that you have passed our little test. We couldn't ask for a better man for our daughter. Welcome to the family."

The moral of this story is:

Always keep your condoms in your car.

Young Davey had been having a hard time in math class and got an 'F' on almost all of his report cards. His mum thought he'd be better off if he went to a private Catholic school. The very first day of school, Davey came home, went straight to his room and began working until he finally just fell asleep on his bed.

This continued for a long time until he got his first report card from the new school and his mum was so proud when he got an 'A' in maths. She said, "I knew you'd do better in a private school. But how did you do so well?"

"Well", said Davey, "when I walked in and saw the guy nailed to the plus sign, I knew they meant business."

FUNNY INTELLIGENT OBSERVATIONS

Do twins ever realize that one of them is unplanned?

If poison expires, is it more poisonous or is it no longer poisonous?

Which letter is silent in the word "Scent," the S or the C?

Why is the letter W, in English, called double U? Shouldn't it be called double V?

Every time you clean something, you just make something else dirty.

The word "swims" upside-down is still "swims".

100 years ago, everyone owned a horse and only the rich had cars. Today   everyone has cars and only the rich own horses.

If you rip a hole in a net, there are actually fewer holes in it than there were before.

Your fingers have fingertips but your toes don't have toetips.
Yet you can tip toe but not tipfinger.

When you transport something by car it is called a shipment.
But when you transport something by ship it is called cargo.

English is the only language where you drive in parkways and park in driveways.

It's also the only language where you recite in a play and play in a recital.

A female Australian news journalist heard about a very old Jewish man who had been going to the Western Wall to pray, twice a day, every day, for a long, long time. So she went to check it out. She went to the Western Wall and there he was, walking slowly up to the holy site. She watched him pray and after about 45 minutes, when he turned to leave, using a cane and moving very slowly, she approached him for an interview.

"Pardon me sir, I'm Rebecca Smith. I'm a news journalist from Australia. What's your name?"

"Moshe Feinberg", he replied.

"Sir, how long have you been coming to the Western Wall and praying?"

"For about 60 years."

"60 years! That's amazing! What do you pray for?"

"I pray for peace between the Christians, Jews, and the Muslims."

"I pray for all the wars and all the hatred to stop."

"I pray for all our children to grow up safely as responsible adults and to love their fellow man."

"I pray that politicians tell us the truth and put the interests of the people ahead of their own interests."

"And finally, I pray that everyone will be happy."

"How do you feel after doing this for 60 years?"

"Like I'm talking to a Brick wall!"

A door-to-door vacuum salesman goes to the first house in his new territory.

He knocks. A real mean and tough looking lady opens the door, and before she has a chance to say anything, he runs inside and dumps cow patties all over the carpet.

He says, "Lady, if this vacuum cleaner don't do wonders cleaning up that horse crap, I'll eat every chunk of it."

She turns to him with a smirk and says, "You want tomato sauce with that?"

The salesman says, "Why do you ask?"

She says, "We just moved in and we haven't got the electricity turned on yet."

A lawyer, a priest, and a young boy were in a plane that was going to crash, yet they only had 2 parachutes. The lawyer proclaimed that since he was the smartest and the most important man on the plane, that he deserved to survive. He grabbed the closest chute and jumped. The priest looks at the young boy, and reflecting back on his life, told the young boy to take the last parachute since he had already lived a wonderful and full life. The boy replied, "You can have the other chute 'Father', the smartest man on this plane just jumped out with my schoolbag!"

A guy goes to the Post Office to apply for a job. The interviewer asks him, "Are you allergic to anything?" He replies, "Yes, caffeine. I can't drink coffee." "OK, have you ever been in the military service?" "Yes", he says, "I was in Iraq for one tour." The interviewer says, "That will give you 5 extra points toward employment." Then he asks, "Are you disabled in any way?" The guy says, "Yes. A bomb exploded near me and I lost both my testicles."

The interviewer grimaces and then says, "Okay. You've got enough points for me to hire you right now. Our normal hours are from 8:00 am to 4:00 pm. You can start tomorrow at 10:00 am, and plan on starting at 10:00 am every day."

The guy is puzzled and asks, "If the work hours are from 8:00 am to 4:00 pm, why don't you want me here until 10:00 am?"

"This is a government job", the interviewer says.

"For the first two hours, we just stand around drinking coffee and scratching our balls. No point in you coming in for that........"

Recent reports indicate the Japanese banking crisis shows no signs of improving. If anything, it's getting worse. Following last week's news that Origami Bank had folded, it was today learned that Sumo Bank has gone belly up. Bonsai Bank plans to cut back some of its branches. Karaoke Bank is up for sale and is going for a song. Meanwhile, shares in Kamikaze Bank have nose-dived and 500 jobs at Karate Bank will be chopped. Analysts report that there is something fishy going on at Sushi Bank and staff there fear they may get a raw deal.

An office manager had the unenviable task of shedding staff. Of the six staff he needed to get rid of, he had already laid off five and needed to lay off one more. He had reduced his choice down to one of two people, Jill the dim witted receptionist or Jack the idiot from accounts.

Unsure of how to approach the subject he chose to give it to them straight. He called Jill, the dim wit, into his office and said, "Jill, I am going to have to lay you or Jack off." To which the dim wit replied, "Well I'm afraid you will just have to jack-off because I have a really rotten headache."

An Irishman goes to the Doctor with botty problems....
"Dactor, it's me ahrse. Oi'd like ya ta teyk a look, if ya woot".
So the doctor gets him to drop his pants and takes a look.
"Incredible", he says, "there is a £20 note lodged up here."
Tentatively he eases the twenty out of the man's bottom, and then a £10 note appears.
"This is amazing!" exclaims the Doctor. "What do you want me to do?"
"Wull fur gadness sake teyk it out, man!" shrieks the patient.
The doctor pulls out the tenner and another twenty appears, and another and another and another, etc.....
Finally the last bill comes out and no more appear.
"Ah Dactor, tank ya koindly, dat's moch batter. Joost out of interest, how moch was in dare den?"
The Doctor counts the pile of cash and says "£1,990 exactly."
"Ah, dat'd be roit," says the Irishman, "Oi knew Oi wasn't feelin' two grand."

WITTY ONE LINERS

Two blondes walk into a building....you'd think at least one of them would have seen it.

Phone answering machine message - ...If you want to buy marijuana, press the hash key...

A guy walks into the psychiatrist wearing only Clingfilm for shorts. The shrink says, "Well, I can clearly see you're nuts."

I went to buy some camouflage trousers yesterday but I couldn't find any.

I went to the butcher's the other day and I bet him 50 bucks that he couldn't reach the meat off the top shelf. He said, "No, the steaks are too high."

My friend drowned in a bowl of muesli. A strong currant pulled him in.

A man came round in hospital after a serious accident. He shouted, "Doctor, doctor, I can't feel my legs!" The doctor replied, "I know you can't, I've cut your arms off."

I went to a seafood disco last week...and pulled a muscle.

Two Eskimos sitting in a kayak were chilly. They lit a fire in the craft, it sank, proving once and for all that you can't have your kayak and heat it.

Our ice cream man was found lying on the floor of his van covered with hundreds and thousands. Police say that he topped himself.

Man goes to the doctor, with a strawberry growing out of his head. Doc says, "I'll give you some cream for that."

"Doc I can't stop singing The Green, Green Grass of Home". "That sounds like Tom Jones syndrome." "Is it common?" "It's not unusual."

You know, somebody actually complimented me on my driving today. They left a little note on the windscreen. It said, 'Parking Fine.' So that was nice.

Guy goes into the doctor's. "Doc, I've got a cricket ball stuck up my backside." "How's that?" "Don't you start."

A man reported that his girlfriend was really a ghost. He said that he had his suspicions the moment she walked through the door.

So I was getting into my car, and this bloke says to me, "Can you give me a lift?" I said, "Sure: you look great, the world's your oyster, go for it."

Police arrested two kids yesterday, one was drinking battery acid, and the other was eating fireworks. They charged one and let the other one off.

You know, somebody actually complimented me on my driving today. They left a little note on the windscreen. It said, 'Parking Fine.' So that was nice.

Two nuns were riding their bicycles down the street. The first nun says, "I've never come this way before." The second nun says, "Yeah, it's the cobblestones!"

Crazy Mike the Biker walks into a pharmacy and says to the pharmacist, "Listen, I have three girls coming over tonight. I've never had three girls at once, and I need something to keep me horny...keep me potent."
The pharmacist reaches under the counter, unlocks the bottom drawer and takes out a small cardboard box marked with a label, "Viagra Extra Strength", and says, "Here, if you take this, you'll go NUTS for 12 hours!"
Then Crazy Mike says, "Give me three boxes."
The next day, Crazy Mike walks into the same pharmacy, right up to the same pharmacist and pulls down his pants. The pharmacist looks in horror as he notices the man's penis is black and blue, and the skin is hanging off in some places.
Crazy Mike says, "Give me a tube of full strength Finalgon cream with eucalyptus."
The pharmacist replies, "FULL STRENGTH FINALGON? You're not going to put Finalgon on that are you?"
Crazy Mike says, "Hell no. It's for my wrists. The girls didn't show up."

It's the Spring of 1957 and Bobby goes to pick up his date. He's a pretty hip guy with his own car.

When he goes to the front door, the girl's father answers and invites him in. "Carrie's not ready yet. Why don't you have a seat?"

Carrie's father asks Bobby what they're planning to do. Bobby replies politely that they will probably just go to the soda shop or a movie.

"Why don't you two go out and screw? I hear all the kids are doing it!"

Naturally, this comes as a quite a surprise to Bobby — so he asks Carrie's dad to repeat himself.

"Yeah", says Carrie's father, "Carrie really likes to screw; she'll screw all night if we let her!"

A few minutes later, Carrie comes downstairs in her little poodle skirt and announces that she's ready to go.

Almost breathless with anticipation, Bobby escorts his date out the front door.

About 20 minutes later, Carrie rushes back into the house, slams the door behind her, and screams at her father, "Dad, you stupid git, it's called the TWIST!"

An Italian chef died.
He pasta way.
I never sausage a tragic thing.
He is now a pizza history.
Sending olive my support to his family.
We cannoli do so much though.
I feel for his wife. Cheese still not over it.
He died fusilli reasons
It was a farfalle from grace
Here today, gone tomato
I guess he just ran out of thyme.

So, this Italian American couple from New York, Luigi and Virginia, took the train from Grand Central Station all the way to Florida.

This was a really special trip for them, the trip of a lifetime, because it was their honeymoon.

After returning from his honeymoon in Florida with his new wife, Virginia, Luigi stopped by his old barber shop in New Jersey to say hello to his friends.

Giovanni the barber said, "Hey Luigi, how wasa da treep?"

Luigi said, "Everyting wasa perfecto except for da train ride down."

"Whata you mean, Luigi?" asked Giovanni.

"Well, we boarda da train at Grana Central Station. My beautiful'a wife Virginia, she pack a biga basket a food. She broughta da vino, some nice cigars for me, and we were lookina forward to da trip.

Everyting wasa Okey Dokey till we getta hungry and open upa da luncha basket. The conductore comea by, wagga his finger at us anda say, 'no eat indisa car. Musta use a dining car.'

"So, me and my beautiful Virginia, we go to a dining car, eat a biga lunch and starta ta open da bottle of a nice a vino!

Conductore walka by again, wagga his finger and say, 'No drinka in disa car! Musta use a cluba car.'

"So, we go to cluba car. While a drinkina da vino, I starta to lighta my biga cigar. The conductore, he waga his finger again and say, 'No a smokina disa car. Musta go to a smokina car.'

"We go to a smokina car and I smoke a my biga cigar. Then my beautiful Virginia and I, we go to a sleeper car anda go to bed.

We just about to have'a da' boom didi boom and the conductore, he walka through da hall shouting ata da top of his a voice................ 'Nofolka Virginia! Nofolka Virginia!'

"Nexta time, I'ma just gonna take a da bus!!"

IVAN SKAVINSKI SKAVAH

The maidens of Russia are fair to behold
But the prostitutes are better by far
And the best one to mount was owned by a count
Count Ivan Skavinski Skavah.

A traveling brothel once came to town
'Twas owned by a Turk from afar
And he often did brag that he could out shag
Count Ivan Skavinski Skavah.

So a day was set for the spectacle great
A holiday proclaimed by the Tsar
And the streets were aligned with the harlots assigned
To Ivan Skavinski Skavah.

They arrived at the track with their tools on the slack
The starters gun punctured the air
And midst the cheers and sighs the prick did arise
Of Abdul Abulbul Amare.

The fannys were shorn no frangers were worn
And Abduls arse revved like a car
But he could not compete with the sure steady beat
Of Ivan Skavinski Skavah.

Now Ivan had won and was polishing his gun
But as he bent down to polish his pair
Something red hot up his back passage shot
It was Abdul Abulbul Amare.

The women turned green, the men shouted "Queen!"
They were ordered apart by the Tsar
But t'was bloody bad luck poor Abdul was stuck
Up Ivan Skavinski Skavah.

The cream of the joke is when apart they were broke
Was laughed at for years by the Tsar
Because Abdul poor fool had left three parts of his tool
Up Ivan Skavinski Skavah.

A man enters the confessional and says, "Bless me father for I have sinned. It has been one month since my last confession. I've had sex with Fannie Green every week for the last month."
The priest tells the sinner, "You are forgiven. Go out and say three
Hail Mary's."
Soon, another man enters the confessional. "Father, it has been two months since my last confession. I have had sex with Fannie Green twice a week for the last two months."
This time the priest asks, "Who is this Fannie Green?"
"A new woman in the neighborhood", the sinner replies.
"Very well", says the priest. "Go and say ten Hail Mary's."
The next morning in church, the priest is standing at the front of the altar preparing to deliver his sermon when a gorgeous, tall woman enters the church.
All the men's eyes fall upon her as she slowly sashays up the aisle and sits down in a pew right in front of the altar.
    Her dress is bright emerald green and very short, with matching shiny emerald green shoes. The priest and altar boy gasp as the woman sits down with her legs slightly spread apart.
The priest turns to the altar boy and whispering asks,
    "Is that Fannie Green?"
The altar boy replies, "No Father, I think it's just the reflection off her shoes."

A Greek and an Irishman were sitting in a Starbucks one day comparing their two cultures.

Over a double latte, the Greek mentions, "We built the Parthenon, you may recall, along with the Temple of Apollo." "Well, it was the Irish that discovered the Summer and Winter Solstices", replied the Irishman. "But it was the Greeks who gave birth to advanced mathematics." "Granted, but it was the Irish who built the first timepieces." Knowing that he's about to deliver the coup de grace, the son of Athens points out with a note of finality, "Keep in mind that it was the ancient Greeks who invented the notion of sex as a pleasurable activity!" "True enough,…" replied the son of Erin, "But it was the Irish who got women involved."

Ireland 's worst air disaster occurred early this morning when a small two-seater Cessna plane crashed into a cemetery. Irish search and rescue workers have recovered 1826 bodies so far and expect that number to climb as digging continues into the night!

FUNNY REALLY GOOD INSULTS

I love what you've done with your hair. How do you get it to come out of the nostrils like that?

The only way you'll ever get laid is if you crawl up a chicken's ass and wait.

Scientists say the universe is made up of neutrons, protons and electrons. They forgot to mention morons.

Your only purpose in life is as an organ donor.

Hey, you have something on your chin... no, the 3rd one down

You are proof that evolution can go in reverse.

It's better to let someone think you're stupid than open your mouth and remove all doubt.

Everyone has the right to be stupid, but you're just abusing the privilege.

The jerk store called. They're running out of you.

If my dog had a face like yours, I would shave its butt and make it walk backwards.

Some people bring joy wherever they go. You bring joy whenever you go.

A man in a bar sees a friend at a table, drinking by himself. Approaching the friend he comments, "You look terrible. What's the problem?" "My mother died in August", his friend replied," and left me $25,000. Then in September my father died, leaving me $90,000."

"Losing both parents in two months. No wonder you're depressed."
"And last month my aunt died, and left me $15,000," his friend continued. "Three close family members lost in three months? And as if that was not sad enough, then this month", concluded, the friend, "nothing, abso' bloody 'lutely nothing!"

A man visited the pastor and his wife, a couple well known for their charitable impulses.
"Pastor", he said in a broken trembling voice,
"I wish to draw your attention to the terrible plight of a poor family in this neighbourhood.
The father is dead, the mother is too ill to work, and the nine children are starving.
They are about to be turned into the cold, empty streets unless someone pays their rent, which amounts to $900."
"How terrible!" exclaimed the preacher's wife. "May I ask who you are?"
The sympathetic visitor applied his handkerchief to his eyes, sniffled twice and said,
"I'm the landlord."

WITTY IDIOSYNCRACIES

One tequila, two tequila, three tequila...... floor.

If man evolved from monkeys and apes, why do we still have monkeys and apes?

I went to a bookstore and asked the saleswoman, "where's the self- help section?" she said if she told me, it would defeat the purpose.

What if there were no hypothetical questions?

If someone with multiple personalities threatens to kill himself, is it considered a hostage situation?

Where do forest rangers go to "get away from it all?"

What do you do when you see an endangered animal eating an endangered plant?

If a parsley farmer is sued, can they garnish his wages?

Would a fly without wings be called a walk?

Why do they lock petrol station toilets? Are they afraid someone will break-in and clean them?

If a turtle doesn't have a shell, is he homeless or naked?

Can vegetarians eat animal crackers?

How do they get deer to cross the road only at those yellow road signs?

One nice thing about egotists: they don't talk about other people.

Does the little mermaid wear an algebra?

Do infants enjoy infancy as much as adults enjoy adultery?

How is it possible to have a civil war?

If one synchronized swimmer drowns, do the rest drown too?

If you ate both pasta and antipasto, would you still be hungry?

If you try to fail, and succeed, which have you done?

Whose cruel idea was it for the word 'lisp' to have 's' in it?

Why are hemorrhoids called "hemorrhoids" instead of "assteroids"?

Why is there an expiration date on sour cream?

If you spin an oriental man in a circle three times, does he become disoriented?

Why do shops have signs, 'guide dogs only', the dogs can't read and their owners are blind?

The other day, a truly dreadful dilemma occurred in the Jewish community in the market place in downtown Jerusalem.
A sign advertised 'Half Priced Bacon'.

A piece of string walks into a bar with a few friends and orders a beer. The bartender says, "You're a piece of string aren't you?"
The piece of string says, "Yes, I am." The bartender says, "We don't serve pieces of string here. Get out."
The string walks away a little upset and sits down with his friends. A few minutes later one of his string friends goes back to the bar and orders a beer. The bartender, looking a little exasperated, says, "Listen, I've already told your mate. We don't serve pieces of string here. Get out."
So the string goes back to his table. Then the third string gets an idea. He ties himself in a knotted loop and then he pulls apart and frays all the top of his hair. Then he walks back up to the bar and orders a beer.
A different bartender squints at him and says, "Hey, you're a piece of string aren't you?"
And the string says, "Nope, I'm a frayed knot."

An American, an Australian and an Irishman were stranded on a deserted island. One day while walking on the beach they espied a strange lamp. They picked it up, gave it a polish and 'POOF' a genie flew out.
"Oh thank you for releasing me", she said. "For that, I can give you one wish each."
The American was first and said, "This island is the pits. I come from New York with the night clubs, bars,

girls, Broadway shows. I WISH I was back in New York."
And 'poof' he was gone.

The Australian was next and said, "I agree with the Yank. This island is really the pits. I come from Sydney. Ah, beautiful beaches, girls, cold beer. I WISH I was back in Sydney."

And 'poof' he was gone.

One wish to go and the genie said, "Come on hurry up. I have to go and catch up on three thousand years of living. What is it you want?"

The Irishman looked around at the deserted beach and said in a panicked tone, "Oh no, my pal Bob from New York is gone. My pal Bluey from Sydney is gone. I'm here all on my own. Gee! I WISH they were back here with me."

An old pensioner couple had just bought a nice three tier cake complete with loads of cream and six candles to signify their sixty years of marriage. The elderly husband said to his wife, "You go ahead and open the car door and I'll follow with the cake."

The elderly wife waddled off to the car. Several metres from her target she stepped in a large dogs turd and fell flat on her back. She picked herself up just as her husband came shuffling along with the cake. He stepped in the same dogs turd and fell flat on his back just like his wife did.

He looked up at his wife who said, "I just did that." To which the elderly man replied, "Filthy woman. I should jolly well rub your nose in it."

There's this blonde out for a walk. She comes to a river and sees another blonde on the opposite bank "Yoo-hoo", she shouts, "How can I get to the other side?" The second blonde looks up the river then down the river and shouts back,
"You ARE on the other side."

A married couple was in a terrible accident where the woman's face was severely burned. The doctor told the husband that they couldn't graft any skin from her body because she was too skinny. So the husband offered to donate some of his own skin.

However, the only skin on his body that the doctor felt was suitable would have to come from his buttocks.

The husband and wife agreed that they would tell no one about where the skin came from, and requested that the doctor also honor their secret. After all, this was a very delicate matter.

After the surgery was completed, everyone was astounded at the woman's new beauty. She looked more beautiful than she ever had before! All her friends and relatives just went on and on about her youthful beauty!

One day, she was alone with her husband, and she was overcome with emotion at his sacrifice. She said, "Dear, I just want to thank you for everything you did for me. How can I possibly repay you?"

"My darling", he replied, "I get all the thanks I need every time I see your mother kiss you on the cheek."

Paddy walks into the site office carrying a flask.
Murphy: "What you got there 'den?"
Paddy: "Tis me new flask."
Murphy: "What's it to do 'den?"
Paddy: "It keeps hot tings hot and cold tings cold."
Murphy: "So what you got in 'dem 'den?"
Paddy: "Two cups of coffee and an ice cream."

A drunk guy went out hunting. He had all the gear, the jacket, the boots and the double-barrelled shotgun. As he was climbing over a fence, he dropped the gun and it went off, multiple shotgun pellets peppering his penis with tiny holes. Obviously, he had to see a doctor.

When he woke up from surgery, he found that the doctor had done a marvelous job repairing it. As he got ready to go home, the doctor gave him a business card. "This is my brother's card. I'll make an appointment for you to see him."

Expectantly, the guy says, "Is your brother a doctor, a plastic surgeon maybe?"

"No", Doc replies, "he's a piccolo player and he will show you where to place your fingers so you don't piss in your eye."

Two old drunks in a bar. The first one says, "Ya know, isn't it amazing how your body changes as you get older. For instance, when I was 30 and got a hard-on, I couldn't bend it with either of my hands. By the time I was 40, I could bend it about 10 degrees if I tried really hard. By the time I was 50, I could bend it about 20 degrees, no problem. I'm gonna be 70 next week, and now I can almost bend it in half with just one hand."

"So", says the second drunk, "what's your point?"

"Well", says the first, "It just seems to me, that the older I get, the stronger my arm gets."

A farmer had his arm full length up the back-end of a pregnant cow helping her give birth when he noticed his four-year-old son standing at the fence with wide eyes, taking in the whole event. The man thought to himself, 'Great, he's four years old and I'm going to have to start explaining the birds and bees now. No need to jump the gun. I guess I'll let him ask and then I'll answer.'
After everything was over and the new born calf was stumbling around, the man walked over to his son and said, "Well son. Do you have any questions?"
"Just one", gasped the wide-eyed lad. The farmer thought, 'Excellent. Only four years old and already seems to have a good grasp of what has just happened.' So anticipating an intelligent reply because, as he kept telling his wife the boy was a clone of himself, he says to the young boy, "So tell me son, what is that question?" To which the boy replied, "Tell me dad. How fast do you reckon that calf was going when he ran into the back of that cow?"

A 10-year-old girl asked her mother, "Mum, how was I born?"
The mother smiled at her precious little child and replied, "Well, once upon a time, me and your father decided to plant a wonderful little seed. Dad put it in the earth and I took care of it every single day. After a while that little seed started to grow more and more. Lovely leaves started blooming and in a few months it turned into a beautiful healthy plant.
So, we took the plant, dried it, smoked it, and got so stoned that we forgot to wear a condom."

A man worked hard all day digging the garden and felt very stiff and sore.

His wife fluttered about him, pleased with the amount of work he had done and anxious to get him to do some more.

"Have a nice soak in the bath and I'll bring you a drink", she suggested smiling.

"Good idea", says the husband looking forward to being waited on.

He's in the bath when she comes in with a nice glass of Scotch which he accepts happily.

"If there's anything else you'd like just call", says the wife as she leaves the bathroom.

When she got halfway along the landing the husband relaxes completely and lets off an enormous long burbling fart in the bath.

A few minutes later, despite it being a very warm summer's evening, the wife comes in with a fluffy bed warmer.

"What the heck is that for?" asks the husband snappily.

"Oh Darling", says the wife, flustered, "I thought I heard you say, 'Whataboutahottawaterbottle.'"

Two foreign female immigrants have just arrived in the United States by boat and one says to the other, "I hear that the people of this country actually eat dogs."

"Odd", her companion replies, "but if we shall live in America, we might as well do as the Americans do."

Nodding emphatically, one of the immigrants points to a hot dog vendor and they both walk toward the cart.

"Two dogs, please", she says. The vendor is only too pleased to oblige, wraps both hot dogs in foil and hands them over the counter.

Excited, the companions hurry to a bench and begin to unwrap their "dogs." One of them opens the foil and begins to blush.

Staring at it for a moment, she turns to her friend and whispers cautiously, "What part did you get?"

One day, on 9/9/99, a man woke up at 9:09 a.m. in the morning, jumped on Bus #99 and went to his favourite restaurant on 9th Street. When the cashier rang up his order, it totaled $9.99.

"Oh, wow, this is an omen!" the man said, so he bought a pair of cheap binoculars at the 99¢ store, pulled out 99 cents in fares and took Bus #99 to the Race Track. As he approached Gate No. 9, he said to the ticket agent: "I would like to bet $999.99 on Horse No. 9 in the 9th race."

"Why those particular numbers?" the ticket agent asked.

"Nine seems to be my lucky number today", the man said excitedly. "I'm really on a roll!"

Feeling confident, he sat through the first eight races until Race No. 9 came up. Sure enough, he was on a roll alright.

The horse came in ninth.

There were some backwoods hillbillies in the Snowy Mountains living across the river from each other, who feuded constantly. Seb hated Clarence with a passion and never passed up a chance to throw rocks across the river at Clarence.

This went on for years until one day the Corps of Engineers came to build a bridge across that river. Seb was elated; he told his wife that finally he was going to get the chance to cross over and whip Clarence.

On the day that the bridge was completed, Seb left the house and returned in a matter of minutes. His wife asked what was wrong, didn't he intend to go over the bridge and whip Clarence?

He replied that he never had really seen Clarence up close and didn't realize his size until he started over the bridge and saw the sign: "CLEARANCE 2.3 METRES"

A guy calls a buddy, who is a horse breeder, and says he's sending a friend over to look at a horse.
The horse breeder asks "How will I recognize him?"
"That's easy, he's a midget with a speech impediment."
The midget goes there, and the breeder asks him if he's looking for a male or female horse.
"A female horth."
He shows him a prized filly.
"Nith lookin horth. Can I thee her eyeth"?
The breeder picks up the midget and he gives the horse's eyes the once over.
"Nith eyeth, can I thee her earzth"?
He picks the little fella up again, and shows him the horse's ears.
"Nith earzth, can I thee her mouf"?
The breeder is gettin' pretty ticked off by this point, but he picks him up again and shows him the horse's mouth.
"Nice mouf, can I see her twat"?
Totally mad as fire at this point, the breeder grabs him under his arms and rams the midget's head as far as he can up the horse's twat, pulls him out and slams him on the ground.
The midget gets up, sputtering and coughing.
"Perhapth I should wefwase that; Can I juth thee her wun awound a widdlebit"?

The Idiot had an interview for a job at a local chemical factory.

The department manager asked him, "Have you worked with chemicals before?"

"Yes of course I have. Don't worry, I know my stuff you know", the idiot replied.

The manager then asked him, "OK. Then can you tell me what nitrate is?"

The Idiot replied, "Well I'm hoping it's going to be time and a half."

At an International meeting, two surgeons were having an argument.

The Indian surgeon was saying, "No no no, I am telling you it is Woomba."

The African surgeon is saying, "No Man, it is hooooooommmmmm."

They go on like this for about 10 minutes. Up comes an English surgeon, and interrupts them. "Excuse me chaps, but I do believe that the word you are trying to say is 'womb'".

After he has gone away, the African turns to the Indian and says, "I bet you he has never even seen a hippopotamus, much less heard one fart under water."

A doctor in a small seaside town North Queensland would finish work every day at 6:00pm and head to his favourite bar for a coconut daiquiri which was made using the scrapings from the inside of a green coconut. He would arrive at the bar at exactly 6:10pm and sit on the same stool where his coconut daiquiri would be ready for him, made at 6:09pm by the barman Dick.

One day there was great panic because there was not a coconut in sight and the doctor was due any moment. Being a most creative fellow, the barman Dick grabbed a packet of hickory nuts from the nut bar and grated some on the top of the daiquiri and set it down on the bar just as the doctor walked in.

The doctor picked up his drink, took a sip, had a sniff of his drink, thought about it for a moment and said to the barman, "Excuse me, is this a coconut daiquiri Dick?." To which the barman replied, "No, it's a hickory daiquiri Doc."

A woman walks into a bar in Longreach, Queensland, and sits down next to a cowboy.
She asks him, "Are you a REAL cowboy?"
He replies, "Well, Maam, I brand calves, I rope steers, I mend fences, ride the plains. I also think about cows a lot of the time. Yep, I guess I'm a real cowboy alright."
The woman replies, "I'm a lesbian. I think about women all day, all evening, all the time. I think about making love with women pretty much non-stop."
The two of them sat there sipping their beers for a while, then a man walked in and sat down on the other side of the cowboy.
He leaned over towards the cowboy and said, "Are you a REAL cowboy?"
The cowboy paused for a minute and responded, "Well, I thought I was, but I just found out that I'm really a lesbian."

A 90-year-old man checked into a posh hotel to celebrate his birthday. As a surprise, some friends sent a call girl to his room. When the man answered his door, he saw before him a beautiful scantily clad young woman. "I have a present for you", she breathlessly told him.
"Really?" replied the bewildered man.
"I'm here to give you super sex." she sighed again.

He considered this for a moment and then said, "That's very nice dear. If it's all the same to you, I think I'll have the soup."

The priest of a small Irish church said to his congregation, "Anyone who has *special needs* who wants to be prayed over, please come forward to the front by the altar."

So Seamus got in line and when it was his turn, the priest said to him, "Seamus, what do you want me to pray about for you?"

Seamus replied, "Father, I need you to pray for help with my hearing."

So the priest put one finger of one hand in Seamus's ear, then placed his other hand on top of Seamus's head, and then prayed and prayed and prayed.

He prayed for special consideration from God for Seamus, and the whole congregation joined in with great enthusiasm.

After a few minutes, the priest removed his hands, stood back and asked, "Seamus, how is your hearing now?"

Seamus answered, "I don't know. It ain't 'til next week."

An elderly couple was watching a show where a preacher was talking about the healing powers of God. "To all of those who are ailed by some sickness, place one hand on the screen and your other hand on your afflicted body part and I will heal you!" the preacher intoned.

The old lady, who was having some stomach problems, placed one hand on the TV screen and the other on her stomach.

The old man placed his hand on the T.V. as well, then stuck his hand deep into his pants.

His wife looks over at him and says, "Gordon, the preacher is talking about healing the sick, not raising the dead you daft old git."

A couple were very delighted at the birth of their long awaited baby. The problem was that it had no body, arms or legs. Just a head. They didn't care because it was precious and it was theirs. So they called it… 'Head'. And every morning they would prop Head at the window so he could see what was going on. One day his mother came running in all excited and said to Head, "Head, guess what really important day it is today?"

Head gave her a blank stare and she said, "Head, it's your birthday."

To which Head replied, "Damn! More bloody hats."

After many years sitting on the window sill and watching all the kids in the park running and jumping, Head got very dejected and wished he could be just like them. Next moment there was a flash of bright light and a tiny fairy stood next to him.

"Head, I am your fairy godmother and I'm here to grant you your wish of being like the other children." And with a sweep of her wand, Head suddenly had legs, feet, arms, the lot. He was so excited he jumped off the sill, ran out the door across the road to the park but a big truck came roaring down the road, ran over him and killed him.

The moral to the story: "Quit while you're a Head."

Three prisoners, an American, a German, and an Irishman, are
scheduled to be executed by firing squad. They bring out the American
and stand him in front of the pole. He points and shouts, "Tornado!"

They all look and the American runs away. Next, they place the German in front of the firing squad. He yells, "Earthquake!" They all hit the dust and the German escapes. Next up is the Irishman. He looks around and shouts, "Fire!"

Two guys were working at a sawmill one day when one of the guys got too close to the blade and cut off his arm. His buddy put the severed arm in a plastic bag and rushed it down to the hospital to get re-attached. The next day he goes to see his chum, and finds him playing tennis. "Incredible", says his friend. "Medical science is amazing."

Another month goes by and the same two guys are again at the sawmill working when the same guy gets too close to the spinning blade and this time his leg gets cut off. Again, his buddy takes the leg, puts it in a plastic bag and takes it to the hospital to get re-attached. The next day, he goes down to see his chum and finds him outside playing football. "Incredible", says his friend. "Medical science is amazing!"

Another month goes by and again the same two friends are at the mill cutting wood when suddenly the same guy bends down too close to the blade and off comes his head. Well, his friend takes the head, puts it in a plastic bag, and heads to the hospital to get it re-attached. The next day he goes to see his friend but can't find him. He sees the doctor walking down the hall and says, "Doc, where is my friend? I brought him in yesterday." The doctor thinks for a minute and says, "Oh yeah, some idiot put his head in a plastic bag and he suffocated."

An idiot went into his local library, stormed up to the front desk and said, "I have a complaint!"

"Yes, Sir?" replied the clerk.

The idiot man continues, "I borrowed a book last week and it was horrible!"

"What was wrong with it?" the clerk asked.

"It had way too many characters and there was no plot whatsoever!" the idiot man replied.

The librarian nodded and said, "Ahh, now I understand, so you must be the person who took our phone book."

One bright sunny day a man was traveling down St Kilda Road in Melbourne with his fat ugly nagging wife at his side. He hated her. Suddenly a police car signaled them to pull over. The police officer walked to the driver's window and said to the man, "Can I see your license please sir?"

"What did he say?" squawked the ugly nagging wife.

"He said he wants to see my license", sneered the husband.

"You know you were doing 90 kilometres an hour in a 60 zone", said the policeman.

"What did he say?" squawked the ugly nag.

"He asked if I knew I was doing 90 in a 60 zone", sneered the husband again.

"I see you come from Dandenong, is that right?" asked the policeman.

"What did he say?" the ugly nag squawked.

"He said he noticed we come from Dandenong", the increasingly detesting husband hissed.

"I used to go out with a girl from Dandenong", mused the policeman.

"What did he say?" squawked the ugly nag again.

"He said he used to go out with a girl from Dandenong", the man again hissed.

"Yeah!" mused the policeman again. "You know she was the fattest, ugliest, worst root I ever met."

"What did he say?" demanded the wife.

The man turned to his wife and loudly yells, "HE SAID HE THINKS HE KNOWS YOU."

I was in an inner city tavern last night, at the bar waiting for a beer, when a big o'l, butt-ugly heifer came up behind me and slapped me on the butt.

She said, "Hey sexy, I dig old guys -- how about giving me your number."

I looked at her and said, "Have you got a pen?"

She enthusiastically said, "I sure do honey."

I said, "Well you better get back into it before the farmer notices you're missing."

My dental surgery is on Monday.

An Irishman is stumbling through the woods, totally drunk, when he comes upon a preacher baptizing people in the river. He proceeds into the water, subsequently bumping into the preacher. The preacher turns around and is almost overcome by the smell of alcohol, whereupon, he asks the drunk, "Are you ready to find Jesus?" The drunk shouts, "Yesh, I am."

So the preacher grabs him and dunks him in the water. He pulls him back and asks, "Brother, have you found Jesus?" The drunk replies, "No, I haven't found Jesus!"

The preacher, shocked at the answer, dunks him again but for a little longer. He again pulls him out of the water and asks, "Have you found Jesus, brother?" The drunk answers, "No, I haven't found Jesus!"

By this time, the preacher is at his wits end and, eager to have a new convert, dunks the drunk again -- but this time holds him down for about 30 seconds, and when he begins kicking his arms and legs about, he pulls him up. The preacher again asks the drunk, "For the love of God man, have you found Jesus?"

The drunk staggers upright, wipes his eyes, coughs up a bit of water, catches his breath, and slurs, "Tell me preacher, are you sure thish is the spot where you lost him."

A drunk was sitting at the bar of a very noisy, very smoky and very crowded inner city hotel in Melbourne. The drinkers were all young and hippy like. A young girl in a thin floral cut away sleeveless hippy dress, forced her way to the crowded bar and stood along side the drunk with her arm in the air trying to get the waiters attention. The drunk slowly turned his head to her and was confronted by a hairy armpit not 6 inches from his face.

"Hey waiter", he slurred, "get the ballerina a drink."

This was done and not 10 minutes later the hippy girl was back, arm in the air, armpit in the drunks face and trying to get the waiters attention.

"Hey waiter", slurred the drunk again, "get the ballerina a drink."

After the girl had left, the waiter said to the drunk, "So you know her do you?"

"Never sheen her 'afore in me loif", slurred the drunk.

"Then how do you know she's a ballerina?" asked the waiter.

"Becaush", slurred the drunk, "any girl who can lift her leg that high, hash got to be a ballerina."

It was a country Aussie Rules football match and the side was short of players, so just for the one match the coach enlisted a visiting rugby player to fill the numbers.

The coach dragged the rugby player aside and said, "I know you don't know much about our game and you will probably get tired quickly, so I'll let you have a run around down in the back pocket, and then I'll pull you off at quarter time."

The eyes of the rugby player lit up and he said, "Gee that's a lot better than rugby. All we ever got there at quarter time was half an orange."

A man who aspired to be an actor, finally managed to get a small part in a Broadway play. All he had to do was strut on to the stage at the appropriate moment, wait for a loud bang and recite, "Hark! I hear a pistol shot."

So he went home and practised every conceivable way of saying the one line in the most dramatic way. This was his big chance and no way was he going to stuff up.

The big opening night arrived and the theatre was packed with dignitaries and important people. The actor was ready but incredibly nervous. His big moment arrived to strut on to the stage and as he did, he glanced at the huge audience and immediately his nervousness rose ten fold. He took his place and right on cue a loud bang was heard from the side of the stage.

The actor puffed out his chest, put a hand to his ear and announced, "Hark! I hear a shistol pot, shostol pit, postol shit. Ah cowshit, bullshit, duckshit, I didn't want to be in the stupid play in the first place!"

Every day, a male co-worker walks up very close to a lady standing at the coffee machine, inhales a big breath of air and tells her that her hair smells nice.

After a week of this, she can't stand it anymore and takes her complaint to a supervisor in the personnel department and states that she wants to make a sexual harassment grievance against him.

The Human Resources supervisor is puzzled by this decision and asks", What's sexually threatening about a co-worker telling you your hair smells nice?"

The woman replies, "It's Frank, the dwarf."

A lady rushes into a pharmacist asking, "Are you a pharmacist?"
He said, "Yes I am."
"Will you please tell me something about Viagra?" she asked.
The pharmacist said, "I would be glad to. Well, it is a prescription medication used for men who are having sexual problems. Your doctor has to write a prescription for this medication."
He also further states, "It's a great medication, I even take it at times."
The lady then interrupts to ask, "Can I get it over the counter?"
"If I take two," says the pharmacist.

THE PIG: A PROBLEM OF HIGHER MATHEMATICS

If a pig drinks a quart of milk before it starts
Then runs one mile before it farts
And the further it runs the worse it gits
How far will it run before it shits?

Well in order to work this out I bet
We must go back to where the fart was let
Now a farmer said he saw the pig pass
With butterfat squirting out of its arse.

The farmer was a mile from where the pig started
And the pig passed the farmer just after it farted
It was so darned funny the farmer had to laugh
The pig had then run a mile and a half.

Now if the pig is lucky and controls its gas
And runs one mile with a puckered ass
It would seem to me if he keeps his wits
He'll do five miles before he shits.

The Pastor entered his donkey in a race and it won.

The Pastor was so pleased with the donkey that he entered it in the race again and it won again.

The local paper read: PASTOR'S ASS OUT FRONT. The Bishop was so upset with this kind of publicity that he ordered the Pastor not to enter the donkey in another race. The next day the local paper headline read: BISHOP SCRATCHES PASTOR'S ASS.

This was too much for the Bishop so he ordered the Pastor to get rid of the donkey. The Pastor decided to give it to a Nun in a nearby convent. The local paper, hearing of the news, posted the following headline the next day: NUN HAS BEST ASS IN TOWN.

The Bishop was furious. He informed the Nun that she would have to get rid of the donkey so she sold it to a farm for $10. The next day the paper read: NUN SELLS ASS FOR $10.

This was definitely way too much for the Bishop so he ordered the Nun to buy back the donkey and lead it to the plains where it could run wild. The next day the headlines read: NUN ANNOUNCES HER ASS IS WILD AND FREE.

A guy takes his wife out for the night. They end up at a disco where there's a guy on the dance floor giving it large – break dancing, moonwalking, back flips, every dance move going.

The wife turns to her husband and says, "See that guy on the dance floor? 25 years ago, he proposed to me and I turned him down."

The husband replies, "It looks like he's still celebrating."

After having their 11th child, an Irish couple decided that that was enough, as they couldn't afford another bed. So the husband went to his doctor and told him that he and his wife didn't want to have any more children.

The doctor told him there was a procedure called a vasectomy that would fix the problem but it was expensive. A less costly alternative was to go home, get a large firecracker, light it, put it in a beer can, then hold the can up to his ear and count to 10.

The husband said to the doctor, "B'Jayzus, I may not be the smartest guy in the world, but I don't see how putting a firework in a beer can next to my ear is going to help me with my problem."

"Trust me, it will do the job", said the doctor.

So the Irishman went home, lit a cracker and put it in a beer can. He held the can up to his ear and began to count: "1, 2, 3, 4, 5, … ", at which point he paused, and placed the beer can between his legs so he could continue counting on his other hand.

This procedure also works in New Zealand and Tasmania.

A guy comes home from the pub, three sheets to the wind and all three sheets ripping badly. Stale beer sloshing around in his belly like a keg adrift in a roiling sea.

He sloshes through the door and is met by his wife, who is scowling, figuring he's been out jumping some young hussey.

"Where the hell you been all night?" she demands.

"At this fantastic new saloon", he says. "The Golden Saloon. Everything there is golden."

"Bullshit! There's no such place!"

Guy says, "Sure there is! Joint's got huge golden doors, a golden floor. Hell, even the urinal's gold!"

The wife still doesn't believe his story, and the next day checks the phone book, finding a place across town called the Golden Saloon. She calls up the place to check her husband's story. "Is this the Golden Saloon?" she asks when the bartender answers the phone.

"Yes, it is", bartender answers.

"Do you have huge golden doors?"

"Sure do."

"Do you have golden floors?"

"Most certainly do."

"What about golden urinals?"

There's a long pause, then the woman hears the bartender yelling, "Hey, Duke, I think I got a lead on the guy who pissed in your saxophone!"

There is a medical distinction between Guts and Balls. We've heard colleagues referring to people with Guts or with Balls. Do they, however, know the difference between them?

Here's the official distinction; straight from the British Medical Journal: Volume 323; page 295; published August 2021

GUTS - Is arriving home late, after a night out with the lads, full of booze and bad manners, being met by your wife with a broom, and having the Guts to ask: "Are you still cleaning, or are you flying off somewhere?"

BALLS - Is coming home late after a night out with the lads, full of booze and bad manners, smelling of perfume and cigarette smoke, lipstick on your collar, slapping your wife on the butt and having the Balls to say:

"You're next, Chubby"

I trust this clears up any confusion.

Medically speaking, there is no difference in the outcome; both are fatal.

An elderly, but hardy cattleman from the Gulf country of North Queensland, once told a young female neighbour, if she wanted to live a long life, the secret was to sprinkle a pinch of gunpowder on her oatmeal each morning.

So when the young lady got married she took this advice and did this religiously every day and lived to the age of 103.

She left behind 14 children, 30 grandchildren, 21 great-grandchildren, five great-great-grandchildren and a 10 metre wide hole where the crematorium used to be.

A wealthy man was driving his BMW737 limo down Toorak Road in Melbourne, heading home to his palatial Georgian mansion in Landsell road.

He stopped at a pedestrian crossing in South Yarra, and noticed 2 men kneeling down on all fours, nibbling grass.

Intrigued, he pulled his car to the sidewalk and called them over. He asked them what they were doing and one of them said, "Sir! We don't have any money to buy food. All we can do is eat this free grass in the park."

Astonished that this should happen in such an affluent city he said, "Come on. Hop in the car. I will take you home to my place and make sure you are well fed."

"But sir, we are here with our wife's and two children. They are over there also eating grass."

"Not a problem. Everybody in the car." So, they all got in the big limo and headed down Toorak Road.

Feeling good like he had helped the less fortunate of this world, the pompous business man turned to his passengers and said, "You guys don't know how lucky you are. You are going to be so well fed at my home. You are going to love it. The grass on the front lawn is almost half a metre high."

Ageing Mildred was a 93 year-old woman who was particularly despondent over the recent death of her husband Earl.

She decided that she would just kill herself and join him in death.

Thinking that it would be best to get it over with quickly, she took out Earl's old Army pistol and made the decision to shoot herself in the heart since it was so badly broken in the first place.

Not wanting to miss the vital organ and become a vegetable and a burden to someone, she called her doctor to inquire as to just exactly where the heart would be.

"On a woman"" the doctor said, "your heart would be just below your left breast."

Later that night, Mildred was admitted to the hospital..... with a gunshot wound to her left knee.

GRANPARENTS ANSWERING MACHINE

"Good morning ... at present we are not at home, but please leave your message after you hear the beep ... beeeeeppp ...

If you are one of our children, dial 1 and then select the option from 1 to 5 in order of "birth arrival" so we know who it is.

If you need us to stay with the children, press 2

If you want to borrow the car, press 3

If you want us to wash your clothes and do ironing, press 4

If you want the grandchildren to sleep here tonight, press 5

If you want us to pick up the children at school, press 6

If you want us to prepare a meal for Sunday or to have it delivered to your home, press 7

If you want to come to eat here, press 8

If you need money, press 9

If you are going to invite us to dinner or take us to the theatre, start talking .... we are listening ..!"

"**M**um", said little Johnny, "If I promise to be good, can I have five dollars?"
To which his mother replied, "Why can't you be good for nothing, just like your father?"

My grandfather who's as tough as leather
Loves tickling his balls with a feather
But the thing he likes best
While having a rest
Is just simply knocking them together.

Mick, from county Cork, died in a fire and was burnt pretty bad and the morgue needed someone to identify the body. So, his two best friends, Seamus and Sean, also from county Cork, were sent for. Seamus went in and the mortician pulled back the sheet. Seamus looked at the front of the body and said, "Yup, he's burnt pretty bad. Roll him over." So the mortician rolled him over and Seamus looked and said "Nope, it ain't Mick."
The mortician thought that was rather strange and then he brought Sean in to identify the body. Sean took a look at the front of the body and said, "Yup he's burnt real bad, roll him over." The mortician rolled him over and Sean looked down and said, "Nope, it ain't Mick."
The mortician asked, "How can you tell?" Sean said, "Well, Mick had two assholes." "What!, He had two assholes?" said the mortician. "Yup, everyone knew he had two assholes. Every time the three of us went into town, folks would say, "Look! Here comes Mick with them two assholes…."

After retiring, I went to the Social Security office to apply for Social Security. The woman behind the counter asked me for my driver's license to verify my age. I looked in my pockets and realized I had left my wallet at home. I told the woman that I was very sorry, but I would have to go home and come back later.

The woman said, "Unbutton your shirt"

So I opened my shirt revealing my curly silver hair.

She said, "That silver hair on your chest is proof enough for me", and she processed my Social Security application.

When I got home, I excitedly told my wife about my experience at the Social Security office. She said, "You should have dropped your pants. You would have gotten disability too."

A man walks out of a pub in Sydney, stumbling back and forth with a key in his hand.

A cop on the beat sees him and approaches, "Can I help you?"

"Yesss, sssshombody stole me car!" the man slurred.

The cop asks, "Well now, where was your car the last time you saw it?"

"It wash at the end of this key."

About this time the cop looks down to see that the mans member is being

exhibited for all to see. He then asks, "Are you aware that you are exposing yourself?"

The drunk looks down woefully and moans, "OOOH GOD... they got me girlfriend too!!"

A drunk stumbles out of the bar and phones the police to report that thieves had been in his car. "They've stolen the dashboard, the shteering wheel, the brake pedal, the radio, and even the bloody shelerator. Bastards!!", he slurs. However, before the police investigation could start, the police station phone rings a second time and the same voice came over the line. "Never mind", he said with a hiccup, "I got in the bloody back seat by mishtake."

Four old-timers were playing their weekly game of golf.
One remarked how nice it would be to wake up on Christmas morning, roll out of bed and without an argument go directly to the golf course, meet his buddies and play a round.
His buddies all chimed in said, "Let's do it! We'll make it a priority -
figure out a way and meet here early, Christmas morning."
Months later, that special morning arrives, and there they are on the golf course. The first guy says, "Boy this game cost me a fortune! I bought my wife a diamond ring that she can't take her eyes off of."
The second guy says, "I spent a ton too. My wife is at home planning the cruise I gave her. She was up to her eyeballs in brochures."
The third guy says "Well my wife is at home admiring her new car, reading the manual."
They all turned to the last guy in the group who is staring at them like they have lost their minds.
"I can't believe you all went to such expense for this golf game. I slapped my wife on the bum and said, 'Well babe, Merry Christmas! It's a great morning - golf course or intercourse?"
She said, "Don't forget your hat.'"

One day, a man staggers into the emergency room with a concussion, multiple bruises, and a five iron golf club wrapped around his neck.

Naturally the doctor is curious and asks him what happened to him.

"Well, it was like this" says the man. "I was enjoying a quiet round of golf with my wife. We were playing the fifth hole which is really difficult and we both sliced our drives into a field full of cows. We went into the field to look for our balls, and while I was searching, I noticed that one of the cows had something white stuck up its backside. So, I went over, lifted up the cow's tail, and sure enough, there was a golf ball with my wife's monogram on it stuck right in the middle of the cow's butt. That's when I made my big mistake."

"Why, what did you do?", asks the doctor.

The man says, "Well, I lifted the cows tail, pointed, and shouted to my wife, 'Hey! This looks like yours!'"

Paddy and Murphy drive their pickup truck into a Bunnings lumberyard.

Paddy walks in the office and says to the man on the desk, "We need some four by twos."

The clerk said, "You mean two by fours, don't you?"

Paddy said, "Just a minute, I'll go check", and he went back to the pickup truck to consult with Murphy.

He returns a minute later, and says, "Yeah, I meant two by fours."

"Allright", says the clerk, "How long do you need them?"

Paddy pauses for a minute, and says, "I'd better go check."

So off Paddy goes to the pickup truck again to consult with Murphy.

After a while, Paddy returns to the office and says, "We will need them for quite a long time. We're gonna build a house."

GETTING OLD

For seventy odd years I've been buggered
With all sorts of horrible pains
I've had every ailment I reckon
From ulcers to varicose veins.

I've spent a small fortune at chemists
And lain months in hospital beds
And the stuff that I've taken to shift me
Has torn my old arsehole to shreds.

I've a neurotic nerve as a torture
They say I have a murmuring heart
While I strain like a bloody great carthorse
And all I squeeze out is a fart.

I've got rheumatic gout in my fingers
It's made them all sizes and shapes
And the piles that I have in my rectum
Hang down like a great bunch of grapes.

My diet is god awful putrid
If I have a square meal I feel sick
And there's also a funny sensation
Like rats gnawing holes in my prick.

Uric acid they say is my trouble
So I do not mind telling you this
I've to whistle 'The last Rose of Summer'
Just to get the old doodle to piss.

And as for a first class erection
The idea is simply absurd
For my cocks like an undersized maggot
And as soft as a night commode turd.

I spend all day in the shithouse
Or moaning and groaning in bed
While my bowels simply murmur in passing
It's time the poor bastard was dead.

It was the day of O'Rourke's wife's funeral and together with his family and friends he was at his wife's graveside for the burial.

The funeral service had barely finished, when there was a massive clap of thunder, which was followed by a tremendous bolt of lightning, then accompanied by even more thunder rumbling away in the distance.

O'Rourke looked at the pastor and calmly said, "Well, she's there. It's God's problem now and the very best of luck with that."

Two old men, Murphy and Sean, were contemplating life when Murphy asked, "If you had to get one or the other, would you rather get Parkinson's or Alzheimer's?"

"Sure, I'd rather have Parkinson's", replied Sean.

"Why would ye say that?" asked Murphy.

"Very simple", said Sean, "'Tis better to spill a couple of ounces of Jameson whiskey than to forget where you keep the bloody bottle!"

Jack, age 92, and Marg, age 89, living in Auckland, are all excited about their decision to get married. They go for a stroll to discuss the wedding, and on the way they pass a chemist shop and Jack suggests they go in.

Jack addresses the man behind the counter:

"Are you the owner?"

The pharmacist answers, "Yes."

Jack: "We're about to get married. Do you sell heart medication?"

Pharmacist: "Of course we do."

Jack: "How about medicine for circulation?"

Pharmacist: "All kinds "

Jack: "Medicine for rheumatism?"

Pharmacist: "Definitely."

Jack: "How about suppositories?"

Pharmacist: "You bet!"

Jack: "Medicine for memory problems, arthritis, and Alzheimer's?"

Pharmacist: "Yes, a large variety. The works."

Jack: "What about vitamins, sleeping pills, antidotes for Parkinson's disease?"

Pharmacist: "Absolutely."

Jack: "Everything for heartburn and indigestion?"

Pharmacist: "We sure do..."

Jack: "You sell wheelchairs and walkers and canes?"

Pharmacist: "All speeds and sizes."

Jack: "Adult incontinence pants?"

Pharmacist: "Sure."

Jack: "Then we'd like to use this store for our wedding presents list."

A doctor and his wife are having a fight at the breakfast table. Husband gets up in a rage and says, "And you are no good in bed either", and storms out of the house. After sometime he realizes he was nasty and decides to make amends and calls home.

She comes to the phone after many rings and the irritated husband says, "What took you so long to answer the phone?"

She says, "I was in bed."

"In bed this late, doing what?" shouts the doctor.

"Getting a second opinion!"

The grade two teacher was organizing the end of year concert where every student had to perform on stage either in a group or alone. She asked each student what they might like to do and the first one, little Jennifer, said she would sing Three Blind Mice. Another one, little Timmy said he would recite a nursery rhyme. The last student was sweet and shy little Megan. "Now what would you like to do Megan?" asked the teacher.

"Can't do nuffin" said sweet, shy little Megan.

"Oh come now", said the teacher, "let's see what you can do. You live on a farm don't you? Perhaps you could imitate some sounds you have heard on the farm?"

This was a good idea for Megan and a week later the concert was on. Sweet and shy little Megan was a perfect picture. Mum had curled her long hair with little pink bows. She had new shoes and a pretty new pink frock to go with her pink bows.

The school hall was packed to the rafters. Little Jennifer sang her song. Little Timmy recited his poem and all the other students did their thing. Then it was time for sweet and shy little Megan. The teacher stood in front of the microphone and condescendingly sickly sweet said, "And now we have little Megan. Megan lives on a farm and tonight, Megan is going to do some farm calls that she has heard on her farm."

Sweet and shy little Megan strode over to the microphone, tilted her head back, cupped her hands to her mouth and in a big loud voice that everyone could hear, she yelled, "GET OFF THE BLOODY TRACTOR!!!!!"

There was a young girl from Madras
Who had a most beautiful ass
Not round and pink
As you would probably think
But was grey had big ears and ate grass.

A guy goes to hell and is met by the devil, who explains that the punishments are changed every thousand years and he is to select his first punishment. So, the devil takes the man on a quick tour, showing him the three examples of what is available. The first room has a young guy on the wall being whipped. The new guy, not keen on this, asks to see the next room. The next room has a middle-aged guy being tortured with fire. The new guy immediately asks to see the third room. It has a group of people standing waist deep in a pool of stinking sewage drinking cups of tea. Now this looks more civilized, the guy thinks, and chooses it and jumps into the pool. Just then, a bell rang, and the devil yelled out loud, "OK you lot, tea break is over for another day, get back standing on your heads."

A man came home from the food factory and explained to his wife that he had been sacked because he got caught sticking his willie in the gherkin cutter.
"What happened to the gherkin cutter?" asked his wife.
"Oh, she got the sack as well."

A guy walks in to a bar with a pet crocodile at his side. He puts the croc up on the bar. He turns to the astonished patrons.
"I'll make you a deal. I'll open this crocodile's mouth and place my genitals inside. The croc will close his mouth for one minute. He will then open his mouth and I will remove my unit unscathed. In return for witnessing this spectacle, each of you will buy me a drink."
The crowd murmured their approval. The man stood up on the bar, dropped his trousers, and placed his privates in the crocodiles open mouth. The croc closed his mouth

as the crowd gasped.

After one minute, the man grabbed a beer bottle and whacked the crocodile hard on the top of its head. The croc opened its mouth and the man removed his genitals - unscathed as promised.

The crowd cheered and the first of his free drinks was delivered. The man stood up again and made another offer.

"I'll pay anyone $100 who is willing to give it a try."

A hush fell over the crowd. After a while, a hand went up in the back of the bar. A skinny unattractive middle aged woman timidly spoke up.

"I'll try, but you have to promise not to hit me on the head with the beer bottle."

A minister was completing a temperance sermon. With great emphasis he said, "If I had all the beer in the world, I'd take it and pour it into the river."

With even greater emphasis he said, "And if I had all the wine in the world, I'd take it and pour it into the river."

And then finally, shaking his fist in the air, he thundered, "And if I had all the whiskey in the world, I'd take it and pour it into the river."

Sermon complete, he sat down. The song leader stood very cautiously and announced with a smile, nearly laughing, "For our closing song, let us sing Hymn #365, 'Shall We Gather at the River.'"

In the garden of Eden lay Adam
Gently caressing his madam
And he smiled with great mirth
Because he knew that on earth
There was only one set of balls and he had'em.

A big time Gangster finds out that his personal accountant, Robert, has cheated him out of 5 million bucks. His accountant is deaf. That was the reason he got the job in the first place. It was assumed that Robert would hear nothing that he might have to testify about in court.

When the Gangster goes to confront Robert about his missing five million, he takes along his lawyer who knows sign language.

The Gangster tells the lawyer, "Ask him where the 5 million bucks are, that he stole from me."

The lawyer, using sign language, asks Robert where the money is. Robert signs back, "I don't know what you are talking about."

The lawyer tells the Gangster, "He says he doesn't know what you are talking about."

The Gangster pulls out a pistol, puts it to Robert's temple and says, "Ask him again!"

The lawyer signs to Robert, "He'll kill you if you don't tell him."

Robert signs back, "OK. You win! The money is in a black bag, hidden in the cupboard at my nephew's house.!"

The Gangster asks the lawyer, "What did he say?"

The lawyer replies, "He says you don't have the guts to pull the trigger."

_Prince Charles was 22 years old and was in Australia doing his Royal duties of visiting the colonies for the first time.

He was invited to attend and open the Birdsville Annual Race Day in the central Australian Outback.

His plane touched down on the dusty earthen strip of dirt that served as the runway.

The temperature was a hot 37 degrees centigrade.

Charles emerged from the air-conditioned plane to the

warm greetings of the gathered dignitaries, local station owners, ringers and numerous pastoralists.

He was of course, resplendent in a tweed jacket, Saville Row slacks, paisley shirt and tie, topped off by perfectly polished shoes. But on his head was a hairy type of hat with a hairy tail attached and it was obviously made from the pelt of a fox.

One of the dignitaries welcomed him and then asked him what was he wearing on his head in this hot dusty place. Charles, in his pompous English accent said, "Well, I didn't know what to wear, so I rang mummy and asked her opinion. And she asked me, 'Where are you going?' And I said 'I'm going to Birdsville.'

And she said, 'Where the focs 'at'. So I did."

While in England, Murphy walks into a pub and has a couple of pints. As he starts to leave, the bartender tells him he owes nine quid. "But I paid, don't you remember?" says Murphy. "Fair enough", says the bartender. "If you said you paid, you did." Murphy walks outside and sees his friend Sullivan and tells him the bartender can't keep track of whether his customers have paid. So Sullivan rushes in, orders a couple of beers and later pulls the same stunt. The barkeep says, "If you say you paid, I'll take your word for it." Sullivan goes into the street and meets O'Reilly and tells him how to get free drinks. O'Reilly hurries into the bar and orders whiskey. After a while the bartender leans over and tells O'Reilly, "You know, a funny thing happened in here twice tonight. Two men had some drinks, neither paid, and both claimed that they did. The next guy who tries that stunt is going to get punched right in the nose!"

"Don't bother me with your troubles", responds O'Reilly, "Just give me my change and I'll be on my way."

FUNNY THOUGHTS AND OBSERVATIONS

As I have grown older, I have learned that pleasing everyone is impossible, but pissing everyone off is a piece of cake.

Condoms don't guarantee safe sex anymore.....
A friend of mine was wearing one when he was shot by the woman's husband.

I think it is just terrible and disgusting how everyone has treated Lance Armstrong, especially after what he achieved, winning 7 Tour de France races, whilst on drugs. When I was on drugs, I couldn't even find my damn bike.

A guy broke into my apartment last week. He didn't take my TV, just the remote. Now he drives by and changes the channels. Sick bastard.

On the morning that Daylight Savings Time ended I stopped in to visit my aging friend. He was busy covering his penis with black shoe polish. I said to him, "You better get your hearing checked - you're supposed to turn your clock back".

Just got scammed out of $25. Bought Tiger Woods DVD entitled 'My Favourite 18 Holes'. Turns out it's all about golf. Absolute waste of money. Pass this on so others don't get scammed.

Doctor asks pregnant prostitute, "Do you know who the father is?" "Hey dumb ass, if you ate a can of beans, would you know which one made you fart?"

Murphy's Law: For every sock you lose in the dryer, you gain a Tupperware lid in the kitchen cabinet.

Is an argument between two Vegans still called a 'Beef'.

As I was standing there watching a dog chase its tail, I thought how stupid and easily amused dogs were. Then I realised I was standing there watching a dog chase its tail

Old Chinese Saying: Happiness is a warm bum and a dry fart.

I can't dance to save my life.
But when I step in dog shit, I can moonwalk better than Michael Jackson.

Men at 25 play football.
Men at 40 play tennis.
Men at 60 play golf.
Have you noticed how as you get older, the balls you play with get smaller?

She was so bow legged and he was so knock kneed, that when they stood next to each other, they spelt the word OX.

The difference between 'light' and 'hard' is: you can go to sleep with a light-on.

The graduate with a Science degree asks, "Why does it work?"
The graduate with an Engineering degree asks, "How does it work?"
The graduate with a Commerce degree asks, "How much will it cost?"
The graduate with an Arts degree asks, "Do you want fries with that?

The groomsman at the wedding of his best mate, was reading out the obligatory telegrams.
He got to one that came from the French Embassy. Not being at all familiar with the French language, he read the telegram which to him said, "To ze beeutifull bride on ze occasion of your vedding, ve vish you a penis. Oh, sorry, I think that should be 'appiness."

Four nuns were standing in line at the gates of heaven.
    Peter asks the first if she has ever sinned. "Well, once I looked at a man's penis", she said. "Put some of this holy water on your eyes and you may enter heaven", Peter told her.
    Peter then asked the second nun if she had ever sinned. "Well, once I held a man's penis", she replied. "Put your hand in this holy water and you may enter heaven", he said.
    Just then the fourth nun pushed ahead of the third nun. Peter asked her, "Why did you push ahead in line?"
    "Because", she said, pointing to the nun behind her, "I wanted to make sure I got to gargle that water before she sticks her arse in it!"

THE FIRST TIME I TRIED IT

I remember the first time I tried it
I was just a green kid of fifteen
And although she was a little bit younger
She was far more composed and serene.

It was down in the barn I remember
At the close of a fine summers day
The evening was scented of clover
And the fragrance of new mown hay.

I remember I spoke to her softly
And the touch of her body was warm
As she moved up lovingly toward me
And nestled her head in my arm.

I was eager but awkwardly backward
Uncertain of how to proceed
But a sense of purpose possessed me
As I prepared to do the deed.

Later I found myself standing
Uncertain to stay or to run
But a feeling of joy came over me
As I knew the job was well done.

Thirty years have gone by since that day
And I will never forget I vow
The thrill and the joy I felt as a boy
On the day............that I first milked a cow.

There were four brothers, Somebody, Nobody, Brain and Mad. One day Somebody got angry and killed Nobody, then Brain went in the toilet crying. Mad then phoned the police and said, "Somebody killed Nobody". The Police said, "Where is your brain". Mad said, "He is in the toilet."

My wife came home from the doctors today and was looking all pleased with herself, so I asked her why she was so happy.
She said, "The doctor said that for a 45 year old woman, I've got the breasts of an 18 year old."
I said, "Oh yeah, and what did he say about your 45 year old arse?"
She said, "Your name never came up in conversation."

There was an incident this morning when five Germans in an Audi Quattro arrived at the Italian border.
The Italian customs officer stopped them and told them:
"Itsa illegala to putta 5 people in a Quattro!"
"Vot do you mean, it's illegal?" the German driver asked.
"Quattro means four!" replied the Italian official.
"Quattro iz just ze name of ze fokken automobile", the Germans retorted in disbelief. "Look at ze dam paperz: Ze car is dezigned to carry 5 people!"
"You canta pulla thata one on me!" replied the Italian customs officer. "Quattro meansa four. You havea five-a people ina your car and you are therefore breaking the law!"
The German replied angrily, "You ideeiot! Call ze zupervizor over! … Schnell! I vont to spik to zumvun viz more intelligence!"
"Sorry", responded the Italian customs officer, "He canta comea … He'sa busy witha two guys in a Fiat Uno."

There was a young man from Newcastle
Who received quite a remarkable parcel
In a box with two locks
Were two cocks with the pox
Two balls and the rim of an arsehole.

A first-grade teacher, Ms. Brooks, was having trouble with one of her students. The teacher asked, "Harry, what's your problem?" Harry answered, "I'm too smart for the 1st grade. My sister is in the 3rd grade and I'm smarter than she is! I think I should be in the 3rd grade too!"

Ms. Brooks had enough. She took Harry to the principal's office. While Harry waited in the outer office, the teacher explained to the principal what the situation was. The principal told Ms. Brooks he would give the boy a test. If he failed to answer any of his questions he was to go back to the 1st grade and behave. She agreed. Harry was brought in and the conditions were explained to him and he agreed to take the test.

Principal: "What is 3 x 3?"

Harry: "9."

Principal: "What is 6 x 6?"

Harry: "36"

And so it went with every question the principal thought a 3rd grader should know. The principal looks at Ms. Brooks and tells her, "I think Harry can go to the 3rd grade."

Ms. Brooks says to the principal, "Let me ask him some questions?"

The principal and Harry both agreed.

Ms. Brooks asks, "What does a cow have four of that I have only two of?"

Harry, after a moment: "Legs."

Ms. Brooks: "What is in your pants that you have but I do not have?"

The principal wondered why would she ask such a question!

Harry replied: "Pockets."

Ms Brooks: "What does a dog do that a man steps into?"

Harry: "Pants."

Ms. Brooks: "What starts with a C, ends with a T, is hairy, oval, and contains thin, whitish liquid?"

Harry: "Coconut."

The principal sat forward with his mouth hanging open.

Ms Brooks: "What goes in hard and pink and then comes out soft and sticky?"

The principal's eyes opened really wide and before he could stop the answer, Harry replied, "Bubble gum."

Ms. Brooks: "What does a man do standing up, a woman does sitting down and a dog does on three legs?"

Harry: "Shake hands."

The principal was trembling.

Ms. Brooks: "What word starts with an 'F' and ends in a 'K' that means a lot of heat and excitement?"

Harry: "Firetruck."

The principal breathed a sigh of relief and told the teacher, "Put Harry in the fifth-grade, I got the last seven questions wrong "

A kindergarten teacher asks her students what animals provide us.

She said, "What does the chirping little chicken give us?" and the students replied, "Eggs". She then asked, "What does the big pink pig give us?" and the students replied a joyous, "Bacon". Finally she asked, "What does the fat old cow give us?" and before anyone could answer, little Johnny yelled, "Homework".

WITTY FIFTY SHEDS OF GREY

We tried various positions – round the back, on the side, up against a wall.
But in the end, we came to the conclusion that the bottom of the garden was the only place for a good shed.

She stood before me, trembling in my shed.
"I'm yours for the night," she gasped, "You can do whatever you want with me."
So I took her to Bunnings Hardware store.

She knelt before me on the shed floor and tugged gently at first, then harder until finally it came. I moaned with pleasure. Now for the other boot.

Ever since she read THAT book, I've had to buy all kinds of ropes, chains and shackles. She still manages to get into the shed, though.

Calmly I instructed her, "Put on this rubber suit and mask."
"Mmmm, kinky" she purred.
"Yes", I said, "You can't be too careful with all that asbestos in the shed roof."

"I'm a very naughty girl", she said, biting her lip. "I need to be punished."
So I invited my mum to stay for the weekend.

"Harder", she cried, gripping the workbench tightly.
"Harder."
"Okay", I said. "What's the gross national product of Nicaragua?"

I lay back exhausted, gazing happily out of the shed window. Despite my concerns about my youthful inexperience, my rhubarb had come up a treat.

"Are you sure you can take the pain?", she demanded, brandishing stilettos.
"I think so", I gulped.
"Here we go, then", she said, and showed me the receipt.

"Hurt me" she begged, raising her skirt as she bent over my workbench.
"Very well", I replied. "You've got a fat arse and no dress sense."

"Are you sure you want this?", I asked. "When I'm done, you won't be able to sit down for weeks." She nodded.
"Okay", I said, putting the three-piece lounge furniture on eBay.

"Punish me" she cried. "Make me suffer like only a real man can!"
"Very well", I replied, leaving the toilet seat up.

"Newspaper headline: Modena, Italy..... The Ferrari Formula 1 Team fired their entire Pit Crew yesterday." The announcement followed Ferrari's decision to take advantage of the skills of black African Americans who were all unemployed youths. The decision to hire them was brought on by a recent documentary on how African American youths were able to remove a set of car wheels in less than 7 seconds without proper equipment, whereas Ferrari's existing crew can only do it in 8 seconds with millions of dollars worth of high-tech gear. This was thought to be an excellent yet bold move by Ferrari Management.

As most races are won and lost in the pits, Ferrari would have an advantage over every team.

However, Ferrari got more than they bargained for as, during the African American crew's first practice session, not only were the new pit crew able to change the tyres in under 6 seconds, but within 12 seconds they had resprayed, rebadged and sold the vehicle over to the McLaren Team for a case of Schlitz malt liquor, a gram of coke and a quick glimpse at Hamilton's girlfriend in the shower.

A woman who was rather on the large side turned up at the theatre just before the performance was due to start. She handed the usher two tickets.

The usher asked, "Where's the other party?"

The woman blushed. "Well, you see one seat's a bit small for me and rather uncomfortable so I bought two. But they're both really for me."

"That's fine with me, Ma'am", the usher replied, scratching his head.

"There's just one problem. Your seats are numbers 23 and 72."

I was on the bus the other day and after a large meal of beans, I really needed to fart, often.

Luckily the music was really loud so I timed my farts with the beat, and after a couple of songs I began to feel better.

As I left the bus though, I noticed everyone was starting at me in disgust.

That's when I remembered I was listening to my iPod.

It was a hot summer day and two nuns were painting a room in the convent.

As there was no air conditioning the heat soon became unbearable. The first nun said that they should remove their clothes so that they would be cooler.

The second said, "What if someone should come?"

The first said, "We'll lock the door and then we'll be safe."

So they lock the door and continue painting when there is a knock on the door.

The first nun asks who it is and the reply comes back, "It is just the old blind man from the village."

The two nuns confer and decide that the blind man can't see anything so they let him in. The door opens, the blind man comes in, takes one look at the naked nuns and says, "G'day. Great tits. Now where shall I put the blinds?"

A French policeman near the city of Lyon, stops an Englishman's car and asks if he has been drinking.

With great difficulty, the Englishman admits that he has been drinking all day, that his daughter got married that morning, and that he drank champagne and a few bottles of wine at the reception, and consumed many single malt scotches there-after.

The policeman proceeds to breath test the Englishman and verifies that he is indeed completely inebriated, far beyond tolerable standards for public safety.

The French Policeman asks the Englishman if he knows why, under French law, he is going to be arrested.

The Englishman answers with a bit of humour, "No sir, I do not! But while we're asking questions, do you realize that this is a British car and my wife is driving on the other side?"

FUNNY IRISH BEING IRISH

Reilly went to trial for armed robbery. The jury foreman came out and
announced, "Not guilty."
"That's grand!" shouted Reilly. "Does that mean I can keep the money?"

Murphy told Quinn that his wife was driving him to drink.
Quinn thinks he's very lucky because his own wife makes him walk.

Mrs Feeney shouted from the kitchen, "Is that you I hear spittin' in
the vase on the mantel piece?"
"No", said himself, "but I'm gettin' closer all the time."

Finnegin: "My wife has a terrible habit of staying up 'til two o'clock in
the morning. I can't break her out of it."
Keenan: "What on earth is she doin' at that time?"
Finnegin: "Waitin' for me to come home!"

Slaney phoned the maternity ward at the hospital. "Quick!" he said.
"Send an ambulance, my wife is goin' to have a baby!"
"Tell me, is this her first baby?" the intern asked.
"No you daft idiot, this is her husband, Kevin, speakin'."

Did you hear about the Irish newly-weds who sat up all night on their honeymoon waiting for their sexual relations to arrive?

Paddy took two stuffed dogs to the Antiques Roadshow.

"OH!", gushed the presenter. "This is a very rare breed indeed. Do you have any idea what they would fetch if they were in good condition?"

"Sticks!", replied Paddy.

Murphy was complaining that nothing was made in Ireland any more. In fact he just bought a new T.V. that said, 'Built in antennae' and he had no idea where that even was.

THE CORMORANT

The common cormorant or shag
Lays eggs inside a paper bag
The reason you will see no doubt
It is to keep the lightning out.

But what these unobservant birds
Have not noticed is that herds
Of wild bears may come with buns
And steal the bags to hold the crumbs.

A Russian, an American, and a Blonde were talking one day.

The Russian said, "We were the first in space."

The American said, "We were the first on the moon."

The Blonde said, "So what? We're going to be the first on the sun."

The Russian and the American looked at each other and shook their heads.

"You can't land on the sun, you idiot, you'll burn up." said the Russian.

To which the Blonde replied, "Oh Yeah! Well we're not stupid you know. We're going at night."

WITTY ERUDITE THOUGHTS

I'd kill for a Nobel Peace Prize.

Borrow money from pessimists -- they don't expect it back.

Half the people you know are below average.

99% of lawyers give the rest a bad name.

92.73% of all statistics are made up on the spot.

A conscience is what hurts when all your other parts feel so good.

A clear conscience is usually the sign of a bad memory.

If you want the rainbow, you got to put up with the rain.

All those who believe in psycho kinesis, raise my hand.

The early bird may get the worm, but the second mouse gets the cheese

I almost had a psychic girlfriend, ... but she left me before we met.

OK, so what's the speed of dark?

How do you tell when you're out of invisible ink?

If everything seems to be going well, you have obviously overlooked something.

Depression is merely anger without enthusiasm.

When everything is coming your way, you're in the wrong lane.

Ambition is a poor excuse for not having enough sense to be lazy.

Hard work pays off in the future; laziness pays off now.

I intend to live forever.... so far, so good.

If Barbie is so popular, why do you have to buy her friends?

Eagles may soar, but weasels don't get sucked into jet engines.

What happens if you get scared half to death twice?

My mechanic told me, "I couldn't repair your brakes, so I made your horn louder."

Why do psychics have to ask you for your name?

If at first you don't succeed, destroy all evidence that you tried.

A conclusion is the place where you got tired of thinking..

Experience is something you don't get until just after you need it.

The hardness of the butter is proportional to the softness of the bread

To steal ideas from one person is plagiarism; to steal from many is research.

The problem with the gene pool is that there is no lifeguard.

The colder the x-ray table, the more of your body is required to be on it.

Everyone has a photographic memory; some just don't have film.

If at first you don't succeed, skydiving is not for you.

If your car could travel at the speed of light, would your headlights
work?

I woke up one morning, and all of my stuff had been stolen… and replaced by exact duplicates.

Paddy had been drinking at his local Dublin pub all day and most of the night celebrating St Patrick"s Day. Mick, the bartender says, "You'll not be drinking anymore tonight, Paddy".

Paddy replies, "OK Mick, I'll be on my way then". Paddy spins around on his stool and steps off. He falls flat on his face. "Shoite", he says and pulls himself up by the stool and dusts himself off.

He takes a step towards the door and falls flat on his face, "Shoite, Shoite !"

He looks to the doorway and thinks to himself that if he can just get to the door and some fresh air he'll be fine. He belly crawls to the door and shimmies up to the door frame.

He sticks his head outside and takes a deep breath of fresh air, feels much better and takes a step out onto the sidewalk and falls flat on his face.

"Bi'Jesus… I'm fockin' focked", he says.

He can see his house just a few doors down, and crawls to the door, hauls himself up the door frame, opens the door and shimmies inside.

He takes a look up the stairs and says, "No fookin' way."

He crawls up the stairs to his bedroom door and says, "I can make it to the bed."

He takes a step into the room and falls flat on his face.

He says, "fook it", and falls into bed.

The next morning, his wife, Jess, comes into the room carrying a cup of coffee and says, "Get up Paddy. Did you have a bit to drink last night ?"

Paddy says, "I did, Jess. I was fookin" pissed. But how did you know?"

"Mick phoned .. . . You left your wheelchair at the pub you daft fool."

A man who had a lot of trouble attracting women, decided to go to a psychologist to see if he could identify what it was that he was doing wrong.

He found a Chinese psychologist and thought, "These Orientals seem to have some inner higher knowledge of these things so he might be the person to fix me."

The psychologist invited the man in, and he told the Chinese psychologist his life's story and all the emotional events that had happened to him and his inability to attract women.

The Chinese man, in his broken English, said "Haw! You must take off aw your crose."

So the man stripped naked and the Chinese man said, "You get on froor on aw fours and you craw to other side of room."

So the man did this and then the Chinese man ordered him to turn around and crawl back to him.

The Chinese man exclaimed, "Haw! I see probrem. You have Esaccery disease."

"I have what? Esaccery disease!!!! What the hell is that?"

"Haw! Velly simple. Your face. Esaccery same as your arsehole."

O'rourke is sitting having a quiet drink in the bar when Murphy walks in cradling a lizard.

O'rourke exclaims, "Bejeezus Murphy, what the hell have you got there? It looks like some mad kind of swivel-eyed dinosaur type of thing?"

Murphy carefully sets his new pet down on the table and replies, "He's a chameleon."

O'rourke lowers his head to the table until he's almost nose to nose with the animal and says, "Go on then, tell me a joke!"

The Archbishop of Canterbury and The Royal Commission for Political Correctness announced today that the climate in the UK should no longer be referred to as 'English Weather'.

Rather than offend a sizeable portion of the UK population, it will now be referred to as: 'Muslim Weather'. Partly Sunni, but mostly Shi'ite.

She was standing in the kitchen, preparing our usual soft boiled eggs and toast for breakfast, wearing only the "T" shirt that she normally slept in. As I walked in, almost awake, she turned to me and said softly, "You've got to make love to me this very moment."

My eyes lit up as I thought, I am either still dreaming or this is going to be my lucky day!

Not wanting to lose the moment, I embraced her and gave it my all, full bore; right there on the kitchen table.

Afterwards she said, "Thanks", and returned to the stove, her "T" shirt still around her neck.

Happy, but a little puzzled, I asked, "What was that all about?"

She explained, "The egg timer's broken and you like yours soft boiled."

Eleven people were hanging on a rope, under a helicopter in flight, 10 men and 1 woman.

The rope was not strong enough to carry them all, so they decided that one had to leave, otherwise they were all going to fall.

They weren't able to choose that person, until the woman gave a very touching speech.

She said that she would voluntarily let go of the rope, because, as a woman, she was used to giving up everything for her husband and kids or for men in general and was used to always making sacrifices with little in return. As soon as she finished her speech, all the men started clapping.

One day, Einstein has to speak at an important science conference.

On the way there, he tells his driver that looks a bit like him:

"I'm sick of all these conferences. I always say the same things over and over!"

The driver agrees: "You're right. As your driver, I attended all of them, and even though I don't know anything about science, I could give the conference in your place."

"That's a great idea!" says Einstein. "Let's switch places then!"

So, they switch clothes and as soon as they arrive, the driver dressed as Einstein, goes on stage and starts giving the usual speech, while the real Einstein, dressed as the car driver, attends it.

But in the crowd, there is one scientist who wants to impress everyone and thinks of a very difficult question to ask Einstein, hoping he won't be able to respond. So, this guy stands up and interrupts the conference by posing his very difficult question. The whole room goes silent, holding their breath, waiting for the response.

The driver looks at him, dead in the eye, and says,

"Sir, your question is so easy to answer that I'm going to let my driver reply to it for me."

A blonde, a brunette and a redhead decided to compete in the Breast Stroke division of the English Channel swim competition.

The brunette came in first and the redhead second.

The blonde finally reached the shore completely exhausted.

After being revived with blankets and a drink she said, "I don't want to complain, but I'm pretty sure those other two girls used their arms."

John Bradford, a Dublin University student, was on the side of the road hitch-hiking on a very dark night and in the midst of a big storm. The night was rolling on and no car went by. The storm was so strong he could hardly see a few feet ahead of him. Suddenly, he saw a car slowly coming towards him and stopped. John, desperate for shelter and without thinking about it, got into the car and closed the door ... only to realise there was nobody behind the wheel and the engine wasn't running. The car started moving slowly. John looked at the road ahead and saw a curve approaching. Scared, he started to pray, begging for his life. Then, just before the car hit the curve, a hand appeared out of nowhere through the window, and turned the wheel. John, paralysed with terror, watched as the hand came through the window, but never touched or harmed him. Shortly thereafter, John saw the lights of a pub appear down the road, so, gathering strength, he jumped out of the car and ran to it. Wet and out of breath, he rushed inside and started telling everybody about the horrible experience he had just had. A silence enveloped the pub when everybody realised he was crying ... and wasn't drunk. Suddenly, the door opened, and two other people walked in from the dark and stormy night. They, like John, were also soaked and out of breath. Looking around, and seeing John Bradford sobbing at the bar, one said to the other, "Look Paddy, 'dere's 'dat fooking ejit 'dat got in 'da car while we was pushin' it!"

Paddy and his missus are lying in bed listening to the next door neighbours dog barking. It had been barking for hours and hours.
Suddenly Paddy jumps up out of bed and says, "I've had enough of this." He goes downstairs.
Paddy finally comes back up to bed and his wife says, "The dog is still barking. What have you been doing?"
Paddy says, "I've put the dog in our yard. Let's see how THEY like it."

Two bowling teams, one of all Blondes and one of all Brunettes, charter a double-decker bus for a weekend bowling tournament on The Gold Coast, Queensland.

The Brunette team rides in the bottom of the bus. The Blonde team rides on the top level.

The Brunette team down below is whooping it up having a great time, when one of them realizes she doesn't hear anything from the Blondes upstairs.

She decides to go up and investigate. When the Brunette reaches the top, she finds all the Blondes frozen in fear, staring straight-ahead at the road, and clutching the seats in front of them with white knuckles.

She says, "What the heck's goin' on up here? We're havin' a grand time downstairs!"

One of the Blondes looks up and with sheer dread in her eyes says, "Yeah, but you've got a driver."

A man was duck shooting on the banks of the river Murray in Victoria when the local wildlife officer pulled up and asked to see the man's shooters license.

"This looks all in order, for Victoria, but you know it's not duck shooting season in New South Wales which is just on the other side of the river. And you have twelve ducks there on the river bank. How do I know some of these ducks aren't New South Wales ducks?"

The man was a bit incredulous and said to the officious fool, 'What are you on about? Ducks is ducks. You have no idea of telling where a duck has come from."

"Oh yes I can"" said the officer. And with that he picked up a duck, held it by the legs, stuck his finger up the ducks arse and then put the finger in his mouth. After a quick taste he said, "Hmmm, just as I thought, cotton seed from the Namoi. This is a New South Wales duck."

He picked up another duck and did the same thing. "Hmmm, Lucerne from Bairnsdale. This is a Victorian duck."

The officer went through all twelve ducks and eventually said, "You're in big trouble mister. You have six New South Wales ducks and six Victorian ducks here."

He then pulled out his note book and pen and said, "OK mister, what's your name?"

A clearly unimpressed and very angry man said, "Name's Jones."

"Jones eh! And tell me Mr Jones. Where do you come from?"

"Where do I come from? You ask me where do I come from!" the angry man said.

With that he put down his beer, undid his belt, pulled down his pants, bent over and bared his backside to the officer and said,

"You want to know where I come from. Well here mate, you're so bloody smart, you tell me."

Two married buddies are out drinking one night when one turns to the other and says, "You know, I don't know what else to do. Whenever I go home after we've been out drinking, I turn the headlights off before I get to the driveway. I shut off the engine and coast into the garage. I take my shoes off before I go into the house, I sneak up the stairs, I get undressed in the bathroom. I ease into bed and my wife STILL wakes up and yells at me for staying out so late!"

His buddy looks at him and says, "Well, you're obviously taking the wrong approach. I screech into the driveway, slam the door, storm up the steps, throw my shoes into the closet, jump into bed, rub my hands on my wife's ass and say, 'How about a root? ' ....and you know what, she's always sound asleep."

A guy in a taxi wanted to speak to the driver so he leaned forward and tapped him on the shoulder.

The driver screamed in fright, jumped up in the air and yanked the wheel over.

The car mounted the curb, demolished a lamppost and came to a stop, centimetres from a shop window.

The startled passenger said, "I'm sorry, I really didn't mean to frighten you. I just wanted to ask you something."

The taxi driver said, "It's ok, it's ok, it's not your fault, Sir. You see this is my first day as a cab driver. I've been driving a hearse for the past 25 years."

A blonde was zipping down the highway in her little red sports car when she was pulled over by a traffic cop – who was also blonde.

When asked for her licence the driver dug frantically through her large handbag, couldn't find it and asked, "What does it look like?"

"It's square and has your picture on it."

The driver found a little square hand mirror, looked at it then handed it over.

The traffic cop looked at the mirror, then handed it back, saying, "No penalty this time driver – I didn't realise you were a cop."

There once was a religious young woman who went to Confession. Upon entering the confessional, she said, "Forgive me, Father, for I have sinned."

The priest said, "Confess your sins and be forgiven."

The young woman said, "Last night my boyfriend made passionate love to me seven times."

The priest thought long and hard and then said, "Squeeze seven lemons into a glass and then drink the juice."

The young woman asked, "Will this cleanse me of my sins?"

The priest said, "No, but it will wipe that smile off of your face."

Three obviously wealthy and rather snobbish elderly English women were having afternoon tea and scones and trying to outdo each other, talking about their husbands.

The first snobbish woman said in her upper class accent, "My husband Nigel, is the secretary to the minister for international affairs."

The second, equally snobbish woman said, "Yes well my husband Maynard, is the chairman of the Royal Ascot Racing Club."

The third woman, not to be outdone, huffed in her posh voice, "Yes, well I will have you know that my husband Drambuie......."

One of the old bags cut in and exclaimed loudly, "Drambuie is an exotic liquor."

"Oh, you've met my husband", snorted the third woman.

Late one night the Pope's most intimate council of senior advisors requests admission to His Holiness's bedchamber, bearing news of the greatest urgency. They tell him that it has just been revealed by sacred divinations that unless the Pope sleeps with a woman, his Vatican State – indeed all of Catholicism – will come to a sudden and terrible end.

The Pope thinks it over for a few minutes, and then agrees to go ahead with the profane deed.

Aware of his pious position in the world, with great dignity, spirituality and humbleness, he says, "But, I have three stipulations.

First, she must be blind, so she cannot see where she is being taken.

Second, she must be deaf, so she cannot speak of what happened to her.

And third, she must have big tits."

Diana and Barbara were in the shopping centre. "There's my husband, coming out of the florist with a dozen roses. That means I'm going to have to keep my legs up in the air for three days", said Diana.

"Why?" said Barbara. "Don't you have a vase?"

A man wished to learn how to sky dive so he went to the sky diving school for intuition.

The instructor said, "Very easy really sir. We take you up to three thousand metres, you jump out of the plane, count to ten, pull the rip cord on your left side, your parachute will open and you will float gently to earth."

"Yeah right", the man said. "What if my chute doesn't open. What then?"

"Never happens but just in case, you have an emergency chute which you would activate by pulling the rip cord on your right side, it will open and you will float gently to earth."

Comforted by this, the man donned his outfit, got into the plane, flew to three thousand metres, jumped out, counted to ten and pulled his left cord. Nothing happened. He pulled it again. And again. Panicking, he thought what to do now. He remembered his emergency chute. He counted to ten and pulled his right side rip cord. Nothing. Frantically he pulled hard on both rip cords. Nothing. The earth was fast approaching when he happened to notice a farm house far below and a crowd of people standing around in the back yard.

Just then, a man came flying up from the backyard and as the two men passed in mid air the man with the dodgy parachutes yelled to him, "Hey! Do you know anything about parachutes?" To which the flying man yelled back, "No, don't know much about gas BBQ's either."

When God made man, all the parts of the body argued over who would be boss. The brain explained that since he controlled all the parts of the body, he should be boss. The legs argued that since they took the man wherever he wanted to go, they should be boss.
The stomach countered with an explanation that since he digested all the food, he should be boss. The eyes said that without them, man would be helpless, so they should be boss. Then the asshole applied for the job. The other parts of the body laughed so hard that the asshole become mad and closed up. After a few days the brain went foggy, the legs got wobbly, the stomach got ill, the eyes got crossed and unable to see. They all conceded and made the asshole boss. This proves that you don't have to be a brain to be boss.... just an asshole.

Father O'Malley answers the phone. 'Hello, is this Father O'Malley?'
'It is!'
'This is the Tax Department. Can you help us?'
'I can!'
'Do you know a Ted Houlihan?'
'I do!'
'Is he a member of your congregation?'
'He is!'
'Did he donate $10,000 to the church?'
'He will.'

In a bar, a well-drunk patron insists that the boss serve him a last gin. "Come on, Jack! Give me another drink. You see I'm not so drunk." The bartender replies, "You're kidding, you're only just standing on your legs." "No, Jack! You want proof? Well, look at that dog coming into your bar. From here, I can clearly tell you that he only has one eye. You see, I'm ok." The bartender laughs and says, "Ah yes! I see. But did you know that the dog in question isn't coming into the bar, it's leaving!"

Two leggy dimwits walked up to a perfume counter in a large department store where the first dimwit, Sharon, picked up a sample bottle of perfume, sprayed it on her wrist, smelled it, and said, "Ooh that's nice, don't you think, Tracy?"
Her friend Tracy took a sniff of her friend's wrist and said, "Yeah, that's nice. What's it called, Sharon?"
Sharon said, "It's called *Viens a moi*."
Tracy replied, "*Viens a moi*? What does that mean?"
The woman on the perfume counter, overhearing them, said haughtily, "*Viens a moi*, ladies, is French for 'Come to me.'"
Sharon takes another sniff of the perfume bottle and said, "That doesn't smell like cum to me Tracy. Does it smell like cum to you?"

George was eighty five and not in the best of health so his wife took him to the doctor for a checkup. The Doctor said to him, "George, in order to find out how your body is going, I'm going to have to do some tests of your bodily fluids. So, I will need from you today, a sample of your urine, a sample of your sperm, a sample of your faeces and a sample of your blood."

George, rather deaf, turned to his wife and said, "What did he say?"

To which his wife replied, "I think he wants to have a look in your undies."

In the Australian Outback, south west of Tennant Creek, Mr. Stewart's wife went into labor in the middle of the night, and the doctor was called out to assist in the delivery.

To keep the nervous father-to-be busy, the doctor handed him a lantern and said, "Here, you hold this high so I can see what I'm doing." Soon, a wee baby boy was brought into the world.

"Whoa there Scotty!" said the doctor. "Don't be in a rush to put the lantern down... I think there's yet another wee one to come." Sure enough, within minutes he had delivered another little baby.

"No, no, don't be in a great hurry to be putting down that lantern, young man... It seems there's yet another one besides!" cried the doctor.

The new father scratched his head in bewilderment, and asked the doctor. "Do ye think it's the light that's attractin' them?"

A little old lady had two pet monkeys, a male and a female. She had them for thirty years and was very attached to them. One day, the male mysteriously died and the female was so distraught that she also died several minutes later.

The old lady wanted to keep her long time pets so she took them to the local taxidermist. She told him her story and how much of a family they all were and how she just could not part with them.

The understanding taxidermist said, "How very sweet. Would you like them to be mounted?"

To which the dear old lady replied, "No not really. Just holding hands would be nice though."

An elderly gentleman went to the pharmacist and asked for some Viagra. The pharmacist said, "That's no problem. How many do you want?"

The man answered, "Just a few, maybe 4, but cut each one in 4 pieces."

The pharmacist said, "That won't do you any good."

The elderly gentleman said, "That's alright. I don't need them for sex anymore as I am over 80 years old. I just want it to stick out far enough so I don't pee on my shoes."

Jesus was relaxing in Heaven when he noticed a familiar looking old man. Wondering if the old man was His father Joseph, Jesus asked him, "Did you, by any chance, ever have a son?"

"Yes", said the old man, "but he wasn't my biological son. He was born by a miracle, by the intervention of a magical being from the heavens."

"Very interesting", said Jesus. "Did this boy ever have to fight temptation?"

"Oh, yes, many times", answered the old man. "But he eventually won. Unfortunately, he heroically died at one point, but he came back to life shortly afterwards."

Jesus couldn't believe it. Could this actually be His father? "One last question", he said. "Were you a carpenter?"

"Why yes", replied the old man. "Yes, I was."

Jesus rubbed His eyes and said, "Dad?"

The old man rubbed his eyes and exclaimed, "Pinocchio???"

Joe and John were identical twins.

Joe owned an old dilapidated boat and kept pretty much to himself.

One day he rented out his boat to a group of out-of-staters who ended up sinking it.

He spent all day trying to salvage as much stuff as he could from the sunken vessel and was out of touch all that day and most of the evening.

Unbeknownst to him, his brother John's wife had died suddenly in his absence.

When he got back on shore he went into town to pick up a few things at the grocery store.

A kind old woman there mistook him for John and said, "I'm so sorry for your loss. You must feel terrible."

Joe, thinking she was talking about his boat said, "Hell no!

Fact is I'm sort of glad to be rid of her."
"She was a rotten old thing from the beginning."
"Her bottom was all shriveled up and she smelled like old dead fish."
"She was always holding water. She had a bad crack in the back and a pretty big hole in the front too."
"Every time I used her, her hole got bigger and she leaked like crazy."
"I guess what finally finished her off was when I rented her to those four guys looking for a good time."
"I warned them that she wasn't very good and that she smelled bad, but they wanted her anyway. The damn fools tried to get in her all at one time and she split right up the middle."
The old woman fainted.

A family is at the dinner table. The son asks the father, "Dad, how many kinds of boobs are there?" The father, surprised, answers, "Well, son, a woman goes through three phases. In her 20s, a woman's breasts are like melons, round and firm. In her 30s and 40s, they are like pears, still nice, hanging a bit. After 50, they are like onions." "Onions?" the son asks. "Yes. You see them and they make you cry."

This infuriated his wife and daughter. The daughter asks, "Mom, how many different kinds of willies are there?" The mother smiles and says, "Well, dear, a man goes through three phases also. In his 20s, his willy is like an oak tree, mighty and hard. In his 30s and 40s, it's like a birch, flexible but reliable. After his 50s, it's like a Christmas tree." "A Christmas tree?" the daughter asks. "Yes, dead from the root up and the balls are just for decoration."

A wife is talking to her husband in the evening, "See, James? Men can still be gallant. Today I got on the subway and three young men stood up so I could sit down."
James looks at her and asks drily, "And did you fit?"

The Hollywood talent scout had just heard a young man give a very funny and lively performance.
"That was great!", he said. "What's your name?"
"Penis van Lesbian", said the young comedian.
"Jeez! We'll have to change that. How about we call you Dick Van Dyke?"

Fred: "What did you get your wife for Xmas?"
   Ned: "She told me, 'Nothing would make me happier than a diamond necklace.'"
   Fred: "So you got her diamonds?"
   Ned: "No, I got her nothing."

A man checked into a hotel on a business trip recently, and was a bit lonely so he thought, "I'll call and get one of those girls you see advertised in the phone books under "Escorts and Massages."
He opened the phone book to an ad for a girl calling herself 'Erotique', a lovely girl, bending over in the photo. She had all the right curves, in all the right places, beautiful long wavy hair, long graceful legs all the way up. You know the kind ….
So, he is in his room and figures, what the hell, and he makes a call.
"Hello?" the woman says.
"God, she sounded sexy!" the man thinks.
"Hi, I hear you give a great massage and I'd like you to come to my room and give me one. No, wait, I should be

straight with you. I'm in town all alone and what I really want is sex. I want it hot, and I want it now. I'm talking kinky the whole night long. You name it, we'll do it. Bring implements, toys, everything you've got in your bag of tricks. We'll go hot and heavy all night. Tie me up, cover me in chocolate syrup and whipped cream, anything you want baby. Now, how does that sound?"

She says, "That sounds fantastic sir, but for an outside line, you need to dial '9'.

I came home really drunk last night and my wife wasn't happy at all.

"How much have you had to drink?" she asked sternly, staring at me.

"Nushing", I slurred.

"Look at me!" she shouted angrily. "It's either me or the pub, which one is it?"

I paused for a second while I thought deeply, and said, "It's you. Definitely you. I can tell by the voice."

Reporter: "Excuse me, may I interview you?"

Man: "Yes!"

Reporter: "Name?"

Man: "Abdul Al-Rhazim."

Reporter: "Sex?"

Man: "Three to five times a week."

Reporter: "No no! I mean male or female?"

Man: "Yes, male, female... sometimes camel."

Reporter: "Holy cow!"

Man: "Yes, cow, sheep... animals in general."

Reporter: "But isn't that hostile?"

Man: "Yes, horse style, dog style, any style."

Reporter: "Oh dear!"

Man: "No, no deer. Deer run too fast. Hard to catch."

Little Jack is six years old and goes with his parents to the nudist beach.

He is playing with sand and creates castles or swims in the water. After 30 minutes he comes back to his mum and asks:

"Mum, Mum, why do all the women have different sizes of their breasts?"

Mum answers, "Oh hmm, see my son, the women with small breasts are poor, the ones with big breasts are rich. That's the difference."

Little Jack is satisfied with this answer and goes back to his sand-castle.

After 30 minutes he comes back again to his mother and asks, "Mum, Mum, why have all the men got different sized penises?"

Mum answers, "Oh hmm, see my son, the men with a small penis are not smart, but the ones with a big penis are very intelligent. That's the difference."

Little Jack is satisfied with this answer and goes back to his sand-castle.

After 30 minutes he comes again back to his mother and says, "Mum, Mum, Daddy is talking to a very rich woman and every second he is getting smarter and smarter."

The teacher asks the children to discuss what their dad's do for a living.

Little Mary says, "My Dad is a lawyer. He puts the bad guys in jail."

Little Jack says, "My Dad is a doctor. He makes all the sick people better."

All the kids in the class had their turn except Little Johnny.

Teacher asks, "Johnny, what does your Dad do?"

Johnny says, "My Dad is dead."

"I'm sorry to hear that, but what did he do before he died?"

"He turned blue and fell on the floor."

A male patient is lying in bed in the hospital, wearing an oxygen mask over his mouth and nose. A young student nurse appears and gives him a partial sponge bath.
"Nurse," he mumbles from behind the mask, "are my testicles black?"
Embarrassed, the young nurse replies, "I don't know, Sir. I'm only here to wash your upper body and feet."
He struggles to ask again, "Nurse, please check for me. Are my testicles black?"
Concerned that he might elevate his blood pressure and heart rate from worrying about his testicles, she overcomes her embarrassment and pulls back the covers. She raises his gown, holds his manhood in one hand and his testicles gently in the other. She looks very closely and says, "There's nothing wrong with them, Sir. They look fine."
The man slowly pulls off his oxygen mask, smiles at her, and says very slowly, "Thank you very much. That was wonderful. Now listen very, very closely: "Are - my - test - results - back?"

A blonde pushes her car into a gas station. She tells the mechanic it died.
After he works on it for a few minutes, it is idling smoothly.
She says, "What's the story?"
He replies, "Just crap in the carburettor."
She asks, "Oh yeah. And how often do I have to do that?"

The other night I was invited out for a night with "the girls."
I told my husband I would be home by midnight, guaranteed!
Well, the hours passed oh so quickly and the margaritas went down way too easy, not to mention the vodka tequila cocktails.

Around 3:00am I was basically almost legless, so I got a taxi and headed for home. Just as I got in the front door, the cuckoo clock in the hall started up and cuckooed 3 times. Quickly realizing I would wake my husband up and he would know what time I really got home, I cuckooed another 9 times, making it appear that it was midnight. I was really proud of myself with being so quick witted in my very inebriated state knowing I had averted any potential conflict with him.

Next morning, he asked me what time I got home and I said midnight. He didn't seem phased by this, he just said, "We need a new cuckoo clock."

When I asked him why, he said, "Well last night, our clock cuckooed 3 times, then said 'Oh crap,' cuckooed 4 more times, cleared its throat, cuckooed another 3 times, giggled, cuckooed twice more, and then tripped over the cat and farted."

An archaeologist in Egypt had entered an ancient tomb and with much anticipation of fabulous riches waiting for him, he switched his torch on and shone it around the crypt.

Nothing. All gone. Except for one object about six inches long and about one inch thick.

"AH!", exclaimed the archaeologist, "The perfectly preserved petrified penis of a prehistoric prince."

With great care this was picked up, wrapped up and sent back to England for further examination. Six weeks later, amidst great excitement, the package was returned. All the archaeologists gathered around as the package was opened. A note from the scientists in London was sitting on the top and it read, "Dear Sirs. What you had pontifically presumed to be the perfectly preserved petrified penis of a prehistoric prince, was merely nothing more than the crystallized crap of a creep who crept into the crypt, crapped and crept out again."

A man is walking down the street in Dublin when he sees a sign in the window of a travel agency that says, 'Cruises on Liffey River – $100'.

He goes into the agency and hands the guy $100.

The travel agent then whacks him over the head and throws him in the river.

Another man is walking down the street a half-hour later, sees the same sign and pays the guy $100.

The travel agent then whacks him over the head and throws him in the river.

Sometime later, the two men are floating down the river together and the first man asks, "Do you think they'll serve any food on this cruise?"

The second man says, "I don't think so. They didn't do it last year."

Bruce and Norm are two Aussie cricket tragics – play for the same bush team, travel the country watching every test match, can remember every one of Warnies wickets. One night when they had a few beers, they agree that whoever dies first will come back and tell the other if they play cricket in heaven.

Tragically, the next day Bruce is playing cricket in the back yard, has a heart and dies.

A few nights later, Norm awakes to hear his mate calling him.

"Is that you Bruce?"

"Bloody oath mate it's me" says the disembodied voice.

"So tell me", says Norm. "Do they play cricket in heaven?"

"Well", says the ghostly Bruce. "There is good news and bad news."

"Bloody hell, give me the good news first."

"Well old mate, the good news is that they do indeed play cricket in heaven. Great wicket, helps the seamers on the first couple of days, takes a bit of spin later on."

"You bloody beauty", says Norm. "What's the bad news?"

"I've had a look in St Peters score book", says Bruce. "Seems you are opening the batting tomorrow."

A car full of Irish nuns is sitting at a traffic light in down town Dublin when a bunch of rowdy drunks pull up alongside of them.
"Hey, show us yer teets, ya bluudy penguins." shouts one of the drunks.
Quite shocked, Mother Superior turns to Sister Mary Immaculata and says,
"I don't think they know who we are; show them your cross."
Sister Mary
Immaculata rolls down her window and shouts, "Piss off, ya fookin'
little wankers, before I come over there and rip yer bleedin' balls off." She then rolls up her window, looks back at Mother Superior quite innocently and asks, "Did that sound cross enough?"

Paddy and Mick are walking home late one night after a heavy night on the grog. They've got no money to get a taxi and are staggering all over the place when they find themselves outside a bus depot.

Paddy, being the bright one, says to Mick, "Get in there and steal a bus so we can get home and I'll wait here and look out for the coppers."

Mick duly breaks into the depot and is gone for 20 minutes while Paddy is wondering what the hell he is doing.

Eventually, Paddy sticks his head around a door and sees Mick running frantically around looking at each bus.

"What in hell are you doing Mick. Get a move on before the coppers get here."

To which Mick replies, "I can't find a No 7 anywhere, Paddy."

Paddy, the bright one, throws his hands in the air in disbelief and shouts,

"You idiot Mick, can't you get anything right. Steal a No 9 and we'll jump off at the roundabout and walk the rest of the way."

A Jewish woman in Melbourne decided to prepare her Will and make her final requests. She told her rabbi she had two final requests. First, she wanted to be cremated, and second, she wanted her ashes scattered all over Myer's city store perfumery section. "Why Myer's perfumery?" asked the rabbi. "Then I'll be sure my daughters visit me twice a week."

Once upon a time, two little boys, Sammy and Tim, were sharing a room in the hospital. As they were getting to know each other a little bit, Sammy eventually asked Tim, "Hey Tim, what're you in for?"
"I'm getting my tonsils out -- I'm a little worried", said Tim.
"Oh don't worry about it. I had my tonsils out and it was a blast! I got to eat all the ice cream and jelly I wanted for two weeks!"
"Oh yeah?" replied Tim. "That's not half-bad. Hey, Sammy, how about you? What're you here for?"
"I'm getting a circumcision, whatever that is", Sammy answered.
"Oh my god, circumcision? I got one of those when I was a baby and I couldn't walk for two years!"

John was a clerk in a small pharmacy but he was not much of a salesman. He could never find the item the customer wanted.
Bob, the owner, had about enough and warned John that the next sale he missed would be his last.
Just then a man came in coughing and he asked John for their best cough syrup. Try as he might John could not find the cough syrup. Remembering Bob's warning he sold the man a box of laxatives and told him to take it all at once.
The customer did as John said and then walked outside and leaned against a lamp post.
Bob had seen the whole thing and came over to ask John

what had transpired.

"He wanted something for his cough but I couldn't find the cough syrup. I substituted laxatives and told him to take it all at once" John explained.

"Laxatives won't cure a cough!" Bob shouted angrily.

"Sure it will" John said, pointing at the man leaning on the lamp post.

"Just look at him. He's AFRAID to cough!"

A young man, eager to impress his new girl friend, thought he would invite her around to his place and cook her a lovely meal. Thoughts of fillet steak, seafood or perhaps something exotic filled his mind. Finally, he settled on something French, Coq au Vin. Chicken in red wine.

The night arrived and the aroma of the French dish filled the kitchen. The new girl friend arrived and looked fabulous, ready to impress her new boy friend with her charm, manners and beauty. Savouring the aromas she enthused, "Yum! What are we having tonight?" The boy friend said, "Do you like Coq au Vin?" To which the lovely young woman said excitedly, "OOH, I like both of them."

After having dug to a depth of 10 feet last year, British scientists found traces of copper wire dating back 200 years and came to the conclusion that their ancestors already had a telephone network more than 150 years ago.

Not to be outdone by the British, in the weeks that followed, an American archaeologist dug to a depth of 20 feet, and shortly after, a story published in the New York Times said: "American archaeologists, finding traces of 250-year-old copper wire, have concluded that their ancestors already had an advanced high-tech communications network 50 years earlier than the British."

One week later, Australia 's Northern Territory Times reported the following: "After digging as deep as 30 feet in his backyard in Tennant Creek , Northern Territory ,

Knackers Johnson, a self-taught archaeologist, reported that he found absolutely bugger-all. Knackers has therefore concluded that 250 years ago, Australia had already gone wireless."

Makes ya feel bloody proud to be Australian I reckon.

A cop was on his horse waiting to cross the street when a little girl on her new shiny bike stopped beside him.

"Nice bike", the cop said. "Did Santa bring it to you?"

"Yes Sir", the little girl said, "he sure did!"

The cop looked the bike over and handed the girl a $5 ticket for a safety violation. The cop said, "Next year tell Santa to put a reflector light on the back of it."

The young girl looked up at the cop and said, "Nice horse you've got there, Sir. Did Santa bring it to you?"

Playing along with the girl, he chuckled and answered, "Yes, he sure did."

The little girl looked up at the cop and said, "Next year tell Santa the dick goes underneath the horse, not on top!"

I went into the confessional box after many years of being away from the Catholic Church.

Inside I found a fully equipped bar with Guinness on tap. On one wall, there was a row of decanters with fine Irish whiskey and Waterford crystal glasses. On the other wall was a dazzling array of the finest cigars and chocolates. When the priest came in, I said to him, "Father, forgive me, for it's been a very long time since I've been to confession, but I must first admit that the confessional box is much more inviting than it used to be."

He replied, "You moron, you're on my side."

Sister Mary Holycard was in her 60s, and much admired for her sweetness and kindness to all.
One afternoon early in the spring a young priest came to chat, so she welcomed him into her Victorian parlor.
She then invited him to have a seat while she prepared a little tea.
As he sat facing her old pump organ, the young priest noticed a crystal glass bowl sitting on top of it filled with water, and in the water floated, a condom.
Well, imagine how shocked and surprised he was.
Imagine his curiosity! Surely, he thought, Sister Mary had flipped or something!
When she returned with tea and cookies, they began to chat, and of course, the priest tried to stifle his curiosity about the bowl of water, and the strange floater. Soon it got the better of him and he could resist no longer.
"Sister", he asked, "I wonder if you could tell me about this?" (pointing to the crystal bowl)
"Oh, yes", she replied, "Isn't it wonderful. I was walking downtown last autumn and I found this little package. The directions said to put it on the organ, keep it wet, and it would prevent disease. And you know what, I haven't had a cold all winter!"

Clive Palmer, a rather large and bombastic Australian politician, was being driven by his government chauffeur down a winding dirt road in Clive's country electorate on their way to a community get together.

Running late, Clive urged his driver to go faster because Clive figured the quicker he got there the quicker he could get out of there.

The driver sped around a corner on the dirt road only to be confronted by a very large old male pig ambling across the road. Fearing this may be a prize pig of one of the local electors, the driver did all he could to miss the pig but couldn't control the car, ran straight over the large animal and finished up in a storm water ditch.

Unable to move the car, Clive yelled, "You bumbling fool, look what you've done. I have to be at that electors meeting in 10 minutes. Look, there's a farm house up on that hill. Go up there and get some help from the farmer."

The driver trudged off and left Clive to fume in the car. 20 minutes went by. 40 minutes went by. After more than an hour, the driver came staggering down the road with a bottle of champagne in his hand, a party hat on his head and obviously very drunk.

Furious, Clive yelled at his driver again saying, "Where the bloody hell have you been, rant, rant, rant."

The driver looked at him through his drunken gaze and said, "Well Mishter Palmer, I did as inshtructed. I went up to the farm house, knocked on the door and the farmer came out. I said, 'G'day. I'm Clive Palmer's chauffer and I have just run over the fat pig.' The farmer was so happy about this, he threw a party."

A man was sitting in a bar with his ugly dog when a man with an equally ugly dog sat next to him.

"What sort of miserable dog is that?", asked the first man.

"This is a carpenter dog", said the second man. "It is so smart that if I gave it a piece of wood to chew on, it would chew and chew until it had produced a small table. What sort of ugly useless dog is yours?"

"This is a blacksmith dog", said the other man. "This dog is so smart that I take a piece of steel, heat it up until it is red hot, then turn the dog around and shove it straight up his backside."

"Good heavens", exclaimed the second man, "what does he do then?"

"He will either make a bolt for your nuts or a spring for the door."

One day, someone made the comment that preaching to people isn't really all that hard. A real challenge would be to preach to a bear. One thing led to another and three local men of the cloth decided to do an experiment. They would all go out into the woods, find a bear, preach to it, and attempt to convert it.

Seven days later, they're all together to discuss the experience.

Father Flannery, who has his arm in a sling, is on crutches, and has various bandages, goes first. "Well", he says, "I went into the woods to find a bear. And when I found him I began to read to him from the Catechism. Well, that bear wanted nothing to do with me and began to cuff me around. So I quickly grabbed my holy water, sprinkled him and, Holy Mary Mother of Jesus, he became as gentle as a lamb. The bishop is coming out next week to give him

first communion and confirmation."

Reverend Billy Bob spoke next from his wheelchair, with an arm and both legs in casts, and an IV drip. In his best fire and brimstone oratory he claimed,

" WELL brothers, you KNOW that we don't sprinkle! I went out and I FOUND me a bear. And then I began to read to my bear from God's HOLY WORD! But that bear wanted nothing to do with it. So I took HOLD of him and we began to wrestle. We wrestled down one hill, UP another and DOWN another until we

came to a creek. So I quick DUNKED him and BAPTIZED his hairy soul. And just like you said, he became as gentle as a lamb. We spent the rest of the day PRAISING the Lord."

They both looked down at Rabbi MacNevinovich, who was lying in a hospital bed. He was in a body cast and traction with IV's and monitors running in and out of him obviously in bad shape. The rabbi looks up and says, "Looking back on it, circumcision may not have been the best way to start."

POLISH CHRISTMAS CAKE RECIPE

Ingredients:
1cup of water
1 tsp baking soda
1 cup of sugar
1 tsp salt
1 cup of brown sugar
!/4 cup of lemon juice
4 large eggs
A bowl of mixed nuts
1 litre bottle vodka
2 cups dried fruit

Steps:
Sample the vodka to check quality.
Take a large bowl, check the vodka again.
To be sure it is the highest quality, pour one level cup and drink.
Repeat.

Turn on the electric mixer. Beat 1 cup of butter in a large fluffy bowl.
Add one teaspoon of sugar. Beat again.
At this point it is best to make sure the vodka is still ok.
Try another cup.....just in case.

Turn off the mixerer.
Break two eggs and add to the bowl and chuck in the cup of dried fruit.
Pick fruit off floor.
Mix on the turner.
If the fried druit gets stuck in the beaterers, pry it loose with a sdrewscriver.

Sample the vodka to test for tonsisticity.
Next, sift two cups of salt. Or something. Who giveshz a shit.
Check the vodka.

Now shift the lemon juice and strain your nuts.
Add one table.
Add a spoon of sugar, or somefink. Whatever you can find.
Greash the oven and piss in the fridge.
Turn the cake tin 360 degrees and try not to fall over.
Don't forget to beat off the turner.
Finally, throw the bowl through the window, finish the vodka and kick the cat.

Fall into bed.

CHERRY MISTMAS

Two Irishmen were digging a ditch directly across from a brothel.
Suddenly, they saw a rabbi walk up to the front door, glance around and duck inside.
"Ah, will ye look at that?" one ditch digger said.
"What's our world comin' to when men of th' cloth are visitin' such places?"
A short time later, a Protestant minister walked up to the door and quietly slipped inside.
"Do ye believe that?" the workman exclaimed.
"Why, 'tis no wonder th' young people today are so confused, what with the example clergymen set for them."
After an hour went by, the men watched as a Catholic priest quickly entered the whorehouse.
"Ah, what a pity", the digger said, leaning on his shovel.
"One of th' poor lasses must be ill."

At a travel agency in Shanghai, I asked the Chinese girl behind the counter if she could escort me on a city tour and asked her for her mobile number so I could call her to make arrangements. She gave me a big smile, nodded her head and said, "For sex sex, wan free sex, for tonigh free." I replied, "Wow, you Chinese women are really hospitable!" A guy standing next to me overheard, tapped me on the shoulder and said, "Don't get excited. What she said was: 466 136 4293!"

My husband and I were dressed and ready to go out for a lovely evening of dinner and theatre. Having been burgled in the past, we turned on a 'night light' and then put the cat in the backyard. When our Uber arrived, we walked out our front door and our rather tubby cat had run from the backyard to the front and scooted between our legs inside, then ran up the stairs. Because our cat likes to chase our parakeet, we didn't want to leave them unchaperoned, so my husband ran inside to retrieve her and put her in the back yard again. Because I didn't want the Uber driver to know our house was going to be empty all evening, I explained to him that my husband would be out momentarily as he was just bidding goodnight to my mother. A few minutes later he got into the Uber all hot and bothered and said, to my growing horror and amusement as the car pulled away, "Sorry it took so long, but the stupid bitch was hiding under the bed and I had to poke her arse with a coat hanger to get her to come out! She tried to take off so I grabbed her by the neck and wrapped her in a blanket so she wouldn't scratch me like she did the last time. But it worked! I hauled her fat arse down the stairs and threw her into the backyard.... she had better not shit in the vegetable garden again."

An Australian man was having a coffee and croissants with butter and jam in a cafe when an American tourist, chewing gum, sat down next to him.

The Australian politely ignored the American, who, nevertheless started up a conversation.

The American snapped his gum and said, "You Australian folk eat the whole bread?"

The Australian frowned, annoyed with being bothered during his breakfast, and replied, "of course."

The American blew a huge bubble. "We don't. In the States, we only eat what's inside. The crusts we collect in a container, recycle them, transform them into croissants and sell them to Australia."

The American had a smirk on his face. The Australian listened in silence.

The American persisted, "D'ya eat jam with your bread?"

Sighing, the Australian replied, "of course."

Cracking his gum between his teeth, the American said, "We don't. In the States, we eat fresh fruit for breakfast, then we put all the peels, seeds and the leftovers in containers, recycle them, transform them into jam and sell it to Australia."

The Australian then asked, "Do you have sex in the States?"

The American smiled and said, "Why of course we do."

The Australian leaned closer to him and asked, "And what do you do with the condoms once you've used them?"

"We throw them away, of course!"

Now it was the Australian's turn to smile.

"We don't. In Australia, we put them in a container, recycle them, melt them down into chewing gum and sell them to the United States. Why do you think it's called Wrigley's?"

I met a very attractive young woman at a nightclub the other night. We seemed to be attracted to each other, chatting, dancing and drinking to excess.

She was drinking champagne and I was drinking apple cider. We both wound up back at her place. More champagne and more apple cider and then into bed together. It turned out great for both of us. She finished the night up to her neck in champagne and I finished up to my balls in cider.

A husband and wife were saving for a house and were shopping at the super market and choosing the cheapest goods. Walking down the alcohol aisle the husband sees that VB beer is on special for twenty nine dollars a carton so puts one in his trolley.

"What's that?", snapped the wife.

"It's a carton of beer", the husband says.

"Twenty nine dollars, too expensive. Put it back", she snapped, which he duly did.

The next aisle was the womens beauty accessories. The wife picked up a sixty dollar bottle of cream and put it in the trolley.

"What's that?", snapped the husband.

"It's a bottle of womans face cream and it will make me look beautiful."

The husband looked at the price and said, "Put it back, it's too expensive. We'll go and get the slab of VB instead. That's only twenty nine dollars and I guarantee you, that will make you look real good."

A Ford motor mechanic was installing a cylinder head on a V8 when he spotted a well-known cardiologist in his work shop.

The doctor was there waiting for the service manager to come and take a look at his car when the mechanic shouted across the garage, "Hey doc, do you want to take a look at this?"

The cardiologist, a bit surprised, walked over to where the mechanic was working.

The mechanic straightened up, wiped his hands on a rag and asked, "So doc, look at this engine. I opened its heart, took the valves out, repaired and replaced anything damaged and then put everything back in, and when I finish, it will work just like new. So how is it that I make $48,000 a year and you make $1.7 million when you and I are doing basically the same work?

The cardiologist paused, leaned over and whispered to the mechanic:

"Try doing it with the engine running!"

A priest, a doctor and a golfer are playing golf one morning at the club when they decide to complain to the greenkeeper about the slow threesome in front of them.

The greenkeeper explained, "I realize they're slow, but they are ex-firefighters who were blinded when they saved our clubhouse from a terrible fire, so they play for free."

The priest said, "Oh, my, I will have my entire congregation pray for them on Sunday!"

The Doctor said, "And I will contact an eye surgeon to see if there is any way to bring back sight to those poor blinded heroes!"

And the Golfer said, "Can't you tell them to play at night?

A Jew, an Indian and a Frenchman were travelling across New South Wales when their car broke down. They knocked on a farmers door and asked for accommodation for the night.

"I can only put up two", said the farmer, "one will have to sleep in the barn."

"I will sleep in the barn", said the Jew.

Five minutes later there was a knock on the door. "There's a pig in the barn", said the Jew, "I cannot sleep with a pig."

"O.K., I'll go", said the Indian.

Five minutes later, there was a knock on the door. "There's a cow in the barn", said the Indian, "I am a Hindu, I cannot sleep with a cow."

"I'll go", said the Frenchman.

Five minutes later, there was another knock on the door. It was the pig and the cow.

A big mining company recently hired several cannibals. "You are all part of our team now", said the HR manager during the welcoming briefing. "You get all the usual benefits and you can go to the cafeteria for something to eat,

but please don't eat any of the other employees."

The cannibals promised they would not.

Four weeks later their boss remarked, "You're all working very hard, and I'm satisfied with you. However, one of our Admin girls has disappeared.

Do any of you know what happened to her?"

The cannibals all shook their heads indicating "no".

After the boss had left, the leader of the cannibals confronted the others angrily saying,

"OK! Which one of you stupid idiots ate the young chick from Admin?"

A hand rose hesitantly, to which the leader of the cannibals bellowed, "You moronic idiotic fool!!!!! For four weeks we've been eating Managers and Supervisors and no one noticed anything, but NOOOOO!!!, you had to go and eat someone who was actually important!!!!"

Two older women are sitting on a bench waiting for a bus.
The first lady takes out a cigarette and starts to smoke. A minute later it begins to rain, so she takes out a condom, cuts off the end, and carefully places it over the cigarette to shield it from the rain.
The second lady looks at that and says, "That's such a good idea, but what is that plastic thing?"
"It's a condom", The first lady replies.
"Well, where can you buy those?" the second lady asks.
"Um... Most people buy them at pharmacies." the first lady replies.
So the second lady goes to a pharmacy and walks up to the counter.
"Do you guys sell those condom things?" she asks the pharmacist.
"Why yes we do", the pharmacist says a little confused. "Do you know what size you need?"
So the lady says, "Well it's got to fit a Camel."

A dejected used car salesman was sitting in the corner drowning his problems.
"What's up?" asked the local harlot.
"Things aren't going too well. If I don't sell more cars, I'll lose my arse."
"I know how you feel", said the harlot. "If I don't sell more arse this month, I'll lose my car."

CURRY COOK-OFF COMPETITION

Notes from an inexperienced curry taster named FRANK, from Australia, who was visiting Durban, South Africa.

"Recently I was honoured to be selected as a judge at a curry cook-off. The original person called in sick at the last moment and I happened to be standing there at the judge's table asking directions to the beer wagon when the call came. I was assured by the other two judges (couple of local Indians) that the curry wouldn't be all that spicy, and besides, they told me I could have free beer during the tasting, so I accepted."

Here are the scorecards from the event:
Curry # 1: Manoj's Maniac Mobster Monster Curry

JUDGE ONE: A little too heavy on tomato. Amusing kick.

JUDGE TWO: Nice, smooth tomato flavour. Very mild.

FRANK: Holy shit, what the hell is this stuff? You could remove dried paint from your driveway. Took me two beers to put the flames out. I hope that's the worst one. These Indian fellows are crazy.

_____

Curry # 2: Applesamy's Afterburner Curry

JUDGE ONE: Smoky, with a hint of pork. Slight Jalapeno tang.

JUDGE TWO: Exciting BBQ flavour, needs more peppers to be taken seriously.

FRANK: Keep this out of reach of children! I'm not sure what I am supposed to taste besides pain. I had to wave off two people who wanted to give me the Heimlich manoeuvre. They had to rush in more beer when they saw the look on my face.

_____

Curry # 3: Farouk's Famous Burn Down the Barn curry

JUDGE ONE: Excellent firehouse curry! Great kick. Needs more beans.

JUDGE TWO: A beanless curry, a bit salty, good use of red peppers.

FRANK: Call Colesburg, I've located a uranium spill. My nose feels like I have been snorting Domestos. Everyone knows the routine by now, get me more beer before I ignite. Barmaid pounded me on the back; now my backbone is in the front part of my chest. I'm getting shit-faced from all the beer.

_____

Curry # 4: Barbu's Black Magic

JUDGE ONE: Black bean curry with almost no spice. Disappointing.

JUDGE TWO: Hint of lime in the black beans. Good side dish for fish or other mild foods, not much of a curry.

FRANK: I felt something scraping across my tongue, but was unable to taste it, is it possible to burn-out taste buds? Savathree, the bar maid, was standing behind me with fresh refills; that 300 lb. bitch is starting to look HOT, just like this nuclear waste I'm eating. Is curry an aphrodisiac?

_____

Curry # 5: Laveshnee's Legal Lip Remover

JUDGE ONE: Meaty, strong curry. Cayenne peppers freshly ground, adding considerable kick. Very impressive.

JUDGE TWO: Curry using shredded beef; could use more tomato. Must admit the cayenne peppers make a strong statement.

FRANK: My ears are ringing, sweat is pouring off my forehead and I can no longer focus my eyes. I farted and four people behind me needed hospital treatment. The contestant seemed offended when I told her that her curry had given me brain damage. Savathree saved my tongue from bleeding by pouring beer directly on it from a pitcher. I wonder if I'm burning my lips off?
It really pisses me off that the other judges asked me to stop
screaming.

———

Curry # 6: Vera's Very Vegetarian Variety

JUDGE ONE: Thin yet bold vegetarian variety curry. Good balance of spice and peppers.

JUDGE TWO: The best yet. Aggressive use of peppers, onions, and garlic. Superb.

FRANK: My intestines are now a straight pipe filled with gaseous, sulphuric flames. I shit myself when I farted and I'm worried it will eat through the chair. No one seems inclined to stand behind me except that slut Savathree, she must be kinkier than I thought.
Can't feel my lips anymore. I need to wipe my ass with a snow cone!

———

Curry # 7: Sugash's Screaming Sensation Curry

JUDGE ONE: A mediocre curry with too much reliance on canned peppers.

JUDGE TWO: Ho Hum, tastes as if the chef literally threw in a can of curry peppers at the last moment. I should note that I am worried about Judge Number 3. He appears to be in a bit of distress as he is cursing uncontrollably.

FRANK: You could put a grenade in my mouth, pull the pin, and I wouldn't feel a damn thing. I've lost the sight in one eye, and the world sounds like it is made of rushing water. My shirt is covered with curry which slid unnoticed out of my mouth.
 My pants are full of lava-like shit to match my damn shirt. At least during the autopsy they'll know what killed me. I've decided to stop breathing, it's too painful. Screw it, I'm not getting any oxygen anyway. If I need air, I'll just suck it in
through the 4 inch hole in my stomach.

———

Curry # 8: Hansraj's Mount Saint Curry

JUDGE ONE: A perfect ending, this is a nice blend curry, safe for all, not too bold but spicy enough to declare its existence.

JUDGE TWO: This final entry is a good, balanced curry, neither mild nor hot. Sorry to see that most of it was lost when Judge Number 3 passed out, fell over and pulled the curry pot down on top of himself. Not sure if he's going to make it. Poor Aussie, wonder how he'd have reacted to a really hot curry?

FRANK: --------------(editor's note: Judge #3 was unable to report)

A man and his wife are awakened at 3 o'clock in the morning by a loud pounding on the door.

The man gets up and goes to the door where a drunken stranger, standing in the pouring rain, is asking for a push.

"Not a chance", says the husband, "it's 3 o'clock in the morning!" He slams the door and returns to bed.

"Who was that?" asks his wife.

"Just some drunk guy asking for a push", he answers.

"Did you help him?" she asks.

"No, I didn't! It's 3 o'clock in the morning and it's pouring out there!"

"Well, you have a short memory", says his wife. "Can't you remember about three months ago when we broke down and those two guys helped us? I think you should help him, and you should be ashamed of yourself!"

The man does as he's told, gets dressed, and goes out into the pouring rain.

He calls out into the dark, "Hello, are you still there?"

"Yesh", comes back the slurred answer.

"Do you still need a push?" calls out the husband.

"Yesh, please!" comes the reply from the dark.

"Where the hell are you?" asks the husband.

"Over here on the swing!" replies the drunk.

A woman from Sydney who was a tree hugging, vegetarian and anti-hunter, purchased a piece of native bushland in northern NSW. There was a large gum tree on one of the highest points in her property. She wanted a good view of the natural splendour of her land so she started to climb the big gum.

As she neared the top, she encountered a koala that attacked her. In her haste to escape, the woman slid down the tree to the ground and got many splinters in her crotch.

In considerable pain, she hurried to a local hospital to see a doctor. She told him she was an environmentalist, vegetarian, and an anti-hunter and how she had come to get all the splinters. The doctor listened to her story with great patience and then told her to go wait in the examining room and he would see if he could help her. She sat and waited. And waited. Three hours later the doctor re-appeared. The angry woman demanded, "What took you so long?"

He smiled and then told her, "Well, I had to get permits from the Environmental Protection Agency, Native Vegetation, Parks and Wildlife service, and the Bureau of Land Management before I could remove old-growth timber from a 'recreational area' so close to a Waste Treatment Facility.

.... And ... I'm sorry, they turned you down."

A man suffered a serious heart attack while shopping in a store. The store clerks called 000 when they saw him collapse to the floor. The paramedics rushed the man to the nearest hospital where he had emergency open heart bypass surgery. He awakened from the surgery to find himself in the care of nuns at the Catholic Hospital he was taken to. A nun was seated next to his bed holding a clip board loaded with several forms, and a pen. She asked him how he was going to pay for his treatment.

"Do you have health insurance?" she asked.

He replied in a raspy voice, "No health insurance."

The nun asked, "Do you have money in the bank?"

He replied, "No money in the bank."

"Do you have a relative who could help you with the payments?", asked the irritated nun.

He said, "I only have a spinster sister, and she is a nun."

The nun became agitated and announced loudly, "Nuns are not spinsters! Nuns are married to God."

The patient replied, "Perfect. Send the bill to my brother-in-law."

Three good friends - a Turtle, a Rabbit, and a Buzzard - decide to chip in together to buy some land and start a farm but the soil was of such a poor quality they needed fertilizer for the job.

After much discussion and numerous pathetic excuses from Buzzard and Turtle, it was decided that Rabbit, being swift and strong, would be the best one to go get the fertilizer.

The first town Rabbit went to, the fertilizer was of inferior quality; the next had a shortage of fertilizer; the third, the price was too high; the fourth, the store was closed and so it went for months and months that stretched into years until he came across a farmer pulling a wagon of fresh manure, all of which Rabbit duly purchased.

While he was gone, however, Buzzard and Turtle struck oil and now the land was worth a fortune. Where their shack once stood was now a mansion with lush landscaping.

As Rabbit approached the mansion with his load of manure, he could hardly believe he had the right farm. He checked his map twice, hopped to the double doors of the mansion and rapped loudly. A man, in full butler attire, pulled open both doors and Rabbit asked, "Where is Mr Turtle?"

The butler, in his pompous nasally accent said, "Mister TurTELL is down the WELL."

Rabbit checked his building anger and asked, "Allright. May I speak to Mr Buzzard then?"

The butler replied pompously and dismissively, "Mister BuzzARD is in the YARD."

By now Rabbit is fuming and he explodes,

"Then you go and tell Mister TurTELL who is down the WELL... and Mister BuzzARD who is in the YARD... that Mister RabBIT is here with the SHIT!!"

A man asks a farmer near the field, "Sorry sir, would you mind if I crossed your field instead of going around it? You see, I have to catch the 4:30 PM train."
The farmer says, "Sure, go right ahead. And if my bull sees you, you'll even catch the 4 PM one."

Husband pinches his wife's breast and says,
"If we firm these up, we can get rid of the bra."
Wife grabs his penis and says,
"If we firm THIS up we can ger rid of the lawn mowing man!"

A young lady was playing a social game of golf with a male member of the Golf Club. As she leant over to place the ball on the tee the male noticed she wasn't wearing any knickers. Slightly embarrassed he mentioned this to her but she explained that she had four children to feed, her husband was on a low wage and with bills coming out of her ears she just couldn't afford to buy any underwear for herself.

The man was deeply touched and reached into his pocket and gave her fifty dollars.

Later at home, the young lady thought what a great way to earn some money, so next day she was at the course again without any knickers. She picked a likely male golfer and after he noticed she had no knickers on, she duly went through her routine from yesterday, explaining in her best sorrowful tone about her financial plight.

Upon hearing her story, the man reached into his pocket and pulled out a fifty cent piece and gave it to her. "What the hell is this for?" she demanded.

"Well", he said, "If you can't afford to buy any knickers at least go and buy a comb and tidy yourself up."

An English guy was waiting at the traffic lights when a group of bearded youths pull up alongside yelling abuse about England and the queen and making rude signs. They were revving the engine and took off before the lights changed to green yelling, "Allah akbar." Suddenly a bus came charging through the intersection and squashed the lot of them. The poor guy sat there in his car stunned. "Hell, he thought. That could have been me!" So the next day he went out and got a bus driver's licence.

My wife and I went to the Royal Agricultural Show and one of the first exhibits we stopped at was the breeder bulls. We went up to the first pen and there was a sign attached that said.....
' THIS BULL MATED 50 TIMES LAST YEAR '
My wife playfully nudged me in the ribs .... smiled and said, 'He mated 50 times last year, that's almost once a week.'
We walked to the second pen which had a sign attached that said,
"THIS BULL MATED 150 TIMES LAST YEAR'
My wife gave me a healthy jab and said, 'WOW ~~ that's almost 3 times a week! ....You could learn a lot from him.'
We walked to the third pen and it had a sign attached that said, in capital letters,
'THIS BULL MATED 365 TIMES LAST YEAR'
My wife was so excited that her elbow nearly broke my ribs, and said, 'That's once a day. You could REALLY learn something from this one.'
I looked at her and said, 'Go over and ask him if it was with the same cow...'
My condition has been upgraded from critical to stable and I pray that eventually I'll make a full recovery, after my testicles have returned to their correct spot.

An American couple were enjoying a morning cuppa in Wales in the town of Llanfairpwllgwyngyllgogerychwyrndrobwllllantysiliogogogoch which at 58 letters is the longest named town in the world.

The name of the town was on a sign across from the restaurant they were in and

being unable to even remotely pronounce the name of the town and also just to get the real feel of their stay in Wales, they called over one of the waitresses and pleasantly said to her, "In your lovely lilting Welsh brogue, would you be able to say for us, very slowly, the name of the place we are in."

The young waitress looked at them, smiled and very eloquently and slowly said,

"B U R G E R   K I N G."

Cliff and his buddy Norm were having a few beers and Cliff was trying to explain to his not so bright friend, Norm, about the buffalo theory of beer drinking.

"Well, you see Norm, it's like this...

A herd of buffalo can only move as fast as the slowest buffalo. And when the herd is hunted, it is the lowest and weakest ones at the back that are killed first. This natural selection is good for the herd as a whole, because the general speed and health of the whole group keeps improving by the regular killing of the weakest members. In much the same way, the human brain can only operate as fast as the slowest brain cells. Now, as we know, excessive intake of alcohol kills brain cells. But naturally, it attacks the slowest and weakest brain cells first. In this way, regular consumption of beer eliminates the weaker brain cells, making the brain a faster and more efficient machine.

And that, Norm, is why you always feel smarter after a few beers."

Amen!!!

A soldier was given the job of hunting for buffalo. To help him, he hired an Indian Scout. The two of them set off on their journey to find buffalo. After riding a while, the Indian gets off his horse, puts his ear to the ground and says, "Humm, buffalo come." The soldier scans the area with his binoculars, but sees nothing and hears nothing. He is confused and says to the Indian, "I do not see or hear anything, how do you know buffalo come"? and the Indian replies, "Ear sticky."

This old man and two attractive young women were riding up in a lift together when one of the young ladies took a fancy bottle of perfume out of her bag and sprayed a small amount on her neck. "Yves St Laurent, one hundred and fifty dollars for fifty mil's", she said haughtily. The other young lady similarly took a delicate bottle out of her bag and sprayed a small amount of perfume on her wrist. "Chanel No 5, two hundred and fifty dollars for fifty mil's", she snootily said.
The lift stopped, the doors started to open and as the two young women got ready to leave the lift, the old man leant slightly forward, let rip a loud rumbling fart, smiled and said, "Broccoli, dollar fifty a bunch."

Did anyone else read about that Bulgarian guy that got guillotined yesterday?
Denhis Hedfelof

Bubba, the mountain misfit and general village idiot, decided to save up and get a hang-glider.

He takes it to the highest mountain, and after struggling to the top, he gets ready to take flight. He takes off running and reaches the edge– into the wind he goes!

Meanwhile, Ma and Pa Hicks were sittin' on the porch swing, talkin' 'bout the good ol' days when ma spots the biggest bird she ever seen!

"Look at the size of that bird, Pa!" she exclaims.

Pa raises up, "Git my gun, Ma."

She runs into the house, brings out his pump shotgun. He takes careful aim. BANG…BANG…..BANG…..BANG!

The monster size bird continues to sail silently over the tree tops.

"I think ya missed him, Pa", she says.

"Yeah", he replies, "but at least he let go of Bubba!"

Three friends married women from different parts of the world.

The first man married a Greek girl. He told her that she was to do the dishes and house cleaning. It took a couple of days, but on the third day he came home to see a clean house and dishes washed and put away.

The second man married a Thai girl. He gave his wife orders that she was to do ...all the cleaning, dishes and the cooking. The first day he didn't see any results but the next day he saw it was better. By the third day he saw his house was clean, the dishes were done, and there was a huge dinner on the table.

The third man married a girl from Australia. He ordered her to keep the house cleaned, dishes washed, lawn mown, laundry washed, beer in the fridge at all times and hot meals on the table for every meal.

The first day he didn't see anything, the second day he didn't see anything either but by the third day, some of the swelling had gone down and he could see a little out of his left eye and his arm was healed enough that he could fix himself a sandwich and load the dishwasher. He still has some difficulty when he urinates.

A small restaurant in inner Sydney claimed that no matter what a patron ordered, they could provide it. A man saw the sign out side and decided to test them.

"I would like a stew made from the front legs of an albino rhinocerous", the man ordered.

"Certainly sir", said the waiter and it wasn't long before the dish arrived and it looked like it was as he had ordered. When he raised concerns that this may not be what he had ordered, he was taken into the kitchen and there was a white rhinocerous on the table with its front legs removed.

OK he thought, I'll get them this time so he ordered a plate of giraffe neck steak poached in a 50 year old Albanian red wine. And sure enough a long plate of meat was presented to him. On asking for authenticity, he was taken into the kitchen and there was a giraffe on the table with a hunk of meat taken from its neck and nearby was a bottle of 50 year old Albanian red wine.

Convinced this was an extraordinary restaurant, he called the waiter over and asked if, in their long history, they hade received an order they just had no way of accommodating.

"Sadly, I must say we have had one", said the waiter. "It was about six years ago and a man came in and ordered Braised Bulgarian Bull Drivers balls on toast. And you know what. We didn't have a loaf of bread in the place."

FUNNY IRISH NONSENSE

Bloke at a horse race whispers to Paddy next to him,
"Do you want the winner of the next race?"
Paddy replies, "No tanks, oi've only got a small yard."

Paddy and Mick found 3 hand grenades and decided to
take them to the police station.
Mick says, "What if one explodes before we get there?"
Paddy replies, "We'll lie and say we only found two."

A coach load of paddies on a mystery tour decided to
run a sweepstake to guess where they were going.....
The driver won $94.00.

Paddy finds a sandwich with two wires sticking out of it.
He phones the police and says, "Bejasus I've just found a
sandwich dat looks like a bomb."
The operator asks, "Is it tickin?"
Paddy says, "No, OI tink it's beef."

Mick says to Paddy, "Close your curtains the next time
you're making love to your wife. The whole street was
watching and laughing at you yesterday."
Paddy says, "Well the joke's on them because I wasn't
even at home yesterday."

The Irish have solved their own fuel problems.
They imported 50 million tonnes of sand from the Arabs
and they're going to drill for their own oil.

Paddy says to Mick, "I'm ready for a holiday, only this year I'm going to do it a bit different.
3 years ago I went to Spain and Mary got pregnant.
2 years ago I went to Italy and Mary got pregnant.
Last year I went to Majorca and Mary got pregnant."
Mick asks, "So what are you going to do this year?."
Paddy replies, "I'll take her with me!"

Sean says to Mick, "Christmas is on a Friday this year."
Mick says, "Let's hope it's not the 13th."

Paddy's in the bathroom and Murphy shouts to him, "Did you find the shampoo?"
Paddy says, "Oi did, but it's for dry hair and I've just wet mine."

While being interviewed for a job, the personnel manager said to the Maguire brothers: "We're going to give you a written examination. Ten questions. Whoever gets most right we'll hire."
Papers were produced and the boys set to work answering the general knowledge questions. When the time was up the personnel manager collected and marked the papers.
"Well", said he, "you've both got nine out of ten, but I'm giving Mick the job."
"Why's that?" asked Pat.
"Well", said the manager, "you both got the same question wrong but he had 'I don't know this,' and you had 'Neither do I!'"

A modest young lass had just purchased some lingerie and asked if she might have the sentence 'If you can read this you're too damn close!' embroidered on her panties and bra.

"Yes Madame", said the clerk, "I'm quite certain that could be done. Would you prefer block or script letters?"

"Braille", she replied, innocently lowering her lashes.

It was a terrible winter for the Highlands of Scotland with most of the land being buried under thick snow.

It had been a colder winter than normal and there had been three months of unbroken blizzards. As a result, most of Scotland had been covered in a thick blanket of snow that was far deeper and lasted for much longer than anyone could remember happening before.

McTavish hadn't been seen in the village for weeks, so a Red Cross rescue team was called to try and check if he was ok.

The Red Cross team struggled through the thick snow to his remote shack, which was at the head of the glen, and was completely buried in deep snow. Only the chimney was showing.

"McTavish", they shouted down the chimney. "Are you there?"

"Who is that?" came the crusty answer.

"It's the Red Cross", they called.

"Go away", shouted McTavish. "I bought a bloody flag last year!"

A young woman was walking past the local bookstore, when she saw a pile of books that were wrapped in plain brown paper, on display in the window.

A big sign above the books read "Newly Translated from the Original French: 37 Mating Positions."

Noticing that the books were already wrapped in plain brown paper, she couldn't stop herself from buying one of them.

Once safely at home, all alone, she opened her package in anticipation, and found out that she had just purchased.......... a very expensive book about chess.

Bono, lead singer of the rock band U2, is famous throughout the entertainment industry for being more than just a little self-righteous.

At a recent U2 concert in Glasgow, he asked the audience for total quiet.

Then, in the silence, he started to slowly clap his hands, once every few seconds.

Holding the audience in total silence, he said into the microphone,

"Every time I clap my hands, a child in Africa dies."

A voice with a broad Scottish accent from the front of the crowd pierced the quiet...

"Well, foockin stop doin' it then, ya evil bastard!"

It was the start of World War 2 in London, England, and the Nazi's were relentlessly bombing the British. The British had an early radar detection system in place which alerted the population in advance of an impending raid using air raid sirens. When the sirens blared, no matter what you were doing, you had to just drop it and run for your life to the nearest Underground entrance.

One morning around 9.00am, Fred and Gladys were having a quiet cuppa when the sirens started their screaming warning. Fred and Gladys dropped everything and ran flat strap out the front door, down the road with all the other neighbours, to the Underground entrance. Fred was about to tear down the stairs but thought he better check where Gladys was so he turned around just in time to see Gladys stop, turn around and run in the other direction.

He yelled to her, "Gladys, where the hell are you going? We have to get into the tunnels."

Gladys turned back and yelled. "I forgot me teeth. They're soakin' in the bathroom!"

Over the blare of the sirens Fred yelled back at her and screamed, "You forgot your teeth!!! For Gods sakes Gladys, they're droppin' bombs, not bloody ham sandwiches."

Man goes to a whore house. The Madam is out of women but, since the guy doesn't seem to be too bright, she thinks she can get away with a blow up doll and he will never know the difference. Being a bit nervous because she has never tried this one before, the Madam waits outside the door. The man comes out in five minutes. "How was it?", says the Madam.
"I don't know," says the man, "I bit her on the tit, she farted loudly and then flew out the window!"

A blind man is walking down the street with his seeing-eye dog one day. They come to a busy intersection, and the dog, ignoring the high volume of traffic zooming by on the street, leads the blind man right out into the thick of traffic. This is followed by the screech of tyres and horns blaring as panicked drivers try desperately not to run the pair down.
The blind man and the dog finally reach the safety of the sidewalk on the other side of the street, and the blind man

pulls a Goodo Doggie Bik out of his coat pocket which he offers to the dog. A passerby, having observed the near fatal incident, can't control his amazement and says to the blind man, "Why on earth are you rewarding your dog with a Goodo? He nearly got you killed!"

The blind man turns partially in his direction and replies, "To find out where his head is, so I can kick his arse."

The guys were all in the Outback on a shooting and camping trip. No one wanted to room with Bob, because he snored so badly.

They decided it wasn't fair to make one of them stay with him the whole time, so they voted to take turns.

The first guy slept with Bob and comes to breakfast the next morning with his hair a mess and his eyes all bloodshot.

They said, "Man, what happened to you?"

He said, "Bob snored so loudly, I just sat up and watched him all night."

The next night it was a different guy's turn. In the morning, same thing, hair all standing up, eyes all bloodshot.

They said, "Man, what happened to you? You look awful!"

He said, "Man, that Bob shakes the roof with his snoring. I watched him all night."

The third night was Fred's turn. Fred was a tanned, older cowboy, a man's man.

The next morning, he came to breakfast bright-eyed and bushy-tailed. "Good morning!" he cheerily said.

They couldn't believe it. They said, "Man, what happened?"

He said, "Well, we got ready for bed. I went and tucked Bob into bed, patted him on the butt, and kissed him good night. Bob sat up and kept his eye on me all night."

The Tax Department suspected a fishing boat owner wasn't paying proper wages to his deckhand and sent an agent to investigate him.

Agent: "I need a list of your employees and how much you pay them."

Boat Owner: "Well, there's Clarence, my deckhand, he's been with me for 3 years. I pay him $1,000 a week plus free room and board. Then there's the mentally challenged guy. He works about 18 hours every day and does about 90% of the work around here. He makes about $10 per week, pays his own room and board, and I buy him a bottle of Bacardi rum and a dozen Carlton draught beer every Saturday night so he can cope with life. He also gets to sleep with my wife occasionally."

Agent: "That's the guy I want to talk to - the mentally challenged one."

Boat Owner: "That would be me. What would you like to know"?

A man walked into a sex shop and said, "I want a blow up doll."

"Certainly sir. What sort would you like? A plastic one or a rubber one?"

"I don't know. I just want a blow up doll. What's the difference? A blow up doll is a blow up doll", he said.

"Well", started the girl, "you see the plastic ones are our cheaper ones. Nice, but a bit rough around the edges. Where as the rubber ones are soft and cuddly and have little bits of fur in the right places. If you know what I mean."

"Ok, Ok I'll take the rubber one", he said.

"Certainly sir, now would you like a white one or a black one."

Getting frustrated he said, "Hell I don't know. I just want a blow up doll. What's the difference anyway?"

Being very patient the young girl explained, "The white ones are our Catholic dolls. They are very life like, good price but the problem is you have to buy a separate device to manually inflate them. Not as popular as the black ones"

"Well why are the black ones so popular", queried the man.

"Because they are our Muslim dolls and they blow themselves up."

This man woke up in his hospital bed with the surgeon hovering over him.

"Doc, how did it go?" he asked.

"Well, I have good news and I have bad news", said the Doc.

"I can take it. Give me the bad news first", said the patient.

"OK. The disease was worse than we first thought and we had to amputate both your legs", said the Doc.

Devastated, the athletic young man said, "How could there possibly be any good news after that."

Smiling and beaming the doctor said, "The bloke in the next bed wants to buy your slippers."

A blind cowboy wanders into an all-girl biker bar by mistake...

He finds his way to a bar stool and orders a shot of Jack Daniels.

After sitting there for a while, he yells to the bartender,"'Hey, you wanna hear a blonde joke?"

The bar immediately falls absolutely silent.

In a very deep, husky voice, the woman next to him says, "Before you tell that joke, Cowboy, I think it is only fair, given that you are blind, that you should know five things:

1. The bartender is a blonde girl with a baseball bat.

2. The bouncer is a blonde girl with knuckle dusters.

3. I'm a 1.9 metre, 85 klilogram blonde woman with a black belt in karate.
4. The woman sitting next to me is blonde and a professional weight lifter.
5. The lady to your right is blonde and a professional wrestler.
Now, think about it seriously, Cowboy ... do you still wanna' tell that blonde joke?"
The blind cowboy thinks for a second, shakes his head and mutters, "No ... not if I'm gonna' have to explain it five times."

Marg told Patricia, "I think that I just blew my diet." Patricia inquired, "What did you do?" "Marg replied, "I had three large eggs for breakfast." "Scrambled?" "No, Cadbury."

A married woman had lunch with 2 of her unmarried friends.
One was engaged, one was a mistress, and the married woman had been married for 20+ years.
They were chatting about their relationships and decided to amaze their men by greeting them at the door wearing a black bra, stiletto heels and a mask over their eyes.
They agreed to meet in a few days to exchange notes. Here's how it all went.
The Engaged friend:
The other night when my boyfriend came over, he found me with a black leather bodice, tall stilettos and a mask. He saw me and said, "You are the woman of my dreams. I love you." Then we made passionate love all night long.
The Mistress:
Me too! The other night I met my lover at his office and I was wearing a raincoat, under it only the black bra, heels and mask over my eyes.
When I opened the raincoat. he didn't say a word, but he

started to tremble and we had wild sex all night.
Then the married woman had to share her story that went like this:
"When my husband came home I was wearing the black bra, black stockings, stilettos and a mask over my eyes. When he came in the door and saw me, he said:
"What's for dinner, Zorro?"

There were two Catholic bishops together in bed.
Which one was wearing the frilly panties, lace negligee, and make-up?
Mrs Bishop.

A bloke wins the lottery and decides to buy himself a Harley Davidson. He goes down to his local bike shop and after purchasing a top of the range bike, the owner of the shop tells him to coat the bike in Vaseline every time it looks like raining. That night he goes and picks his girlfriend up on his new toy and heads over to her parents house for the first time. As they arrive there, she explains to him that whenever they have dinner, don't talk.
"If you talk," she tells him, "you have to do the pots." The man is astounded as he walks into the house as it is a complete mess. Anyway, the family all sit down for dinner not saying a word. The man decides to take advantage of the situation by groping his girlfriend's tits, yet there is not a sound from anyone.
So he decides to shag his bird on the table, and still there is not a word. He then proceeds to do his girlfriend's mum over the table, but still, amazingly, there's not a word from anyone. Just at that moment, there was a clap of thunder and rain starts pelting down on the kitchen window. He remembers his precious new motorbike, so he reaches into his pocket and flops the Vaseline out.
At which point his girlfriend's dad leaps up and shouts, "Okay! Okay! Enough! Enough! I'll do the bloody pots!"

John O'Reilly hoisted his beer in toast and said, "Here's to spending the rest of me life, between the legs, of me wife!"

That won him the top prize at the pub for the best toast of the night!

He went home and told his wife, Mary, "I won the prize for the Best toast of the night."

She said, "Aye, did ye now. And what was your toast?"

John said, "Here's to spending the rest of me life, sitting in church, beside me wife."

"Oh, that is very nice indeed, John!" Mary said.

The next day, Mary ran into one of John's drinking buddies on the street corner. The man chuckled leeringly and said, "John won the prize the other night at the pub with a toast about you, Mary."

She said, "Aye, he told me, and I was a bit surprised myself. You know, he's only been in there twice in the last four years. Once I had to pull him by the ears to make him come, and the other time he fell asleep."

There was a young man called Paul
Who was born with a rectangular ball
The cube of his date
By penis length plus eight
Was three fifths of five eights of bugger all.

A young woman had been taking golf lessons. She had just started playing her first round of golf when she suffered a bee sting. Her pain was so intense that she decided to return to the clubhouse for help and to complain.

Her golf pro saw her come into the clubhouse and asked, "Why are you back in so early? What's wrong?"

"I was stung by a bee," she said.

"Where?," he asked.

"Between the first and second hole," she replied.

He nodded knowingly and said, "Then your feet were too far apart."

A bear walks into a bar in Bendigo, Victoria and sits down. He bangs on the bar with his paw and demands a beer. The bartender approaches and says, "We don't serve beer to bears in bars in Bendigo." The bear, becoming angry, demands again that he be served a beer. The bartender tells him again, more forcefully, "We don't serve beer to belligerent bears in bars in Bendigo." The bear, very angry now, says, "If you don't serve me a beer, I'm going to eat that lady sitting at the end of the bar." The bartender says, "Sorry, we don't serve beer to belligerent, bully bears in bars in Bendigo." The bear goes to the end of the bar, and, as promised, eats the woman. He comes back to his seat and again demands a beer. The bartender states, "Sorry, we don't serve beer to belligerent, bully bears in bars in Bendigo who are on drugs." The bear says, "I'm NOT on drugs." The bartender says, "You are now. That was a barbitchyouate."

Bloke goes into a pub, and the barmaid asks what he wants.

"I want to bury my face in your cleavage and lick the sweat from between your tits" he says.

"You dirty bastard!" shouts the barmaid, "get out before I get my husband."

The bloke apologizes and promises not to repeat his gaffe. The Barmaid accepts this and asks him again what he wants.

"I want to pull your pants down, spread yoghurt between the cheeks of your arse and lick it all off."

She says, "You dirty filthy pervert! You're banned. Get out!!" Again, the bloke apologizes and swears never ever to do it again.

"One more chance", says the barmaid, "Now - what do you want?"

"I want to turn you upside down, tear your knickers off and fill your pussy with Guinness, and then drink every last drop from the hairy cup."

The barmaid is furious at this personal intrusion, and runs upstairs to fetch her husband, who's sitting quietly watching the TV.

"What's up love?" he asks.

"There's a bloke in the bar who wants to put his head between my tits and lick the sweat off", she says.

"I'll kill him.. Where is he?" storms the husband.

"Then he said he wanted to pour yoghurt down between my arse cheeks and lick it off", she screams.

"Right. He's dead!" says the husband, reaching for a baseball bat.

"Then he said he wanted to turn me upside down, fill my fanny with Guinness and then drink it all", she cries!

The husband puts down his bat and returns to his armchair, and switches the TV back on.

"Aren't you going to do something about it?" she cries hysterically.

"Look love, I'm not messing with any bloke who can drink 15 pints of Guinness..."

One day a father, on his way home from work suddenly remembers that it's his daughter's birthday. He pulls over to a Toy Shop and asks the sales person, "How much for one of those Barbies in the display window?" The salesperson answers, "Which one do you mean, Sir? We have: Work Out Barbie for $19.95, Shopping Barbie for $19.95, Beach Barbie for $19.95, Disco Barbie for $19.95, Astronaut Barbie for $19.95, Skater Barbie for $19.95, and Divorced Barbie for $265.95."

The amazed father asks: "It's what? Why is the Divorced Barbie $265.95 and the others only $19.95?"

The annoyed salesperson rolls her eyes, sighs, and answers:

"Sir..., Divorced Barbie comes with: Ken's Truck, Ken's House, Ken's Fishing Boat, Ken's Furniture, Ken's Dog, Ken's Computer, one of Ken's Friends, and a key chain made from Ken's testicles."

A man staggered home one evening, clearly the worse for wear. Shoes in hand to avoid waking his wife, he tip toed upstairs, but misjudged a step and fell.

He landed heavily on his rump, breaking a whiskey bottle he had in each hip pocket. Managing to suppress a yelp of pain, he sprang up and examined his bleeding and lacerated backside in a nearby mirror. Then, finding a packet of Band Aids, he tried to patch himself up before making his way to bed.

Next morning, he awoke in searing pain and noticed his wife staring at him from across the room.

"You were drunk last night" she said.

"Now, dear", he protested, "why could you possibly say such a thing?"

"Well", she said, "Three reasons. Firstly, it could be the glass at the bottom of the stairs, or secondly, it could be the stench of spilt whiskey on the carpet, but thirdly and mostly, it's all those Band Aids stuck on the downstairs mirror."

As a bagpiper, I play many gigs. Recently, I was asked by a funeral director to play at a graveside service for a homeless man. He had no family or friends, so the service was to be at a pauper's cemetery in Western Sydney.
As I was not familiar with the suburbs, I got lost and being a typical man, I didn't stop for directions. I finally arrived an hour late and saw the funeral guy had evidently gone and the hearse was nowhere in sight. There were only the diggers and crew left and they were eating lunch.
I felt badly and apologised to the men for being late. I went to the side of the grave and looked down. The vault lid was already in place. I didn't know what else to do, so I started to play. The workers put down their lunches and began to gather around. I played out my heart and soul for this man with no family and friends. I played like I've never played before for this homeless man. And as I played 'Amazing Grace,' the workers began to weep. They wept, I wept, and we all wept together. When I finished, I packed up my bagpipes and started for my car. Though my head hung low, my heart was full.
As I opened the door to my car, I heard one of the workers wistfully say, "I never seen nothing like that before...... and I've been putting in septic tanks for twenty years."
Apparently, I'm still lost.

Moshe was sitting at the bar staring at his drink when a large, trouble-making biker steps up next to him, grabs his drink and gulps it down in one swig.
Moshe burst into tears.
"Come on, man," the biker says, "I didn't think you'd CRY. I can't stand to see a man crying. What's your problem?"
"This is the worst day of my life", Moshe says. "I'm a complete failure. I was late to a meeting and my boss fired me. When I went to the parking lot, I found my car had been stolen and I don't have any insurance. I left my wallet in the cab I took home.

I found my wife in bed with the postman and then my dog bit me.

So, I came to this bar to work up the courage to put an end to it all.

I buy a drink; drop a capsule in and sit here watching the poison dissolve. Then you show up and drink the whole thing!

But enough about me, how's your day going?"

Muldoon lived alone in the Irish countryside with only a pet dog for company. One day the dog died, and Muldoon went to the parish priest and asked, "Father, me dog is dead... Could ya' be sayin' a mass for the poor creature?"

Father Patrick replied, "I'm afraid not; we cannot have services for an animal in how do I the church.... But there are some Baptists down the lane, and there's no tellin' what they believe. Maybe they'll do somethin' for the creature."

Muldoon said, "I'll go right away Father. Do ya' think $5,000 is enough to donate to them for the service?"

Father Patrick exclaimed, "Sweet Mary, Mother of Jesus! Why didn't ya' tell me the dog was Catholic?"

A gentleman is preparing to board a plane, when he hears that the Pope is on the same flight. "This is exciting," thinks the gentleman. "Perhaps I'll be able to see him in person." Imagine his surprise when the Pope sits down in the seat next to him. Shortly after take-off, the Pope begins a crossword puzzle. Almost immediately, the Pope turns to the gentleman and says, "Excuse me, but do you know a four letter word referring to a woman that ends in 'unt?" 'Only one word leaps to mind' thought the man, 'but my goodness, I can't tell the Pope that. There must be another word.' The gentleman thinks for quite a while, and then it hits him. Turning to the Pope, the gentleman says, "I think the word you're looking for is 'aunt.'" "Of course, how silly of me," says the Pope. "Do you have an eraser?"

A man was married to the biggest nag of a woman you could imagine. He realized he would only ever be happy if she wasn't around. That is, dead. He knew he couldn't do it himself so he went to a seedy bar one night and put the word around. After a while a slimy little character came up to him and said in a low raspy voice,

"My name is Arty. Everyone calls me Arty. I hears yous has a job to be done. I will do it for you for one dollar."

Excited at how easy and cheap this was going to be, the man was the happiest he had ever been. Next day he went to work in high spirits and returned home around six o'clock with expectations that Arty had done the deed. And all for only one dollar. He walked into the kitchen and there was his wife. On the floor, dead. Her eyes were bulging, her neck had large blue bruises around it and her tongue was hanging out the side of her mouth. The man was ecstatic and danced into the lounge room only to find his mother in law in exactly the same way. Oh no, not the mother in law as well. He staggered into the dining room and there was the neighbours wife. Same thing.

Three people dead. This was all too much for the man so he called the police. The coroner inspected the scene and promptly pronounced that all three had died from asphyxiation. Cause of death….choking.

Next day, the terrible crime was reported on the front page of every newspaper and in big bold lettering, the headlines read:

"ARTY CHOKES THREE FOR A DOLLAR"

Text of a letter from a kid from a cattle station near Cunnamulla in far west Queensland, to Mum and Dad.

Dear Mum & Dad,

I am well. Hope youse are too. Tell me big brothers Doug and Phil that the Army is better than workin' on the station - tell them to get in bloody quick smart before the jobs are all gone. I wuz a bit slow in settling down at first, because ya don't hafta get outta bed until 6am. But I like sleeping in now, cuz all ya gotta do before brekky is make ya bed and shine ya boots and clean ya uniform. No bloody horses to get in, no calves to feed, no troughs to clean - nothin'. Ya haz gotta shower though, but it's not so bad, coz there's lotsa hot water and even a light to see what ya doing.

At brekky ya get cereal, fruit and eggs but there's no kangaroo steaks or goanna stew like wot Mum makes You don't get fed again until noon and by that time all the city boys are buggered because we've been on a 'route march' - geez its only just like walking to the windmill in the bullock paddock.

This one will kill me brothers Doug and Phil with laughter. I keep getting medals for shootin' - dunno why. The bullseye is as big as a bloody dingo's arse and it don't move and it's not firing back at ya like the Johnsons did when our big scrubber bull got into their prize cows before the Ekka last year. All ya gotta do is make yourself comfortable and hit the target - it's a piece of p..... You don't even load your own cartridges, they comes in little boxes, and ya don't have to steady yourself against the rollbar of the roo shooting truck when you reload.

Sometimes ya gotta wrestle with the city boys and I gotta be real careful coz they break easy - it's not like fighting with Doug and Phil and Jack and Boori and Steve and Muzza all at once like we do at home after the muster.

Turns out I'm not a bad boxer either and it looks like I'm the best the platoon's got, and I've only been beaten by this one bloke from the Engineers - he's 6 foot 5 and 15 stone and three pick handles across the shoulders and as ya know I'm only 5 foot 7 and eight stone wringin' wet, but I fought him till the other blokes carried me off to the boozer.

I can't complain about the Army - tell the boys to get in quick before word gets around how bloody good it is.

Your loving daughter,
Susan

An Arab family was considering putting their grandfather, Abdullah, in a nursing home. All the Arab Facilities were completely full, though, so they had to put him in an Italian home.

After a few weeks in the Italian facility, they came to visit Grandpa.

"How do you like it here?" asked the grandson,

"It's wonderful! Everyone here is so courteous and respectful". said grandpa.

"We're so happy for you. We were worried that this was the wrong place for you since you are a little different from everyone."

"Oh, no! Let me tell you about how wonderfully they treat the residents". Abdullah said with a big smile.

"There's a musician here - he's 85 years old. He hasn't played the violin in 20 years, and everyone still calls him Maestro!

There is a judge in here - he's 95 year old. He hasn't been on the bench in 30 years and everyone still calls him Your Honor.

There's a dentist here - 90 years old. He hasn't fixed a tooth for 25 years, and everyone still calls him Doctor."

"And Me – I haven't had sex for 45 years, and they still call me The F…king Arab."

Paddy was on his way to the pub for his end of day imbibe when he happened upon a leprechaun in distress, caught in some brambles and unable to get free.

Paddy managed to untangle him. The little fella was most appreciative and offered Paddy two wishes.

Paddy thought long and hard, and being a drinker said, "Oi wish oi 'ad a bottle of Baileys Irish Cream that never got empty."

And pft! There was immediately said bottle. Paddy couldn't believe his good fortune and immediately ripped the top off the bottle and began sculling the delicious liquid. As soon as he had finished the bottle, pft! It was full again. The leprechaun said, "OK Paddy, what's your second wish? Hurry up now I have lots of work to do."

Paddy was in no hurry and continued drinking his second bottle. The leprechaun, getting agitated, said sternly to a now very intoxicated paddy, "Last chance to get your second wish Paddy. I want it now."

So, Paddy took the bottle from his lips, thought hard about his good luck and said, "Ok! Ok! Oi wish, Oi wish, Oi wish I 'ad another bottle jush like thish one."

John, woke up after the annual office Christmas party with a pounding headache, cotton-mouthed and utterly unable to recall the events of the preceding evening. After a trip to the bathroom, he made his way downstairs, where his wife put some coffee in front of him.
"Louise", he moaned, "tell me what happened last night. Was it as bad as I think?"
"Even worse", she said, her voice oozing scorn. "You made a complete arse of yourself. You succeeded in antagonizing the entire board of directors and you insulted the president of the company, right to his face."
"He's an arsehole", John said. "Piss on him."
"You did", came the reply. "And he fired you."
"Well, screw him!" said John.
"I did. You're back at work on Monday."

There was a young girl from Ballarat
Had triplets Nat, Pat and Tat
Breeding time was swell
But feeding time was hell
'Cos she found she had no tit for Tat.

A married Irishman went into the confessional and said to his priest, 'I almost had an affair with another woman.'
The priest said, 'What do you mean, almost?'
The Irishman said, 'Well, we got undressed and rubbed together, but then I stopped.'
The priest said, 'Rubbing together is the same as putting it in. You're not to see that woman again. For your penance, say five Hail Mary's and put $50 in the poor box.'
The Irishman left the confessional, said his prayers, and then walked over to the poor box.
He paused for a moment and then started to leave.
The priest, who was watching, quickly ran over to him saying, 'I saw that. You didn't put any money in the poor box!'
The Irishman replied, 'Yeah, but I rubbed the $50 on the box, and according to you, that's the same as putting it in!'

Little Johnny's mother decided to give her son an anatomy lesson one day, so she took off all of her clothes and pointed to her vagina, and said, "Johnny. This is where you come from."
Johnny went to school the next day smiling and insisting all his friends now refer to him as "Lucky Johnny."
"Why?" one asked.
Johnny held his fingers an inch apart and said, "Because I came this close to being a turd."

There was an Australian man who lived in Korea and when he was there he had a lot of sex and never once used a condom the entire time he was there. Then he returned to Australia and one morning he woke up and noticed bright green and purple dots on his penis. The man freaked out. He went to the doctor.

The doctor said, "I have never seen anything like this before. We will need to run some tests. Come back in 3 days for your test results."

The man came back in 3 days and the doctor said, "I have some really bad news. You have a disease called Pongolion HP. I'm sorry sir but we will need to amputate your penis."

The man was horrified. He went to a Korean doctor thinking he would know more about it. "Haw yes, Pongolion HP, velly ware. Yes", said the Korean Doctor.

"The Australian doctor wants to amputate my penis", cried the Aussie.

"Stupid 'Stralian doctah, make more money that way, no need amputate."

"Oh thank god" said the man feeling greatly relieved.

"Haw, wait 2 weeks, fall off by itself."

A man and his wife go to their honeymoon hotel for their 25th anniversary. As the couple reflected on that magical evening 25 years ago, the wife asked the husband, "When you first saw my naked body in front of you, what was going through your mind?"
The husband replied, "All I wanted to do was to screw your brains out, and suck your tits dry."
Then, as the wife undressed, she asked, "What are you thinking now?"
He replied, "It looks as if I did a pretty good job."

An elderly man was quite unhappy because he had lost his favorite hat.

Instead of buying a new one, he decided he would go to church and swipe one out of the vestibule.

When he got there, an usher intercepted him at the door and took him to a pew where he had to sit and listen to the entire sermon on "The Ten Commandments."

After church, the man met the preacher in the vestibule doorway, shook his hand vigorously, and told him, "I want to thank you preacher for saving my soul today. I came to church to steal a hat and after hearing your sermon on the Ten Commandments, I decided against it."

Preacher: "You mean the commandment 'I shall not steal' changed your mind?"

Old Man: "No, the one about adultery did. As soon as you said that I remembered where I left my old hat!"

A DRINKING TOAST

Here's to the breezes
That blows through the treeses
And lifts the girls tweezers
Above their bare kneeses
And shows us the creases
That oozes and squeezes
And teases and pleases
And gives us diseases
Be Jesus,
TO THE BREEZES!!!

WITTY ALCOHOL PUNS

Did you know that wine and beer doesn't make you fat?
It makes you lean….
Against tables, chairs, floors, walls and ugly people.

I drank so much wine last night that when I walked across
the dance floor to get another glass, I won the dance
competition.

I can't wait for the day when I can drink wine with my kids
instead of because of them.

Every box of raisins is a tragic tale of grapes that could
have been wine.

I am giving up drinking alcohol for the month of January.
Sorry, that was a typo: I am giving up. Drinking alcohol for
the month of January.

When I drink alcohol, people call me alcoholic. But when
I drink Fanta, no one calls me fantastic…

I'm not an alcoholic, I only drink on days that have the
letter "R' in it. Friday, Saturday, Sundray, Mondray…..

I feel sorry for people who don't drink. They wake up in
the morning and that's the best they're going to feel all
day.

I cook with wine. Sometimes I even add it to the food.

Lips that touch liquor shall never touch mine. No, not my
lips, my liquor.

Wine improves with age. The older I get, the more I like it.

I enjoy a glass of wine each night for its health benefits. The other glasses I consume are for my witty comebacks, intelligent conversation and my flawless dance moves.

I just read an article on the dangers of drinking alcohol. Scared the crap out of me.
So that's it. After today…No more reading!!

Two men had been totally lost in the Canadian wilderness for eight days.
"If we ever get out of here, what is the first thing you will do?" asked one of the men.
"I'm going to have a very hot shower, eat the biggest steak I can find, drink 2 bottles of superb wine and then sleep for two days", said the man.
The second man said, "Well I'm going to screw the first woman I lay my eyes on."
That afternoon they stopped on a rocky rise and there below them was a gorgeous naked Indian maiden taking a dip in a waterfall rock pool. The second man couldn't control himself and true to his vow, he was off, only to be dragged back by his comrade who said, "You can't go down there and molest that woman. What about the RCMP?"
"Who?" queried the second man.
"The RCMP. You know. The Royal Canadian Mounted Police", explained the first man.
"Bugger them", said the randy man and he was off, only to be dragged back again by his comrade who said, "You can't go down there. What about the RCFR?"
"Who?" queried the man again.
"The RCFR. You know. The Royal Canadian Forest Rangers", the first man said.

"Bugger them", the panting second man said and he was off. About an hour later he returned. Two black eyes, a broken arm, a broken nose, three teeth knocked out and all his clothes ripped apart.

"What happened to you?", exclaimed the first man.

"The FBI was there", the clearly hurting man said.

"What! You mean the **F**ederal **B**ureau of **I**nvestigation?" asked the first man.

"No, a **F**riggin' **B**ig Indian."

A Briton, a Frenchman, and a Russian are standing and staring at a portrait of Adam and Eve.

"Look at their calm, their reserve", says the Briton. "Surely they must be British!"

"Nonsense!" replies the Frenchman. "They are beautiful. Surely they must be French!"

The Russian finally speaks, "They have no clothes, no shelter, only an apple to eat, and are being told this is paradise. They are Russian."

A highway patrolman pulled alongside a speeding car on the freeway.

Glancing at the car, he was astounded to see that the blonde behind the wheel was knitting.

Realizing that she was oblivious to his flashing lights and siren, the trooper cranked down his window, turned on his bullhorn and yelled, "PULL OVER."

"NO!" the blonde yelled back, "IT'S A SCARF."

A wife decides to take her husband to a strip club for his birthday.

They arrive at the club and the doorman says, "Hey, Dave! How ya doin'?"

His wife is puzzled and asks if he's been to this club before.

"Oh, no", says Dave. "He's on my bowling team."

When they are seated, a waitress asks Dave if he'd like his usual and brings over a Victoria Bitter beer.

His wife is becoming increasingly uncomfortable and says, "How did she know that you drink V.B.?"

"She's in the Ladies Bowling League, honey. We share lanes with them."

A stripper then comes over to their table, throws her arms around Dave, and says, "Hi Davey Wavey. Want your usual table dance, big boy?"

Dave's wife, now furious, grabs her purse and storms out of the club.

Dave follows and spots her getting into a cab. Before she can slam the door, he jumps in beside her. He tries desperately to explain how the stripper must have mistaken him for someone else, but his wife is having none of it. She is screaming at him at the top of her lungs, calling him every name in the book.

The cabby turns his head and says, "Looks like you picked up a real bitch tonight, Dave."

Bob was in trouble. He forgot his wedding anniversary. His wife was really crapped off.
She told him, "Tomorrow morning, I expect to find a gift in the
driveway that goes from 0 to 200 in 6 seconds AND IT BETTER BE THERE !!"
The next morning he got up early and left for work. When his wife woke up, she looked out the window and sure enough there was a box gift-wrapped in the middle of the driveway.
Confused, the wife put on her robe and ran out to the driveway, and brought the box back in the house.
She opened it and found a brand new bathroom scale.
Bob has been missing since Friday.

A shark was swimming in the cold waters of the English Channel off the coast of Scotland when he espied a rather sluggish squid.
The shark asked the squid why the long face and the squid replied that the waters were so cold he could hardly move and felt dreadful.
The shark said, "What you need is some nice warm water to swim around in, like the Mediterranean Sea. Come on, jump on top of me and I will take you there."
Three days later they arrived off the coast of Sicily and the water was just divine. The squid was really tired and still sluggish from the long journey and not feeling very well at all.
A very large barracuda swam up to the shark and the shark, recognizing the large fish as his old friend, said, "I told you last time we met that I always pay my money debts. So, here's the sick squid I owe you."

One day, in line at the company cafeteria, Joe says to Mike,

"My elbow hurts like hell. I guess I'd better see a doctor."

"Listen, you don't have to spend that kind of money", Mike replies.

"There's a diagnostic computer down at Aldi's. Just give it a urine sample and the computer will tell you what's wrong and what to do about it.

It takes ten seconds and costs ten dollars. A lot cheaper than a doctor."

So, Joe deposits a urine sample in a small jar and takes it to Aldi's.

He deposits ten dollars and the computer lights up and asks for the urine sample.

He pours the sample into the slot and waits. Ten seconds later, the computer ejects a printout:

"You have tennis elbow. Soak your arm in warm water and avoid heavy activity.

It will improve in two weeks. Thank you for shopping at Aldi."

That evening, while thinking how amazing this new technology was, Joe began wondering if the computer could be fooled. He mixed some tap water, a stool sample from his dog, urine samples from his wife and daughter, and just to really mess things up, a sperm sample from himself, just for good measure.

Joe hurries back to Aldi's, eager to check the results.

He deposits ten dollars, pours in his concoction, and awaits the results.

The computer prints the following:

1. Your tap water is too hard. Get water softener. (Aisle 9)
2. Your dog has ringworm. Bathe him with anti-fungal shampoo. (Aisle 7)
3. Your daughter has a cocaine habit. Get her into rehab.
4. Your wife is pregnant. Twins. They aren't yours. Get a lawyer.
5. If you don't stop wanking yourself, your elbow will never get better.

Thank you for shopping at Aldi.

A doctor in Dublin wanted to get off work and go fishing, so he approached his assistant. "Murphy, I am going hunting tomorrow and don"t want to close the clinic I want you to take care of the clinic and take care of all me patients".
"Yes, sir!" answers Murphy.
The doctor goes fishing and returns the following day and asks: "So,Murphy, how was your day?"
Murphy told him that he took care of three patients.
"The first one had a headache so he did, so I gave him Paracetamol."
"Bravo Murphy lad, and the second one?" asks the doctor.
"The second one had indigestion and I gave him Gaviscon, so I did sir" says Murphy.
"Bravo, bravo! You"re good at this and what about the third one?" Asks the doctor
"Sir, I was sitting here and suddenly the door flies open and a young gorgeous woman bursts in so she does. Like a bolt outta the blue, she tears off her clothes, taking off everything including her bra and her panties and lies down on the table, spreading her legs and shouts: "HELP ME for the love of St Patrick! For five years I have not seen any man!"
"Tunderin' lard Murphy, what did you do?" asks the doctor.
"I put drops in her eyes!"

Two little kids, aged six and eight, decide it's time to learn how to swear. So, the eight-year-old says to the six-year-old, "Okay, you say `arse' and I'll say `hell'". All excited about their plan, they troop downstairs, where their mother asks them what they'd like for breakfast. "Aw, hell", says the eight-year-old, "give me some Vegemite toast." His mother backhands him off the stool, sending him bawling out of the room, and turns to the younger brother. "What'll you have?"
"I dunno", quavers the six-year-old, "but you can bet your arse it ain't gonna be Vegemite toast."

AUSTRALIAN ETIQUETTE

IN GENERAL

1. Never take an open stubby of beer to a job interview.
2. Always identify people in your paddocks before shooting at them.
3. It's tacky to take an Ice Cooler full of beer to church.
4. If you have to vacuum the bed, it's time to change the sheets.
5. Even if you're certain you're included in the will, it's rude to take your
   4X4 truck and trailer to the funeral.

DINING OUT
1. When decanting wine from the 2 litre box, tilt the paper cup and pour slowly so   as not to bruise the wine.
2. If drinking directly from the bottle, hold it with only one hand.

ENTERTAINING IN YOUR HOME
1. A centre piece for the table should never be anything prepared by a taxidermist.
2. Don't allow the dog to eat at the table, no matter how good his manners.

PERSONAL HYGIENE
1. While ears need to be cleaned regularly, this should be done in private, using one's OWN 4X4 truck keys.
2. Even if you live alone, deodorant isn't a waste of money.
3. Extensive use of deodorant can only delay bathing by a few days.
4. Dirt and grease under the fingernails is a no-no, it alters the taste of finger foods and if you are a woman it can draw attention away from your jewellery.

DATING
1. Always offer to bait your date's hook - especially on the first date.
2. Be assertive. Let her know you're interested: "I've been wanting to go out with you ever since I read that stuff on the dunny door two years ago."
3. Establish with her parents what time she's expected back. Some will say 1:00 PM, others might say "Monday." If the latter is the answer, it's the man's responsibility to get her to school on time.

THEATRE ETIQUETTE
1. Crying babies should be taken to the lobby and picked up after the movie ends.

2. Refrain from yelling abuse at characters on the screen. Tests have proven they can't hear you.

WEDDINGS
1. Livestock is a poor choice for a wedding gift.
2. Kissing the bride for more than five seconds may cause a drop in your popularity. (Excessive use of the tongue is also considered out of place)
3. For the groom, at least, rent a tux. A tracksuit with a cummerbund and a clean football jumper can create a tacky appearance.
4. Though uncomfortable, say "yes" to socks and shoes for the occasion.

DRIVING ETIQUETTE
1. Dim your headlights for approaching vehicles, even if your gun is loaded and the roo is in your rifle sight.
2. When entering a roundabout, the vehicle with the largest roo bar doesn't always have the right of way.
3. Never tow another car using panty hose and duct tape.
4. When sending your wife down the road with a petrol can, it's impolite to ask her to bring back beer too.

A zebra died and went to heaven and was met at the pearly gates by St Peter. On seeing all the lush green grass, the zebra couldn't wait to get in. "Hold on a minute", said St Peter, "we are a bit full today so we are only taking whites. Now, look at you. What are you? Are you white with black stripes or black with white stripes?"

The zebra was confused and said, "I don't know. How can I find out?"

"Easy", said St Peter. "God appears behind that cloud over there at two o'clock every day to answer any questions. It's almost that time now so go ask him."

Sure enough, at two o'clock a loud booming voice came from within the clouds saying, "What is your question?" The zebra told him his predicament and God said, "You are, what you are." And then in a flash of lightning, God was gone.

The zebra was more confused than ever so he went back to St Peter and told him what happened and that God had simply said 'You are what you are'.

With that the gates were thrown open and St Peter said in a very excitable voice, "Welcome in. As you know, God knows everything. If he said 'You are what you are' then you must be white because if you were black, he would have said in a loud excited Caribbean voice, 'Yea bro! Yo IS what Yo IS!"

Moses is coming down from Mt Sinai with the two tablets. He addresses the people assembled, pointing to the tablets. "I have good news and I have bad news. The good news is I got Him down to ten, the bad news, goddamn it, adultery is still in it"

An Irishman went for an interview with one of the major blue chip computer companies.

When the interview was over the interviewer told him that all applicants had to complete a test. The interviewer took a piece of paper and drew six vertical lines in pairs of two on the paper and placed it in front of the Irishman.

"Could you please show me a clever way to make this into nine?"

After thinking for awhile, the Irishman took the pencil and drew a canopy of leaves on top of the three pairs of lines, and handed the paper back to the interviewer.

The interviewer looked at the drawings and said: "But that is not nine!"

"Oh, yes it is", said the Irishman with a broad Irish accent, "Tree + Tree + Tree make nine!"

The interviewer handed the paper back to the Irishman and asked him to make it 99.

After thinking for a long while the Irishman scribbled up and down the trunks and handed the paper back to the interviewer.

The interviewer looked at the drawings and said: "But that is not ninety-nine!"

"Oh, yes it is", said the Irishman, "Dirty tree + dirty tree + dirty tree make ninety-nine."

The interviewer was now a bit cheesed off so he decided to do the Irishman once and for all, therefore, he handed the paper back to the Irishman and asked him to make it 100.

After thinking for a considerably longer time the Irishman suddenly grabbed the pencil and drew a little 'blop' on the bottom right-hand side of each three and handed the paper back to the interviewer.

The interviewer looked at the drawings and said: "But that is not 100!"

"Oh yes it most certainly is", said the Irishman with a much broader Irish accent,

"Dirty tree and a turd + dirty tree and a turd + dirty tree and a turd, make a 100."

A burglar broke into a house one night. He shone his flashlight around, looking for valuables. When he picked up a CD player to stuff into his sack, he heard a strange disembodied voice come through the darkness: "Jesus is watching you."

He nearly jumped out of his skin! He shut off his flashlight and waited. When he heard nothing more after a bit, he shook his head and resumed searching for more valuables. Just as he disconnected the stereo, he heard again, clear as a bell:

"Jesus is watching you."

Completely freaked, he shone his light around looking for the source of the voice. In a corner of the room the beam came to rest upon an African parrot.

"Did you say that?!" he hissed at the parrot.

"Yep", the bird replied. "I'm just trying to warn you."

The burglar visibly relaxed. "Warn me, huh?! Who the heck are you?"

"Moses", replied the parrot.

The burglar laughed, "What kind of stupid people would name a parrot Moses?"

"Probably", the bird answered, "the same kind of people who would name a rottweiler Jesus."

A newly married couple, both not too bright and both still virgins, go on their honeymoon. Unfortunately, neither knows what to do when they get there. The newlyweds call the groom's mother for advice. The mother says that they should sit on the bed together, snuggle, and things should happen from there. The newlyweds do this, but nothing happens. The groom calls his mother back. She says they should take their clothes off, get under the covers, and nature should take its course. The bride and groom take his mother's advice, but still nothing comes to mind. He calls his mother a third time. Getting frustrated with the situation, she says, "Listen, just take the biggest thing you have and stick it in her hairiest spot!" The groom is quiet for a moment and then asks his mother, "I've got my nose in her armpit, now what?"

Rick volunteers with prison ministries, and in his work has become friends with a pastor of a store front church. The pastor's church is called Almighty God Tabernacle. On a Saturday night several weeks ago, this pastor was working late, and decided to call his wife before he left for home. It was about 10:00 PM, but his wife didn't answer the phone. The pastor let it ring many times. He thought it was odd that she didn't answer, but decided to wrap up a few things and try again in a few minutes. When he tried again she answered right away. He asked her why she hadn't answered before, and she said that it hadn't rung at their house.

They brushed it off as a fluke and went on their merry ways. The following Monday, the pastor received a call at the church office, which was the phone that he'd used that Saturday night. The man that he spoke with wanted to know why he'd called on Saturday night.

The pastor couldn't figure out what the guy was talking about. Then the guy said, "It rang and rang, but I didn't answer." The pastor remembered the mishap and apologized for disturbing him, explaining that he'd intended to call his wife. The man said, "That's OK. Let me tell you my story. You see, I was planning to commit suicide on Saturday night, but before I did, I prayed, 'God if you're there, and you don't want me to do this, give me a sign now.' At that point my phone started to ring. I looked at the caller ID, and it said, 'Almighty God'. I just got the courage today to call back.

A wife says to her husband, "How would you describe me?"

Her husband replies, "ABCDEFGHIJK."

The wife asks, "What does that mean?"

The husband says, "Adorable, Beautiful, Cute, Delightful, Elegant, Fashionable, Gorgeous, and Hot."

The wife is pleased, "Aw, thank you, but what about IJK?"

The husband says, "I'm Just Kidding!"

Several men were in the locker room of the gym when a cell phone on a bench rang and a man put it on speaker and begins to talk.

Everyone in the room stopped to listen.

Man: Hello!

Woman: Hi honey, it's me. Are you at the club?

Man: Yes.

Woman: I'm at the shops now and found this beautiful leather coat. Its only $2000: is it OK if I buy it?

Man: Sure, go ahead if you like it that much.

Woman: I also stopped by the Lexus dealership and saw the new models. I saw one that I really liked.

Man: How much?

Woman: $90,000

Man: OK, but for that price I want it with all options.

Woman: Great! Oh, and one more thing. I was just talking to Jane and found out that the house I wanted last year is back on market. They are asking $980,000 for it.

Man: Well, then go ahead and offer $900,000. They'll probably take it. If not, we can go to the extra $80,000 if that's what you really want.

Woman: OK. See you later! I love you too much!

Man: Bye, I love you too.

The man hung up. The other men in the locker room were staring at him in astonishment, mouths wide open.

He turned and asked: Anyone know whose phone is this?

A young Arab boy asks his father, "What is that strange hat you are wearing?"
The father said, "Why, my son, it is a 'chechia.' In the desert it protects our heads from the intense heat of the sun."
"And what is this clothing you are wearing?" asked the boy. "This long flowing robe seems so…"
"Oh, my son!" exclaimed the father. "It is very simple. This is a 'djbellah.' As I have told you, in the desert it is not only very hot but the sand is always blowing. My djbellah protects the entire body."
The son then asked, "But Father, what about those ugly shoes you have on your feet?"
"These are 'babouches' my son", the father replied. "You must understand that although the desert sands are very beautiful, they are also extremely hot. These 'babouches' keep us from burning our feet."
"So tell me then", added the boy...
"Yes, my son…"
"Why are you living in London and still wearing all this ridiculous shit?"

An artist talks to his curator about his recent sales
Artist: "So? Did I sell anything?"
Curator: "You won't believe this: a man came by and asked if the value of the paintings will rise after the artist's death. I told him that I think so. So he bought the entire gallery."
Artist: "Wow! That's great! who was he?"
Curator: "It was your doctor."

An Englishman, Scotsman and an Irishman are in France during World War II, they have been cut off from their unit and seek refuge in a barn. Later that night they hear a German patrol coming round, so they need to hide. In the barn there are three large sacks, so they all agree to try hiding in them. No sooner are they all in their sacks when the Germans burst in the door, they see the three sacks and view them suspiciously.

They approach the sack with the Englishman inside and kick it, quick-witted the Englishman says "woof" in his best dog impression, and the Germans shrug and walk to the next one.

Reaching the sack with the Scotsman inside they kick that one, and following the Englishman's example the Scotsman says "meow" in his best cat voice and the Germans leave it be.

Then they approach the sack with the Irishman inside, as with the others they kick it and the Irishman says, "potatoes".

In the middle of the night Mary woke up to find Paddy standing over their baby's crib. She watched him silently as Paddy stood looking down at the sleeping infant, his face going through a mixture of emotions: disbelief, doubt, delight, amazement, enchantment, scepticism. Mary was touched by this unusual display and the deep emotions it aroused, and with eyes glistening she slipped her arm around her husband. "A penny for your thoughts", she whispered. "It's amazing!" Paddy replied. "I just can't see how anybody can make a crib like that for only $46.50."

Before performing a baptism, the priest approached the young father and said solemnly, "Baptism is a serious step my son. Are you prepared for it?" "I think so", the man replied. "My wife has made all the appetisers herself and we have a caterer coming in to provide plenty of sandwiches and cakes for all of our guests." "I don't mean that", the priest responded. "I mean, are you properly prepared, spiritually?" "Oh, hell yeah!" came the reply. "For the men I've got a keg of beer plus whiskey, gin and brandy and a couple of bottles of Baileys Irish Cream for the women. That should do the trick."

Riots in Birmingham England last month caused over £1 million worth of improvements.

I was walking down the road when I saw an Afghan bloke standing on a fifth floor balcony, shaking a carpet. I shouted up to him, "What's up Abdul, won't it start?"

One day, during lessons on proper grammar, the teacher asked for a show of hands from those who could use the word "beautiful" in the same sentence twice. First, she called on little Suzie, who responded with, " My father bought my mother a beautiful dress and she looked beautiful in it."
"Very good, Suzie", replied the teacher. She then called on little Michael. "My mummy planned a beautiful banquet and it turned out beautifully." She said, "Excellent, Michael!"
Then the teacher reluctantly called on little Johnnie.
"Last night at the dinner table, my 16 year old sister told my father that she was pregnant, and he said 'beautiful, just bloody beautiful!'"

In a murder trial, the defense attorney was cross-examining the coroner:
Attorney: Before you signed the death certificate, had you taken the pulse?
Coroner: No.
Attorney: Did you listen to the heart?
Coroner: No.
Attorney: Did you check for breathing?
Coroner: No.
Attorney: So, when you signed the death certificate, you weren't sure the man was dead, were you?
Coroner: Well, let me put it this way. The man's brain was sitting in a jar on my desk. But I guess it is possible that he could be out there practicing law somewhere.

"Doctor", the embarrassed man said, "I have a sexual problem. I can't get it up for my wife anymore."
"Mr. Garrett, bring her back with you tomorrow and let me see what I can do."
The next day, the worried fellow returned with his wife.
"Take off your clothes, Mrs. Garrett", the medic said. "Now turn all the way around. Lie down please. Uh-huh, I see. Okay, you may put your clothes back on."
The doctor took the husband aside. "You're in perfect health", he said. "Your wife didn't give me an erection either."

FUNNY CHURCH NOTICES

The following announcements were written by church organisers, on old fashioned typewriters, and they appeared on various church bulletin boards or were announced in church.

The Fasting & Prayer Conference includes meals.

Scouts are saving aluminium cans, bottles and other items to be recycled. Proceeds will be used to cripple children.

The sermon this morning: 'Jesus Walks on the Water. 'The sermon tonight: 'Searching for Jesus.'

Ladies, don't forget the rummage sale. It's a chance to get rid of those things not worth keeping around the house. Bring your husbands.

Don't let worry kill you off - let the Church help.

Miss Charlene Mason sang 'I will not pass this way again', giving obvious pleasure to the congregation.

For those of you who have children and don't know it, we have a nursery downstairs.

Next Thursday there will be try-outs for the choir. They need all the help they can get.

Irving Benson and Jessie Carter were married on October 24 in the church. So ends a friendship that began in their school days.

A bean supper will be held on Tuesday evening in the church hall. Music will follow.

At the evening service tonight, the sermon topic will be 'What Is Hell?' Come early and listen to our choir practice.

Eight new choir robes are currently needed due to the addition of several new members and to the deterioration of some older ones.

Please place your donation in the envelope along with the deceased person you want remembered.

The church will host an evening of fine dining, super entertainment and gracious hostility.

Pot-luck supper Sunday at 5:00 PM - prayer and medication to follow.

The ladies of the Church have cast off clothing of every kind. They may be seen in the basement on Friday afternoon.

This evening at 7 PM there will be a hymn singing in the park across from the Church. Bring a blanket and come prepared to sin.

The pastor would appreciate it if the ladies of the Congregation would lend him their electric girdles for the pancake breakfast next Sunday.

Low Self Esteem Support Group will meet Thursday at 7 pm. Please use the back door.

The eighth-graders will be presenting Shakespeare's Hamlet in the Church basement Friday at 7 pm. The congregation is invited to attend this tragedy.

Weight Watchers will meet at 7 pm at the First Presbyterian Church. Please use large double door at the side entrance.

And this one just about sums them all up
The Associate Minister unveiled the church's new
campaign slogan last Sunday:
'I Upped My Pledge - Up Yours.'

AMEN

An English guy is driving with his idiot friend as his
passenger,
when he decides to pull over because he suspects that
his turn signal may not be working. He asks his idiot friend
if he doesn't mind stepping out of the car to check the
lights while he tests them. The idiot steps out and stands
in front of the car.
The English guy turns on the turn signal and asks, "Is it
working?"
To which the idiot responds, "Yes, it's working....No, it's
not working....Yes, it's working....No, it's not working...."

The first grade teacher was in class and getting to
know her new pupils. She said to the first sweet little girl,
"And what is your name?"
    The little girl lisped, "My name is Autumn Leaf. That's
because when I was born my mummy and daddy didn't
know what to call me so one day, we were outside under
a tree and a leaf fell on me. So they called me Autumn
Leaf."
The next pupil was another sweet little girl whose name
was Apple Blossom and was called that because a
blossom fell on her when she was born.
    The teacher then came to a little boy. Red hair, freckles
everywhere and a severely pushed in face and nose.
Screwing up her nose at the kids looks, she asked, "And
what's your name?"
    "Ward Robe."

There was this punk who got on a bus. He sat next to an old man who started staring at him, because the punk was dressed in really colorful clothing.

The punk had all this colorful make-up on, and his hair was spiked up with red, green & yellow spears in the form of feathers.

The punk was getting sick of being stared at so he said to the old man, "Hey, old man, what are you lookin' at, eh? Didn't you ever do anything strange when you were a teenager?"

"Well, yeah", the old man answered. "Once I got so drunk that I screwed a parrot, so I can't help but think that maybe you might be one of my offspring."

A fleeing Taliban, desperate for water, was plodding through the Afghan Desert when he saw something far off in the distance.

Hoping to find water, he hurried toward the oasis only to find a Royal Marine selling regimental ties.

The Taliban asked, "Do you have water?"

The soldier replied, "There is no water, the well is dry. Would you like to buy a tie instead? They are only 5 pounds."

The Taliban shouted, "You idiot infidel. I do not need an over-priced tie. I need water.

I should kill you, but I must find water first."

"OK", said the soldier, "It does not matter that you do not want to buy a tie and that you hate me.

I will show you that I am bigger than that, and that I am a much

better human being than you.

If you continue over that hill to the east for about two miles, you

will find our Officers Mess. It has all the ice cold water you need."

Cursing him, the Taliban staggered away over the hill.

Several hours later he staggered back, collapsed with dehydration and rasped...

"They won't let me in without a tie."

A student visits the principal's office one day.

The principal says to him, "What's your name, son?"

The student replies, "D-d-d-dav-dav-david, sir."

The principal looks up and asks him, "Oh, do you have a stutter?"

The student replies, "No sir, my dad has a stutter but the guy who registered my name was a complete smart arse."

A newly wed couple were spending their honeymoon in a remote log cabin resort way up the mountains. They had registered on Saturday and they had not been seen for 5 days. An elderly couple ran the resort, and they were getting concerned about the welfare of these newlyweds. The old man decided to go and see if they were all right. He knocked on the door of the cabin and a weak voice from inside answered. The old man asked if they were OK. "Yes, we're quite OK."

"We're living on the fruits of love."

The old man replied, "Yes well that might be fine, but would you mind not throwing the peelings out the window ... they're choking my ducks."

"What's your father's occupation?" asked the schoolteacher.

"He's a magician, ma'am", said Little Johnny.

"How interesting. What's his favourite trick?" asked the teacher.

"He saws people in half", answered Little Johnny.

"Wow! That must be amazing to watch", said the teacher. "Do you have any brothers or sisters?"

And Little Johnny said, "One half brother and two half sisters."

There were three guys traveling in Africa, a Frenchman, a Japanese, and an Australian. They are captured by a tribe of fierce head hunters. The witch doctor says to them, "We are going to slaughter you, but you might take some comfort in the fact that we don't believe in waste here, and that therefore every part of your body will go to some use. We will weave baskets out of your hair, we will render your bones for glue, and we will tan your skin and stretch it over wooden frames for canoes. Now we are going to allow you an honourable death, so I will give you each a knife and allow you to say some last words before killing yourselves."

The Japanese guy yells, "Banzai!" and commits hari-kari.

The French guy yells, "Vive la France!" and slits his throat.

Then the Australian guy takes the knife, pokes holes all over his body, and yells, "Up yours pal. There's your bloody canoe!"

Hospital regulations require a wheel chair for patients being discharged. However, while working as a student nurse, I found one elderly gentleman already dressed and sitting on the bed with a suitcase at his feet, who insisted he didn't need my help to leave the hospital. After a chat about rules being rules, he reluctantly let me wheel him to the elevator. On the way down I asked him if his wife was meeting him.

'I don't know,' he said. 'She's still upstairs in the bathroom changing out of her hospital gown.'

Arnold's wife purchased a new line of expensive cosmetics that she saw advertised on television and which guaranteed to make her look years younger. After spending a long time sitting in front of the mirror applying her "miracle" cosmetic products, she asked Arnold, "Darling, honestly, what age would you say I am?" Arnold looked her over carefully and then replied, "Well honey, judging from your skin, I would say twenty. By your hair, eighteen. By your figure, twenty five."

"Oh wow, you old flatterer you!" she said, blushing deeply.

"Wait a minute", Arnold replied, interrupting her. "I haven't added them up yet."

A couple of North Queensland hunters are out in the rain forests when one of them falls to the ground.

He doesn't seem to be breathing, his eyes are rolled back in his head. The other guy whips out his mobile phone and calls 000. He gasps to the operator, "My friend is dead! What can I do?"

The operator, in a calm soothing voice says, "Just take it easy. I can help. First, let's make sure he's dead." There is a silence, then a shot is heard.

The guy's voice comes back on the line. He says, "OK, now what?"

A little boy goes to his father and asks him the difference between hypothetical and a fact.

His father tells him to go ask his mother if she would sleep with the mailman for a million dollars.

The boy asks his mother and she replies, "Hell yeah."

He tells his father what she says and then his father tells him to go ask his sister if she would sleep with the principal for a million dollars.

He asks and his sister replies, "Yes."

He again tells his father what the answer was. The little boy asks "So what's the difference?"

The father replied "Hypothetically we're rich, the fact is, we're just living with a couple of whores."

An Islander boy and his father were visiting the city. They were amazed by two shiny, silver walls that could move apart and then slide back together again. The boy asked, "What is this, Father?"

The father (never having seen an elevator) responded, "Son, I have never seen anything like this in my life, I don't know what it is."

While the boy and his father were watching with amazement, a fat old lady in a wheel chair rolled up to the moving walls and pressed a button. The walls opened and the lady rolled between them into a small room. The walls closed and the boy and his father watched the small circular numbers above the walls light up sequentially. They continued to watch until it reached the last number and then the numbers began to light in the reverse order. Finally the walls opened up again and a gorgeous, voluptuous 24 year old blonde woman stepped out.

The father, not taking his eyes off the young woman, said quietly to his son...

"Go get your mother."

An Australian, an Irishman and a Scot are in a bar. They're staring at another man sitting on his own at a table in the corner.

He's so familiar, but not actually recognising him is driving them mad.

They stare and stare, until suddenly the Irishman twigs: 'My God, it's Jesus!'

Sure enough, it is Jesus, nursing a pint.

Thrilled, they send him over a pint of Guinness, a pint of Fosters and a pint of Bitter. Jesus accepts the drinks, smiles over at the three men, and drinks the pints slowly, one after another. After he's finished the drinks, Jesus approaches the trio. He reaches for the hand of the Irishman and shakes it, thanking him for the Guinness. When he lets go, the Irishman gives a cry of amazement:

'My God! The arthritis I've had for 30 years is gone. It's a miracle!'

Jesus then shakes the Scots hand, thanking him for the Bitter. As he lets go, the man's eyes widen in shock. 'Och Mon! The bad back I've had all me life is completely gone! It's A Miracle.'

Jesus then approaches the Aussie who says, 'Back off, mate, I'm on disability benefit.'

It was the mailman's last day on the job after 35 years of carrying the mail through all kinds of weather to the same neighborhood. When he arrived at the first house on his route, he was greeted by the whole family there, who congratulated him and sent him on his way with a big gift envelope.

At the second house they presented him with a box of fine cigars. The folks at the third house handed him a selection of terrific fishing lures.

At the fourth house he was met at the door by a strikingly beautiful blond woman in a revealing negligee. She took him by the hand, gently led him through the door, which she closed behind him, and led him up the stairs to the bedroom where she blew his mind with the most passionate love he had ever experienced. When he had had enough, they went downstairs, where she fixed him a giant breakfast: eggs, potatoes, ham, sausage, blueberry waffles, and fresh-squeezed orange juice. When he was truly satisfied, she poured him a cup of steaming coffee. As she was pouring, he noticed a dollar coin on the saucer.

"All this was just too wonderful for words", he said, "but what's the dollar for?"

"Well", she said, "last night, I told my husband that today would be your last day, and that we should do something special for you. I asked him what to give you.

He said, 'Screw the postie, give him a dollar', but the breakfast was my idea."

A TV host asked a Spanish guest what was the meaning of the common word used in Spain, 'manyana'. The guest said that the term means "maybe the job will be done tomorrow, maybe the next day, maybe the day after that. Perhaps next week, next month, next year. Who cares?" The host turned to her other guest, Irishman Shay Brennan who was also on the show, and asked him if there was an equivalent term in Irish. "No", replied Brennan. "In Ireland we don't have a word to describe that degree of urgency."

Into a Belfast pub comes Paddy Murphy, looking like he'd just been run over by a train. His arm is in a sling, his nose is broken, his face is cut, and bruised, and he's walking with a limp.
"What happened to you?" asks Sean, the bartender.
"Micheal O'Connor and me had a fight," says Paddy
"That little skinny O'Connor?" says Sean. "How could he do that to you? He must have had something in his hand."
"That he did," says Paddy, "a shovel is what he had, and a terrible beatin' he gave me with it."
"Well," says Sean, "you should have defended yourself ta' same. Didn't you have something in your hand?"
"That I did," said Paddy. "Mrs. O'Connor's left breast. And a thing of beauty it was too, but bloody useless in a fight."

Four brothers all became successful businessmen and lawyers and lived across the country from each other. They met to discuss the 95th birthday party and gifts they were to give their elderly mother.
The first said, "You know I have had a big house built for Mum."
The second said, "And I had a large theatre room built into that house."
The third said, "And I had my Mercedes dealer deliver an

SL600 to her."

The fourth said, "You know how Mum loved reading the Bible and you know she can't read anymore because she can't see very well. I met this Minister who told me about a parrot who could recite the entire Bible. It took ten Ministers almost 8 years to teach him. I had to pledge to contribute $50,000 a year for five years to the church, but it was worth it. Mum only has to name the chapter and verse, and the parrot will recite it."

The other brothers were impressed. After the celebration Mum sent out her "Thank You" notes.

She wrote: "Michael, the house you built is so huge that I live in only one room, but I have to clean the whole house. Thank you anyway."

"Mervin, I am too old to travel. I stay home, I have my groceries delivered, so I never use the Mercedes. The thought was good. Thank you."

"Mark, you gave me an expensive theatre with Dolby sound and it can hold 50 people, but all of my friends are dead, I've lost my hearing, and I'm nearly blind. I'll never use it. Thank you for the gesture just the same."

"Dearest Mitchell, you were the only son to have the good sense to give a little thought to your gift. The Cornish hen was delicious. Thank you so much.
Love, Mum."

A wife was in bed with her lover when she heard her husband's key in the door. "Stay where you are", she said. "He's so drunk he won't even notice you're in bed with me." Sure enough, the husband lurched into bed none the wiser, but a few minutes later, through a drunken haze, he saw six feet sticking out at the end of the bed. He turned to his wife and slurred: "Hey, there are shix feet in thish bed. There should only be four. Wha's goin' on?" 'Nonsense", said the wife. "You're so drunk you miscounted. Get out of bed and try again. You can see better from over there." The husband staggered out of bed and counted. "One, two, three, four. Well bugger me dead. Sshow there are. Sshorry 'bout that."

    A man was taking his wife, who was pregnant with twins, to the hospital when his car went out of control and crashed.
Regaining consciousness, he saw his brother, a relentless practical joker, sitting at his bed side.
He asked his brother how his wife was doing and his brother said, "Don't worry, everybody is fine and you have a son and a daughter.
But the hospital was in a real hurry to get the birth certificates filed and since both you and your wife were unconscious, I named them for you."
The husband was thinking to himself, "Oh no, what has he done now?" and asked with some trepidation, "Well, bro, what did you name them?"
Whereupon, his brother replied, "I named the little girl Denise."
The husband, relieved, said, "That's a lovely name! And what did you come up with for my son?"
The brother winked and replied, "Denephew."

I left the hospital absolutely shattered. Pulling the plug on my mother in law who lived with us for the past 18 years was the hardest thing I've ever done. I had to wrestle the wife, two doctors, a nurse, and a security guy.

Seventy year old George went for his annual physical. All of his tests came back with great results.
Dr. Smith said, "George everything looks great physically. How are you doing mentally, emotionally and are you at peace with yourself and have a good relationship with God?"
George replied, "God and me are tight. We are so close that when I get up in the middle of the night, poof!...the light goes on and I go to the bathroom and then poof! the light goes off!"
"Wow", commented Dr. Smith, "That's incredible!"
A little later in the day Dr. Smith called George's wife.
"Thelma", he said, "George is just fine. Physically he's great. But I had to call because I'm in awe of his relationship with God. Is it true that he gets up during the night and poof! The light goes on in the bathroom and then poof! the light goes off?"
Thelma replied, "Darn fool! He's peeing in the fridge again!"

The boss walked into the office one morning not knowing his zipper was down and his fly area wide open.
His assistant walked up to him and said, "This morning when you left your house, did you close your garage door?"
The boss told her he knew he'd closed the garage door, and walked into his office puzzled by the question.
As he finished his paperwork, he suddenly noticed his fly was open, and zipped it up.
He then understood his assistant's question about his 'garage door.'
He headed out for a cup of coffee and paused by her desk to ask,
"When my garage door was open, did you see my Jaguar parked in there?"
She smiled and said, "No, I didn't. All I saw was an old minivan with two flat tyres..."

Ever since I was a child, I've always had a fear of someone under my bed at night. So I went to a shrink and told him.

"I've got problems. Every time I go to bed, I think there's somebody under it. I'm scared. I think I'm going crazy."

"Just put yourself in my hands for one year", said the shrink. "Come talk to me three times a week and we should be able to get rid of those fears."

"How much do you charge?"

"Eighty dollars per visit", replied the doctor.

"I'll sleep on it", I said.

Six months later the doctor met me on the street. "Why didn't you come to see me about those fears you were having?" he asked.

"Well, eighty bucks a visit three times a week for a year is an awful lot of money! A bartender cured me for $10. I was so happy to have saved all that money that I went and bought me a new pickup!"

"Is that so!" With a bit of an attitude he said, "and how, may I ask, did a bartender cure you?"

"He told me to cut the legs off the bed! Ain't nobody under there now!"

A bus stops and two Italian men get on. They sit down and engage in an animated conversation. The lady sitting next to them ignores them at first but her attention is galvanised when she hears one of them say the following:

"Emma, she comma first. Den I come. Den two asses dey comma together. I comma once-a-more. Two asses dey comma together again. I comma again and pee twice. Then I comma one lasta time."

"You foul-mouthed, sex-obsessed swine", says the lady indignantly. "In this country we don't speak aloud in public places about our sex lives.

"Hey coola down lady", said the man. "Who talkin abouta da sex? I'm justa tellin' my frienda how to spell Mississippi."

LIFE EXPLAINED

On the first day, God created the dog and said, "Sit all day by the door of your house and bark at anyone who comes in or walks past. For this, I will give you a life span of twenty years."

The dog said, "That's a long time to be barking. How about only ten years and I'll give you back the other ten?"

And God saw it was good.

On the second day, God created the monkey and said, "Entertain people, do tricks, and make them laugh. For this, I'll give you a twenty-year life span."

The monkey said, "Monkey tricks for twenty years? That's a pretty long time to perform. How about I give you back ten like the dog did?"

And God again saw it was good.

On the third day, God created the cow and said, "You must go into the field with the farmer all day long and suffer under the sun, have calves and give milk to support the farmer's family. For this, I will give you a life span of sixty years."

The cow said, "That's kind of a tough life you want me to live for sixty years. How about twenty and I'll give back the other forty?"

And God agreed it was good.

On the fourth day, God created humans and said, "Eat, sleep, play, marry and enjoy your life. For this, I'll give you twenty years."

But the human said, "Only twenty years? Could you possibly give me my twenty, the forty the cow gave back, the ten the monkey gave back, and the ten the dog gave back; that makes eighty, okay?"

"Okay", said God, "You asked for it."

So that is why for our first twenty years, we eat, sleep, play and enjoy ourselves. For the next forty years, we slave in the sun to support our family. For the next ten years, we do monkey tricks to entertain the grandchildren. And for the last ten years, we sit on the front porch and bark at everyone.

Life has now been explained to you.

A dad is explaining how things are to his son, "I think it's time you knew, Thomas. You know the Easter Bunny, Santa, and the Tooth Fairy? That's always been me."
"That's OK, daddy, I've known for a long time now that all these fairy creatures were really you. Except for the stork, right? That was uncle Vernon?"

A motorist locked himself out of his car and a passer-by stopped to help him.
"I'll have your door open in no time", he said as he proceeded to rub his bottom against the driver's door.
The motorist found this to be rather odd but very soon the locks sprung open.
"How amazing", cried the relieved driver. "How did you do that?"
"Easy", replied the stranger. "I'm wearing khaki trousers."

Paddy and Seamus, two Irishmen, are traveling to Australia. Before they leave home, one of their dads gives them both a bit of advice: "You watch them Aussie cab drivers. They'll rob you blind. Don't you go paying them what they ask. You haggle." At the Sydney airport, the Irishmen catch a cab to their hotel. When they reach their destination, the cabbie says, "That'll be twenty dollars, lads." "Oh no you don't! My dad warned me about you. You'll only be getting fifteen dollars from me", says Paddy. "And you'll only be getting fifteen from me too", adds Seamus.

TEXT MESSAGE

'Hi, Max. This is Richard, next door. I've been riddled with guilt for a few months and have been trying to get up the courage to tell you face-to-face. When you're not around, I've been sharing your wife, day and night, probably much more than you. I haven't been getting it at home recently. I know that's no excuse. The temptation was just too great. I can't live with the guilt and hope you'll accept my sincere apology and forgive me. Please suggest a fee for usage and I'll pay you. Richard'

Max, enraged and betrayed, grabbed his gun, went next door, and shot Richard dead. He returned home, shot his wife, poured himself a stiff drink, and sat down on the sofa. Max then looked at his phone and discovered a second text message from Richard.

SECOND TEXT MESSAGE:

'Hi, Max. Richard here again. Sorry about the typo on my last text. I assume you figured it out and noticed that the darned Spell-Check had changed "wi-fi" to "wife." Technology, huh? It'll be the death of us all.'

At the National Art Gallery in Dublin, a husband and wife were staring at a portrait that had them completely confused.

The painting depicted three black men totally naked, sitting on a bench. Two of the figures had black penises, but the one in the middle had a pink penis.

The curator of the gallery realized that they were having trouble interpreting the painting and offered his personal assessment.

He went on for over half an hour explaining how it depicted the sexual emasculation of African Americans in a predominately white, patriarchal society.

"In fact", he pointed out, "some serious critics believe that the pink penis also reflects the cultural and sociological oppression experienced by gay men in contemporary society."

After the curator left, an Irishman approached the couple and said, "Would you like to know what the painting is really about?"

"Now why would you claim to be more of an expert than the curator of the gallery?" asked the couple.

"Because, I am the artist who painted the picture", he replied. "In fact, there are no African Americans depicted at all.

They're just three Irish coal miners. The guy in the middle went home for lunch."

Three desperately ill men met with their doctor one day to discuss their options.

One was an Alcoholic, one was a Chain-Smoker, and one was a Homosexual.

The doctor, addressing all three of them, said, "If any of you indulge in your vices one more time, you will surely die."

The men left the doctor's office; each convinced that he would never again indulge himself in his vice.

While walking toward the train station for their return trip to the suburbs, they passed a bar.

The Alcoholic, hearing the loud music and smelling the ale, could not stop himself. His buddies accompanied him into the bar, where he had a shot of whiskey. No sooner had he replaced the shot glass on the bar, he fell off his stool, stone cold dead.

His companions, somewhat shaken, left the bar, realizing how seriously they must take the doctor's words.

As they walked along, they came upon a cigarette butt lying on the ground, still burning.

The Homosexual looked at the Chain-Smoker and said, "You know, if you bend over to pick that up, we're both dead."

An elderly Mormon asked his doctor if he thought he'd live to be a hundred. The doctor asked the man, "Do you smoke or drink?" "No," he replied, "I've never done either." "Do you gamble, drive fast cars, and fool around and marry many women?" inquired the doctor. "No, I've never done any of those things either." "Well then," said the doctor, "what the hell do you want to live to be a hundred for?"

Mary Lou went into a coffee shop and noticed there was a "peel and win" sticker on her coffee cup.
Like any other young person she can't resist the chance to enter a competition and win a prize, so she peeled it off and then started jumping up and down and screaming out in a high pitched hysterical voice:
"I've won a motor-home!"
"I've won a motor-home!"
The waitress went over to her and said, "That's impossible. The biggest prize that you can win is a Free Lunch."
But Mary Lou kept on screaming hysterically and jumping up and down:
"I've won a motor-home!
"I've won a motor-home!"
Finally, the manager went over to her and said, "Mary Lou, I'm sorry, but you're mistaken. You couldn't have possibly won a motor-home because we didn't have that as a prize."
Mary Lou said, "No, it's not a mistake. I've won a motor-home!"
With that, she handed the ticket to the manager and he read…
"W I N A B A G E L"

Two blokes took their wives to the horse races, where they had a few bets.

One of the wives said she had backed No 6 in the sixth race.

The field for the race lined up and they were off.

The horse No 6 went the wrong way but the woman was jumping up and down and excitedly and loudly cheering the horse on.

Her husband said: "You fool, the stupid horse is running the wrong way."

She replied: "Don't worry, I backed it each way."

On their first night of wedded bliss, the groom took off his trousers and asked his new bride to try them on.
"They don't fit", she said.
"And never forget it!", said the husband. "In this house I wear the trousers."
She continued to disrobe. She threw him her frilly knickers and said, "Put those on."
He looked at the scanty briefs and said, "I'll never get into these!"
"You're right", she said. "And if you don't change your attitude, you never will."

I asked old Maud how she lost her husband.
She told me her sad story: "Well, he needed a blood transfusion, but his blood type was not on record, so the doctors asked me if I knew what it was, as they urgently needed to know, in order to save my Norman's life.
Tragically, I've never known his blood type, so I only had time to sit and say goodbye.
 I'll never forget how supportive my Norman was! Even as he was fading away, he kept on whispering to me ... "Be positive ... be positive!"
That was my Norman! Always thinking of others!!"

WITTY WORD PLAYS

You can tune a piano, but you can't tuna fish.

I changed my iPod's name to Titanic. It's syncing now.

England has no kidney bank, but it does have a Liverpool.

Haunted French pancakes give me the crepes.

This girl today said she recognized me from the Vegetarians Club, but I'd swear I've never met herbivore.

I know a guy who is addicted to drinking brake fluid, but he says he
can stop any time.

A thief who stole a calendar got twelve months.

When the smog lifts in Los Angeles, U.C.L.A.

I got some batteries that were given out free of charge.

A dentist and a manicurist married. They fought tooth and nail.

A will is a dead giveaway.

With her marriage, she got a new name and a dress.

Police were summoned to a daycare where a three-year-old was resisting a rest.

A bicycle can't stand alone; it's just two-tired.

The guy who fell onto an upholstery machine last week is now fully recovered.

He had a photographic memory, but it was never fully developed.

When she saw her first strands of gray hair, she thought she'd dye.

Acupuncture is a jab well done. That's the point of it.

Did you hear about the crossed-eyed teacher who lost her job because she couldn't control her pupils?

When you get a bladder infection, urine trouble.

When chemists die, they barium.

I stayed up all night to see where the sun went, and then it dawned on me.

I'm reading a book about anti-gravity. I just can't put it down.

WHY SENIORS NEVER CHANGE THEIR PASSWORD

WINDOWS:
Please enter your new password.

USER:
Cabbage

WINDOWS:
Sorry, the password must be more than 8 characters.

USER:
Boiled cabbage

WINDOWS:
Sorry, the password must contain 1 numerical character.

USER:
1 boiled cabbage

WINDOWS:
Sorry, the password cannot have blank spaces

USER:
50damnboiledcabbages

WINDOWS:
Sorry, the password must contain at least one upper case character

USER:
50DAMNboiledcabbages

WINDOWS:
Sorry the password cannot use more than one upper case character consecutively.

USER:
50damnBoiledCabbagesShovedUpYourArseIfYouDon'tGi
veMeAccessRightBloodyNow

WINDOWS:
"Sorry, that password is already in use."

AGING OBSERVATIONS

SEX AT 73 +???
Just took a leaflet out of my mailbox informing me that I
can have sex at 73.
I'm so happy, because I live at number 71.
So it's not too far to walk home afterwards.
And it's the same side of the street.
I don't even have to cross the road!

Answering machine message,
"I am not available right now, but thank you for caring
enough to call.
I am making some changes in my life.
Please leave a message after the beep.
If I do not return your call, you are one of the changes."

My wife and I had words, but I didn't get to use mine.

Frustration is trying to find your glasses without your
glasses.

The irony of life is that, by the time you're old enough to
know your way around, you're not going anywhere.

A man calls up the hotel manager from his room.
"Please come fast, I am having a raging argument with my wife and she says she will jump from your hotel window."
The manager says in an aloof tone, "Sir, I am sorry, but this is a personal issue. We can't help you here."
The husband heatedly replies, "The hell you can't. The window is not opening, this is a maintenance issue. SO HURRY!!!!"

Young Maria was on her first date. It was with a nice young Italian boy, Antonio, and she was dressed in a flowing dress with a rather revealing neckline.
Papa was proud of his young daughter but slightly apprehensive about her lack of modesty.
She explained they were simply going to the movies and would be home by 11.00pm.
As promised, she was home on time and proceeded to tell papa about the night.
"Well," she said. "He was such a gentleman that he paid for the tickets and even bought a packet of Smarties to nibble on."
Continuing on she said, giggling, "During the movie he put his hand on my waist. It was so funny. Then he slid his hand under my blouse and played with my breasts. So funny. Then he put his hand on my knee, slid it up my leg and into my knickers. So funny."
Horrified and angry, papa exclaimed, "What the hell was so funny about all that?"
To which the innocent young Maria, giggling loudly, blurted out, "The Smarties were in my back pocket."

FUNNY FOOD QUIPS

In Australia, some supermarkets, like Woolworths, have admitted that there is horse meat in their home cooked burgers.
The following Quips would probably be relevant:

I'm so hungry, I could eat a horse. I guess Woolworths just listened!

Anyone want a burger from Woolworths? Yay or neigh?

Not entirely sure how Woolworths is going to get over this hurdle.

Had some burgers from Woolworths for supper last night. I still have a bit between my teeth.

A woman has been taken into hospital after eating horse meat burgers from Woolworths.
Her condition is listed as 'stable'.

Woolworths are now testing all their vegetarian burgers for traces of unicorn.

"I've just checked the Woolworths burgers in my freezer ... "And they're off!"

Woolworths is now forced to deny the presence of zebra in burgers, as shoppers confuse barcodes for serving suggestions.

I said to my spouse, "These Woolworths burgers give me the trots.

THE END

ABOUT THE AUTHOR

Ian Nayda was born and raised in the country town of Waikerie, which sits on the banks of the Murray River in South Australia.

In the 1960's life was simple, with entertainment being derived from radio, some television and numerous concerts and cabarets.
It was the concerts, with music, drama and comedy that appealed to Ian who relished entertaining with a group on stage.

This led to doing stand up comedy, on his own at cabarets and functions, which gave him a rare insight into the art of the funny joke and how to make people laugh.

Ian worked as a computer analyst for forty years and over that period he was able to collect an enormous number of jokes and witty ditty's from the large number of people he worked with.

From his vast collection of jokes, poems, limericks and short witty gags, Ian has chosen the 'best of the best' which have been edited and rewritten with the intention of collating them into a book to be kept for the ages on your bookshelf, and to be shared with everyone who appreciates, or has a yearning for, quality humour.

Ian currently resides with his wife in Melbourne Australia.

Made in the USA
Las Vegas, NV
29 November 2023

81810095R00193